Why I Left the Hebrew Roots Movement

Alexander Larson

Table of Contents

Introduction

I, Alexander Larson, used to associate myself with and adhere to a set of religious beliefs which are referred to as the "Hebrew Roots Movement", also known sometimes as "Messianic Judaism." This position, as the name implies, focuses on returning back to the alleged Hebraic Roots of the Christian faith, and bridging the gap between 1st century Jewish culture and modern, 'corrupt' Christianity. From the summer of 2016 to the summer of 2018, I became deeply involved in this movement, and had very little doubts about whether or not I was right. It seemed like the absolute truth to me at the time, a doctrine which made so much sense. After all, if the Messiah lived in 1st century Israel, why are we using Greek terms and names for people and concepts in the Bible? Why are there supposed parallels between some heathen philosophies and the religion known as Christianity? These were the questions which I pondered.

At first, I was sucked in through the teachings of Messianic "Torah" teachers such as Michael Rood, Arthur Bailey, and others who mostly operated through obscure television and radio stations, or who spread their message on social media platforms such as Youtube. The series by Michael Rood known as "A Rood Awakening!" shook my religious beliefs which had already been in transformtion for quite some time through my own independent study of the Bible. Gradually, throughout the rest of 2016, my life changed slowly to fit that of these supposed teachers and the Hebrew Roots movement. I began to keep and celebrate the holy days of the Torah, I used Hebrew words and phrases, called Jesus by the Hebrew name Yeshua, and scoffed at those who I viewed to be part of pagan "Churchianity."

This was a trap which affected the way I viewed the world in every matter. The thought of perfecting myself through keeping the commandments in the Law of Moses and becoming more and more like a "Hebrew" was my main desire. I began to preach these doctrines myself, and even separated myself from many old friends who disliked my new beliefs. For the next year and a half after converting to this faith, I was convinced that nothing could ever change my mind, that the Hebrew Roots movement was the truth, and a return to God's actual word.

However, I was wrong. When 2018 came, I went down a gradual spiral towards turning away from the beliefs which I had cherished for nearly two years. It all began on accident, on an attempt to prove my own beliefs about justification, and my own doctrines about Torah-keeping. I stumbled across the preaching of God's word by a multitude of fire-breathing, leather-lunged, zealous, soulwinning, independent fundamental Baptists from the King James Bible, laying out the Gospel as clear as can be. Before long, I got saved, on June 25th, 2018, when I personally trusted Jesus Christ alone as my personal saviour, and realized that none of the traditions, none of the ordinances, none of the commandments or my own righteousness, regardless of my ethnicity, regardless of the languages I knew, regardless of who I am, could get me everlasting life, but that it's through the finished work of Christ in his death, burial, and resurrection.

Now I'm grateful that I was saved and delivered out of this false end-times cult which seeks to amalgamate Christianity and Judaism together. Even if those in the Hebrew Roots Movement don't claim to be of the Jewish religion, it was fairly obvious that I and others like me fell into the same pitfalls and false doctrines of the first-century Pharisees through rigorous legalism and strivings about the law, which the Bible commands us not to do.

So, what is Hebrew Roots, how and why did it change my life, and how and why did I manage to break free of it? The Hebrew Roots movement is a fairly new religion which arose out of denominations such as Messianic Judaism and the Armstrongists. Hebert W. Armstrong was a theologian and minister who founded the "Radio Church of God" in 1931 as a member of the Church of God (Seventh-Day), an Adventist group which emphasized keeping the commandments. Armstrong's church was later renamed as the Worldwide Church of God in 1968, which splintered into other groups after his death, such as the United Church of God, Restored Church of God, Global Church of God, and House of Yahweh, among others.

Doctrines which are emphasized in Armstrongism include Sabbatarianism, an obedience to the dietary laws, celebration of the Leviticus 23 feast days, and that obeying these laws and the Ten Commandments results in salvation. They reject the concept of heaven and hell and instead teach the "soul-sleep" doctrine. Armstrongists also believe that being born again is a future event at Jesus' second coming. Together, with the Armstrongists, many other Sabbatarians of the 20th century continued to teach an emphasis of obeying all of God's laws. This worked with the Messianic Judaism movement which arose in the 1960s among Jewish Christians who chose to keep the customs of

Judaism while accepting the beliefs of Christianity. Eventually, by the 1980s-1990s, 'Messianic teachers' of the Torah began to arise, such as Dean Wheelock, Monte Judah, and Michael Rood. Other groups which came out of the Sacred Name Movement, beginning in the 1930s, can also be classified as "Hebrew Roots", such as the Assemblies of Yahweh.

Wherever the Hebrew Roots movement came from, the fact of the matter is that it's in existence today, and growing rapidly. Nobody knows how many people are a part of this new movement, but it wouldn't be unreasonable to say it's in the millions. Although there are different ministries and organizations which may differ in minor beliefs, for the most part, those who identify as part of this group typically believe these following doctrines:

> That obedience to the Torah is not only important, but necessary for salvation (OR, at least, a desire to follow God's commands is, but the grace of God atones for mistakes). This includes not just the Ten Commandments, but all of the 613 commandments in the Torah. Particular emphasis is placed on the Sabbath, and going to church on Sunday is typically rejected as a pagan practice.

> Use of Hebrew words for theological terms, and use of Hebrew names. Most prominently, those in the Hebrew Roots movement will refer to Jesus as Yeshua, Yahshua, Yahushua, or some other pseudo-Hebrew variant. The name of God as YHVH (pronounced as Yahweh, Yehovah, Yahuwah, etc.) is also emphasized. Instead of God, they say Elohim. Other figures in the Bible will also be referred to by their Hebrew names (John as Yochanan, Peter as Kefa, Isaiah as Yeshayahu, etc.).

> For the most part, a rejection of the Trinity doctrine. Many will either accept total unitarianism, claiming that the Father alone is Elohim, or that Yeshua is a created being, although partially divine (similar to Arianism or the Jehovah's Witnesses).

> An emphasis is placed on the importance of the Feast Days, including Passover, the Day of Firstfruits, Shavuot, Yom Teruah, Yom Kippur, and Sukkot. Holidays such a Christmas and Easter are said to have a pagan origin and are entirely avoided.

> The Jewish people are God's chosen people, and the Hebrew culture is God's chosen culture which the original Christians lived in and

practiced. Most of Biblical prophecy centers around this fact, and focuses on the return of the Jewish people to Israel and the modern state of Israel.

At death, there is no heaven or hell, but rather a state of soul-sleep which is shared by both believers and unbelievers. Those who are unsaved will be cast into the Lake of Fire and annihilated at the final judgment, while the saved will be resurrected and enter the kingdom of heaven at the time of Yeshua's second coming.

Although there are many other examples of beliefs which independent ministries may hold, for the most part, these are the main concepts which distinguish the Hebrew Roots from Christianity. The focus and building block of the Hebrew Roots movement is the idea that the Christian religion should be rooted in the Hebrew culture of the 1st-century church and apostles. The Messianic Torah teachers as well as the followers of this belief system truly believe that they are thus restoring the church to its original state, filtering out all of the pagan influences which supposedly exist in modern Christianity. Thus, Hebrew Roots practitioners view Christianity as a heathen religion, corrupted by the lies of Greek, Egyptian, and Roman philosophy and idolatry which mixed in with the truths of the Bible.

In this book, I'll be exploring both how and why I joined this movement, and how it changed my life for nearly two years; followed by why I left the Hebrew Roots movement and why I now strongly believe that the core tenets of this faith are incorrect, and often heretical.

CHAPTER 1: TRANSITION TO THE HEBREW ROOTS MOVEMENT

Early Life in Christianity

As a child, I didn't have that much experience with the worldwide religion known as Christianity. My father was a Christian by profession, a member of the Lutheran church, but not by practice. He had not gone to church for several years prior to my birth. My mother on the other hand, was raised as a Catholic but was by my time an agnostic - one who wasn't even sure whether God existed or not, and who definitely did not attend church. My parents divorced at a young age, and after living with my father for nine months in Missouri, I returned to my home in Arizona to find my mother married to a man, my stepfather, who was an atheist.

As a younger child, the only exposure I had to Christianity was during the holidays: Christmas and Easter. At Christmas time, whenever I would go shopping with my parents, I would see pictures of the Nativity on posters or on the side of boxes which held decorations. Occasionally I'd stumble across a candle or a shrine which depicted Jesus, or Mary, or some other Christian figure. I'd hear talk about God, such as people saying "God bless you" or cursing using the name of God of Jesus Christ. For a few short years, around the age of 6 or 6, my mother made me pray before going to bed 'just in case'. The prayer mentioned angels but not God. My maternal grandmother, who remained a devout Catholic for most of her life, would occasionally mention God or Jesus or Mary.

So, by the age of 7 or 8, I was well aware of who Jesus was, especially through observation and listening to television. However, besides knowing that he was the Son of God and that he died on the cross, I was ignorant of who he was and what he did for mankind. The only time I had ever seen anything close to the Bible was a kid's version of the Bible one of my friends brought to school in 2nd grade. So, by no means was I raised in a "Christian" household.

This changed as I began to develop a closer relationship with my father. Soon after my brother and I had left Missouri to live with our mother again, my dad moved to Georgia, where he rented an apartment. As often as possible, our mother would make sure to get us on the phone with him so we could talk about how we were doing. Eventually, our father decided to move back to

Arizona, where he once again rented an appartment. However, we only got to see him for two weekends of a month, which meant that we still needed to talk to him over the phone during the weeks. I recall one conversation, which was an interview I did of him for a school project. I asked him a variety of questions, including "What religion are you?" to which he replied "Lutheran." I had no idea what that meant, so I inquired a bit more, and learned for the first time that there were different types or denominations of Christianity.

By Christmas 2010, the year my father had moved to Arizona, we spent Christmas eve and morning at his appartment. He told us of his plan a few days in advance - that we would go to church with him that Christmas eve. I had never gone to church before, so I didn't know what it was like. The only idea I had was what I had seen on television - nicely-dressed people sitting in pews, with crosses and altars and the like all around. The church we went to was called St. Peter's Lutheran Church, located in Mesa. When we pulled in, I asked my dad about who St. Peter was, because I had no idea. He told me that Peter was an apostle who held the keys to the kingdom of heaven, and left it at that.

Inside of the church were decorations such as banners hung down near the windows with stars on them and names of people from the Bible, such as David and Abraham. I didn't know who they were, so I again asked my father. During the service, the minister at this church explained exactly what Christmas is and why we celebrated it. Although the church was very traditional, there were still screens mounted high on the walls which displayed the Bible verses he read from. One of them was Isaiah 7:14, which uses the name of Immanuel. Once again, I was confused. This was the first time I got any direct exposure of something from the Bible, and although I had no understanding of half of what the minister said, it interested me. The only part I didn't like was singing, so I just mouthed the words when the time came to sing.

At first, I thought that this experience in church would be the only thing our dad would do to get us more interested in religion. However, on Christmas morning, as I opened up the presents placed under the Christmas tree, I found a pleasant surprise - my father had bought us a Bible. It was an NLT (New Living Translation) version which attempted to organize the stories and writings of the Bible in chronological order. My dad encouraged me to read it, saying that it would only take 15 minutes a day to get through it in a whole year. Because the 1-year reading plan started at the beginning of the year, I waited a week until I started, and on January 1st, 2011, I started reading the "Bible" for the first time, getting through the first few chapters of Genesis.

As a child of 8 years old, things which I didn't understand intrigued me, especially since there was so much to learn. It was a whole new world I was delving into. The book was over 1400 pages long. If I successfully finished it by the end of the year, it would be the longest book I had ever read. For the first few weeks, I did pretty good, reading through the whole book of Genesis, and then through the book of Job and a little bit through Exodus. However, by February, I had gotten to a point where I had just gotten bored, and in addition, school work and other hobbies (such as playing video games) distracted me from my reading. So, I stopped for a bit, and only picked my Bible up occasionally throughout the rest of the year. In addition to this, I would not pick up where I left off, but chose to turn to random places and read for a couple pages. No context, no background, nothing. I read several passages from Judges, Isaiah, and bits and pieces of the epistles of the New Testament. Sometimes I would just read Genesis again. In fact, in my first year of reading the Bible I probably went through the book of Genesis six or seven times.

Part of the reason why was because of the great stories told within Genesis. The entirety of the book took place long ago and far-away, telling of the creation, the flood, and the patriarchs. I enjoyed trying to sound out the Hebrew names which I had never seen before. Doing so greatly improved my skills in reading. On Easter of 2011, we again attended church with our Father, and this time, I got much more information about the crucifixion and resurrection of Jesus. However, with my short attention span and lack of background knowledge of the Gospels, I still didn't know why Jesus died or why he was resurrected, or even much about who Jesus was and why he came to this world. I just assumed that he was raised again because God loved him and wanted to raise him, 'just because.'

We continued to go to church every Christmas and Easter for several years. Eventually we changed churches because St. Peter's Lutheran was too far from my father's apartment. Christmas of 2012, for example, we stumbled into a non-denominational megachurch where a rock band played songs like "Angels We Have Heard on High", and in which the sermon only lasted a quarter of an hour. Both my brother and I hated contemporary services, as did our father, who promised us that we would only go to more traditional services from then on. The following Easter, we settled down at a church called Christ's Greenfield Lutheran Church. By then, I was much more comfortable with singing, but still neglected to pay attention the entire time. I just followed along as best as I could.

One thing which helped grow my love for the Bible, especially the earlier parts of the Bible such as the books of Genesis and Exodus, were films. First, around Easter of 2011, I watched the full 1956 movie "The Ten Commandments." It wasn't the first time I had heard of the movie, because my dad had watched it on television several times in the past while we visited him. Every year during Easter, the movie was replayed at the same time on the same channel, so I watched it. Then, in spring of 2013, a new miniseries, known simply as "The Bible", was aired on the History Channel. My dad informed me about it, knowing that I was more interested in the Bible than my brother and that history was growing to be my favorite subject. I sat down and watched every episode, every week as it aired.

What interested me about the series was that I got to see events recorded in the Bible which I had never actually read about. The first episode, about Noah, Abraham, and Moses, were all familiar to me. However, when it got to the stories of Joshua, Samson, Samuel, David, and the prophets, such as Daniel, I was amazed. Most of the stories were news to me, and they inspired me to learn more about the Bible. So, about this time, when I was in 5th grade and about 10 years old, I started to bring my Bible to school to read it more. I scanned through the first five books of Moses, and discovered something which scared me.

I had known about the ten commandments for some time now, but I had never actually read them. And in addition, I had never heard of the other commandments and statutes given by God in Exodus, Leviticus, Numbers, and Deuteronomy. Upon reading these words, I realized that I was not doing God's will - that there were a lot of commandments I was breaking. In fact, in 2013, I assumed that I would go to hell if I didn't change my life around soon, especially if I didn't go to church more often. After all, I only attended on Christmas and Easter. In my mind, that wasn't enough for serving God.

However, that never happened. In fact, what little church attendance we had I started to get away from, mostly because my dad started to develop health issues. I was heavily upset in the Christmas of 2014 when I learned that we weren't going to go to church on Christmas Eve that year. However, the following Easter and even the following Christmas, we attended once again. All the while, I grew in my own beliefs, developing and forming my own doctrine in my mind. Due to the nature of my exposure to religion, all I knew about Christianity was that Jesus was supposedly born on Christmas and that he died, was buried, and rose again on Easter, and that he did miracles of several sorts. I also had heard talk of "the Rapture" and "the Second Coming", which inspired me to read the Book of Revelation. That only scared me more.

By the age of 13, in early 2015, I strongly believed that I was wrong in God's eyes, and so I wanted to do anything to obey his commandments in the Bible. I greatly misinterpreted the Scriptures and Biblical prophecy, assuming that the 144,000 in Revelation were the only people going to heaven. If I were to make it, I needed to try my best and be as holy as possible. How to do that, since I couldn't learn from church due to our limited number of visits there, I took into my own hands, and intensely studied the books of Exodus and Leviticus, writing down the commandments over and over again, and putting them in my own words so that I could remember them better. I believed in a heavy works salvation, that if I broke what I was learning, I would end up in hell, and end up facing the plagues found in the book of Revelation.

All of that put frightening thoughts into my mind.

Obsession with Archaeology

The next phase of my interest in the Bible began around the age of 13, when I began to develop an increasing interest in ancient history and the study of archaeology. This came, once again, from my love of the Book of Genesis and its stories which seemed so distant. It felt like I was delving into a lost world of things which most people didn't know about. Because of my past of watching "The Bible" series on the History channel, as well as an interest in other historical documentaries I had watched in my 6th grade world history class, I decided to watch the History channel more and more.

One of the shows which I happened to stumble upon was called "Ancient Aliens", a series which revolved around an idea that human history has been guided by extraterrestrials, and that ancient structures such as the Pyramids of Giza and the ziggurats of Sumer were either built by aliens and with the help of alien technology. Although it seemed absurd to me, the concept was still interesting. Furthermore, as I began to watch the series in spring of 2015, I recognized that there was constant reference to ancient civilizations and sites I had never heard of.

Therefore, even though I didn't believe in the "Ancient Astronaut" theory, I still watched the series because it helped me learn about what the world was like long ago. Hearing stories about megalithic and monolothic structures from thousands of years ago led me back to the Bible. Around summer of 2015, I started to develop my own theories and ideas which were partially based on the Ancient Astronaut theory and what I knew about the book of Genesis. Instead of aliens, I believed that there were fallen angels who had guided the antediluvian world, and that such giant structures were created by the giants mentioned in Genesis 6.

Another endeavour which captivated my mind was figuring out the chronology of the Bible. Because I believed the Bible, which in my mind at this point was mostly the first five books of Moses, I did not accept the notion of an Old Earth. However, I was willing to compromise based on what I had heard about ancient civilizations, and thought that surely the earth was older than just 6000 or 7000 years. In a very stretched-out attempt at interpreting Scripture, I took the concept of the "Shemitta" years in Leviticus and applied them to the numbers given in Genesis for the ages of the patriarchs. This led me to the conclusion that the world was about 22,000 years old, and that the flood happened around 7000 BCE, and was only localized to the Middle East. Again, this theory came from Ancient Aliens, which had a whole episode on the deluge stories of the past.

However, I was never satisfied with an exact answer of how old the earth was. I kept adjusting the dates of this chronology I made up as I learned more, and eventually, by 2016, I had completely abandoned the Shemitta theory and accepted a literal interpretation of the Book of Genesis. However, I based my new dates on the Septuagint instead of the Bible which I had, and came to the conclusion that the world was about 7700 years old, and that the flood happened around 3200 BCE. This latter date made sense to me, because that's when civilization seemed to have begun. As I continued to research such topics as the creation of the world, antediluvian civilizations, I became more interested in the topic of the flood itself.

I recall that sometime in 2015, most likely over the summer, I stumbled upon a video; it was a documentary about 2 hours in length. The video was made by the Wyatt family, based on the findings of an amateur archaeologist named Ron Wyatt, who claimed to have found the petrified remains of Noah's Ark in Turkey. I watched the entire documentary, and was startled by the evidence I had seen. This increased my faith in the Bible. I then watched more videos by Ron Wyatt and his supporters, including those on the remains of Sodom and Gomorrah, and those claiming that he had found the Ark of the Covenant. For a few weeks, I kept coming back to these videos and rewatching them, attempting to grow in my knowledge so that I could defend the Bible and my faith even further.

However, for a while, I got away from that. Although I still considered myself a Christian with strong beliefs, in the fall of 2015, I focused on other projects, including trying to make short films and sketches on Youtube with my friends. I briefly discussed the Bible and Christianity with my friend, whose name was coincidentally 'Christian.' He was a Christian, and his dad happened to own one of the original copies of the KJV Bible in his house, which I thought was interesting.

I should not go on without mentioning something that I discovered in the NLT Bible which I owned in 2015. Even though departing temporarily from my obsession with archaeology, I still read my Bible and brought it to school occasionally. I remember one time reading the lists of Hebrew names out loud to my friend to prove to him that I could say them. However, as I read the book of Exodus again, I noticed something in the footnotes of verses 14-16. Although the text said "LORD", in the footnotes it said "Yahweh." I had never heard the term Yahweh before, so I decided to look it up and what it meant. I discovered that this was one of the ways in which people pronounced the Hebrew name of God. Not too long after, as I clicked around on websites and articles about Yahweh, I found the name of Yeshua, which, according to what I found, was the Hebrew name of Jesus.

By the end of 2015, I had started to call God by the name Yahweh, and Jesus by Yeshua, although none of my other beliefs changed. I still considered myself a "Lutheran", even though I didn't know what their main doctrines were, and I still believed myself to be in accordance with most fundamental

Christians. In 2016, we went to Christ Greenfield's Lutheran Church again on Easter. After the service we ate breakfast in a fellowship hall, where my father talked about getting my brother and I baptized with the priest. All the arrangements were set, and my dad planned on getting us baptized as soon as possible. However, as expected, we didn't return to the church anytime soon. In fact, that was the last time I ever went to a Lutheran church. I didn't know it yet, but in a few short months, my beliefs would shift in a completely different direction.

Michael Rood

For the preceding year and a half, I had assumed that I needed to improve my Christian life by starting to go to church and obey more of the commandments. In 2016, there were times when I occasionally picked up my Bible and read from the Law to figure out exactly what I was supposed to do. I started writing documents about how I should live my life as a Christian on my new desktop which I received for Christmas in 2015. For example, I wrote a document about a hypothetical religion which based all of its practices upon the commandments of Yahweh, and listed all of the precepts and rules practiced by this religion in a document on Google Docs which I made in April 2016.

In May and June, I once again listed down all of the laws and commandments I could possibly find in the Bible, and highlighted those things which I did not actively apply to my life, so that I would know which to follow and work on. After all, I needed to be perfect, in my mind. I tried to apply as many commandments as possible which I knew that ordinary Christians didn't do. For example, I started to keep the Sabbath day, or at least, what I thought was the Sabbath day. From midnight to midnight on Saturday, I would try to do as little work as possible; although, because I feared my mother and didn't want anybody to know about my changing beliefs, I gave in whenever my mother told me to do some type of chore or activity on a Saturday.

I also attempted to keep the dietary laws, never ordering any unclean meat at restaurants. However, I once again gave in whenever my mother gave me a ham sandwich or a sausage for dinner or lunch. I ate it anyway, although I really didn't want to. I also started to pray on my own, although I didn't often know what to say, so I simply called out to God or Yahweh and prayed for him to help me obey his laws. That was the extent of my experience in religion before a major turning point, which tied all of my shifting beliefs together.

This next part is quite strange, but the purpose of this chapter is to recount my story exactly as it happened. There may be some factors I have forgotten, but I know for sure that I already held many of the beliefs that those in the Hebrew Roots movement do by summer 2016. I was finally sucked in through music.

Music? Yes, music. Not Hebrew music, which may seem logical (or at least, not yet. I developed an affinity for that a bit later). Rather, it was a specific song which I heard the year before. The early part of 2016 was marked by a growing interest in music for me. I would often spend nights, up until 1 or 2 in the morning on Youtube, finding new songs on Youtube that I could listen to, which ranged across genres. I would place these songs in playlists on a secondary Youtube channel of mine so that I could listen to them when working on schoolwork or writing, a favorite hobby of mine. One of the songs which I added was a piano song called 'Regal Reign' by the Greek Christian pianist Dino Kartsonakis. I initially heard the song at the beginning of the Ron Wyatt documentary which I watched back in July 2015, and loved it.

So, one day, as I scanned through my music playlists in July 2016, I came across 'Regal Reign' once again, and listened to it. That prompted me to go back and find the Ron Wyatt documentary which I had watched. Upon finding it and watching other videos about Biblical archaeology, I noticed in my recommended playlist another video about Ron Wyatt, this time created by a different person. The man in the thumbnail looked peculiar. He had a long gray beard, wore a golden cap on his head, and had a maroon, gold, and white Middle-Eastern looking garment draped over him. I watched the video, which was recorded at a religious seminar organization called the Prophecy Club, and which featured a man named Michael Rood.

Rood stated that he knew Ron Wyatt personally and had personal confirmation that his findings were authentic. I soon found that Michael Rood made videos of a similar fashion, which looked at archaeological findings that confirmed the Bible. His series, which he had produced in the early 2000s, was called "A Rood Awakening! from Israel," the first episode of which dealt with the remains of Sodom and Gomorrah. I watched the entire 25 minute video, then several others, and left completely shocked. I'm not sure of the exact date in which this happened, but it was around July 14th-

16th, 2016.

Although I had no conversion experience that day, my interest in the Bible was renewed and flared tenfold past what it was before. Once again, I had a desire in my heart to defend the Bible and understand my beliefs better. An opportunity came for this only a few days later. As I scanned through videos to watch from Michael Rood once again, I discovered an interview he did with a man named Kent Hovind. Mr. Hovind talked about how he was a former teacher of science, and that he had engaged in numerous debates with evolutionists about creationism and the age of the earth. Immediately, I left Michael Rood for a bit to watch Kent Hovind's debates and seminars. There were quite a bit on Youtube.

From watching these, I learned a lot about creation science, and was now more confident in the young age of the Earth and in the fact that the theory of evolution was unscientific and verifiably false. Because I knew that many people did not believe what the Book of Genesis said about creation, I decided to take it into my hands to seek out people in the comment sections of these videos, as well as videos made by evolutionists and atheists, and expose their lies using the same information which Hovind constantly repeated in his lectures. In the short period of a week, I had managed to post comments on well over two dozen videos and started quite a few flame wars and arguments with non-Christians.

This mostly took place in the week leading up to my first day of high school, after which I knew that I would have to lay back a bit on the debates. However, I spent several hours behind my computer screen, typing as fast as I could and writing virtually whole essays attempting to refute what people said. Some videos did not even deal with the topics of evolution or creationism, but were general attacks against Christianity. At this point, I still considered myself a Christian and used generally Christian-like (although theologically poor) answers. Since most of my comments are now lost, it's difficult to tell whether I actually made good points, or if I, as a 14 year old, was using fallacious arguments. However, I knew that at the time, I believed I was right, and would do anything to get the person replying to me to admit that they were wrong.

I started reading to my brother these arguments and debates. He took so much of an interest in them, that he asked me to talk about it more and more.

I even began to play videos of Kent Hovind's. Within a couple weeks, by the end of July, I had convinced my brother that the theory of evolution was a fraud and that the earth was young. I had now made it my task to defend the Bible at all costs, believing what the books of Moses said with full confidence.

By the end of July, I began to return back to Michael Rood's videos and watch more of the series known as "A Rood Awakening! from Israel." In all of the videos, this strangely dressed man who looked like he came straight from some foreign nation (but who was actually completely American) spoke as if he was an authority on the subject, as if he knew what he was talking about. The purpose of each episode in this series was clearly to try to tear away beliefs which Michael Rood perceived as false, and to, as his ministry's website says, "Restore the Hebrew Roots of the Christian faith."

Past the archaeological videos, I found other episodes such as "The Name of the True God" and "Truth and Tradition" particularly interesting. In these videos, Rood constantly claimed that we have inherited the lies and traditions of men, and that many of the practices of Christians today are corrupted and come from paganism. Among these are calling the name of God 'The LORD' instead of Yahweh. Another one is the celebration of Christmas, which according to Michael Rood, had its origins in the worship of the Persian and Roman sun god 'Mithra.' Much of what he claimed involved stating that the corruption originated from the Roman emperor Constantine, who apparently invented Christianity and mixed in Roman festivals and sun god worship into the religion of the saints.

Torah Teachers

It didn't take long for me to find other people who taught similar things. This completely changed my perception of the world, but since I had already been going down this path, it wasn't difficult for me to accept it as true. Among these other teachers who emphasized the importance of the Torah, or the first five books of Moses, were people like Paul Nison, Zachary Bauer, Nehemia Gordon, and Arthur Bailey, all of which were associated with Michael Rood in some way.

After the week or two of focusing on creationism and evolution, the topics of obeying the Torah continuously came back to my mind. I already believed that my justification was through obedience to the laws of God, but now I felt certain of it. Michael Rood assured that this was the truth, and insisted that the Bible teaches thus, by using as many Scriptures as possible to tell his audience that the Christian idea that the law is done away with is contrary to Yeshua's teaching. He also repeatedly stated that most Christians take the Bible out of context and are unlearned in the Scriptures. Since I didn't have much knowledge of Christianity outside of the very little experience I had in the Lutheran church, I accepted this as fact.

Thus, my gullible 14-year old mind had become part of the Hebrew Roots movement.

Hebrew Traditions and Names

I started rejecting the 'pagan' holidays - firstly Christmas, which was the nearest in time. I swore to myself that I would never celebrate Christmas again because of its pagan origins in the worship of Horus, Mithra, and Sol Invictus. I swore also to never celebrate Easter again, because it apparently came from the worship of the Babylonian goddess Ishtar. Easter and Ishtar sounded similar, so it made sense to me. Instead, I turned my attention to the Feasts of the LORD, as Michael Rood called them - the seven festivals and holy days in the Torah which we are commanded to keep.

I also planned on abandoning the Gregorian calendar. Whenever I spoke about the days of the week, I tried to refer to them as "the first day of the week, second day, etc." instead of by other names, since they came from the names of pagan Germanic gods (for example, Thursday = Thor's Day). The same thing happened with the months. Instead of saying that the new month was August, named after Augustus Caesar, I considered it part of the 4th month of the Biblical calendar, leading into the fifth month.

As for my speech, I completely changed the way I referred to the people in the Bible. I began to write down the Hebrew names of people so that I could remember them and say it correctly. For example, I started to call John 'Yochanan', Isaac 'Yitzhak', Jacob 'Ya'aqov', and Simon Peter 'Shimon Kepha', among others. I thought that these other names were corruptions of their true names, and that somehow Greek inspired pronounciations were more pagan. In addition, as I watched newer videos by Michael Rood, I learned that the pronunciation of the sacred name was Yehovah and not Yahweh, and started to refer to God in that way.

I also began to take keeping the Sabbath much more seriously. Every Friday evening at sunset, if I would have to do a chore like taking care of and feeding our dogs, I'd ask my brother to do it for me. I explained to him why and what I was doing now, and read from the NLT Bible which I owned to show him that that's what I believe we're supposed to do as believers. He accepted, so that for the next month, whenever I had work to do on the Sabbath, my brother would do it for me. My mother didn't notice.

I also started to make a tradition of watching the weekly program called "Shabbat Night Live" on Michael Rood's channel, which aired every Friday evening at about 7 PM. I also went back to older recordings of the Shabbat Night Lives, where I learned about his interpretations of Bible prophecy and keeping the Torah. I started to learn Hebrew terms and phrases for things in the Bible, including calling the old Testament the "Tanakh" and the New Testament the "Brit Chadasha". I truly believed that in Hebrewizing my practices, I was getting closer to God, and thought of myself as higher than other Christians, as a person who knew secrets other people didn't know.

Presentation to Parents

My mother found out one night, on September 2nd, when she asked me to take care of the dogs. My brother, who was with me in the den (the room where we played video games and talked), jumped in and promised to do it for me. My mother asked why he was doing it for me, to which I replied "Because it's the Sabbath." Her initial response, coming from a Catholic background, was that Sunday was the Sabbath, but I explained to her that it wasn't, and that the Sabbath began on Friday evening and ended on Saturday evening.

This confused her, so I went down with my brother while he let the dogs outside and gave them water, and I explained to my mother what I believed concerning the Sabbath and obeying the Torah. She was completely dumbfounded and told me that she had no idea that I had an interest in religion or that I was a religious person. In addition, because she was raised as a Catholic, although non-practicing, she tried to debate my statements. I stood boldly on what I believed was the truth and told her about everything I had recently learned.

For nearly two hours, up until about midnight, my mother and I remained downstairs, as I explained what the Bible says about different subjects, or at least, what I thought it said. I told her that the name of God is Yehovah and that the name of Jesus is really Yahshua, and that the Trinity doctrine is false, and that the symbol of the cross came from paganism. She was too tired to understand most of what I was saying, so she offered to talk about it another time.

At that point, I came up with an idea: I would make a powerpoint on Google Slides, in which I would lay out all of my new beliefs and all of the things which I had 'learned' from Michael Rood, and present it to my family. I started work on this presentation the following week, on September 6th, and finished on September 9th, when I planned to present it that night, which was a Friday night leading into a Sabbath day. My mother told my dad about it, and also my mom's friend and his two daughters and one granddaughter, who joined us with my brother.

We connected my brother's laptop to a big screen television in my mother's bedroom, and I presented the powerpoint to the seven of them. It was awkward for me because I wasn't that great of a speaker, so I simply read off of what the screen said, but I tried not to falter in my words. Whenever somebody had a question, I tried to answer the question boldly as if I knew what I was talking about.

Instead of summarizing the contents of this powerpoint, I feel like it'll be important to simply copy all of the information on there into this book. Therefore, what you are about to see is what I wrote in early September 2016, and what I strongly held to be true in the early stages of my involvement in the Hebrew Roots movement. Some of it may seem useless and unimportant, but these were the things I knew, and things which I felt necessary to regurgitate. Keep in mind also that I no longer hold to many of the things written below (hence why I write this book). It's quite long, so just try to bear through it. Here it is:

> *"In this presentation, I will explain what my "religious beliefs" are. I will also explain why I believe these things as opposed to other religions, why I think other religions are incorrect, and why I'm no longer a Christian. There is no official name for my belief, I just say that it's The Truth. If I had to come up with a name for it, I would call it Torahism (because I try to follow the Torah) or Messianic Hebrewism (because I follow the*

ancient Hebrew religion with an addition to the belief in the Messiah). If you have any questions, please wait until the end of the slide to ask. I'll wait four or five seconds after reading the entire page. If you don't have questions, I'll be moving on.

There are many names associated with the Avrahamic God or gods, all of which are used by multiple religions around the world. All of these names are indistinct and meaningless titles.

- *God*
- *The Lord*
- *Jehovah*
- *Adonai*
- *Yahweh*

I, however, do not agree with any of these names and instead worship the one and only God, YHVH (pronounced YaHoVaH).

The name YHVH is the original name of The Almighty which was revealed to Moses on Mt. Horeb nearly 3400 years ago. The people of ancient Israel used this holy name to worship and pray. YHVH is an English form of the Hebrew letters Yod He Vav He (יהוה). In Proto-Sinaitic, (the writing system used by the Hebrews before 1200 BCE), the individual letters of YHVH mean "Behold Hand, Behold Nail." This is remarkable because of how it relates to the Messiah's crucifixion. The name YHVH also means "He exists," or "I AM WHAT I AM." The holy name of YHVH can be shortened to just "Yah." Yah is used in Hebrew names such as Yirmeyahu (Jeremiah), Yeshayahu (Isaiah), Eliyahu (Elijah), and the name of the Messiah himself (I'll talk about that later).

The Almighty has a name, which should be used instead of meaningless and indirect titles such as The Lord and God. The Lord should not be used as the name of God Almighty. In about 800 BCE, the prophet Eliyahu battled the Prophets of Ba'al on top of Mount Carmel in Israel. They called upon the name of their god, Baal, and nothing happened. Eliyahu called upon the name of YHVH, and fire from heaven came down and consumed his offering. Baal literally means "master, lord, or husband." Crying out to The Lord is the same thing as calling out to Baal. The modern English Bibles say that Elijah was a prophet of The Lord, which is completely incorrect. The name of YHVH is the name which was given to the people of Israel, that will be known across the entire world one day. Jehovah is another mistranslation because the Hebrew language does not contain a J sound. The titles "God Almighty" and "God Most High" are acceptable for use because they distinguish a difference between other gods and because they were titles that Avraham and his family used.

There is only one God, YHVH, but there are other spiritual beings who have higher power than us on Earth. The most famous and obvious is the Son of God, whose name is not Jesus, but Yahshua. Yahshua was born on Earth 2019 years ago to the virgin Miryam. Yahshua lived for 33 years before being arrested and then executed by crucifixion. Yahshua died as a sacrifice for our wrongdoings. The punishment was previously death and only death, but with the crucifixion of Yahshua, we are given a second chance. The death of a completely sinless person was what was needed to lift the weight of our sins off of us.

The name Jesus has existed for about 350 years and began with the invention of the J sound in the English language during the 1600s. The name used in the King James Bible was Iesus, which was translated from the Greek Iesous. The Messiah's original name was Yahshua, which not only has a meaning, but is an actual name that is supported by the rules of the Aramaic language. Every name in Hebrew has a meaning. Yahshua means "YHVH is our salvation," which perfectly describes the purpose of him. ' Christ comes from the Greek word christos, which means "anointed." Yahshua was a Hebrew, he did not have a last name, and especially not a Greek one. He was never called Christ in his lifetime. The first use of the title was in 64 CE when the Roman senator Tacitus wrote the book Annals. Yod he vav shin ayin (Yahshua) is not the same as Iota chi theta upsilon sigma (Ihthous or Iesous).

Yahshua is the Son of God, the Lamb, the Lord of Lords, King of Kings, and the Messiah. He lives in the Kingdom of God with his father YHVH as they prepare the way for the end times. Yahshua is the mediator between man and God Almighty. After the seven bowls of YHVH's wrath are poured upon the Earth, Yahshua will return to reign on Earth with the 144,000 faithful Israelites for one thousand years. Depicting Yahshua as a white man with long brown hair is inaccurate for the area where he lived and for other reasons as well. First, the Bible states that men having long hair is not acceptable, so why would the sinless Yahshua have long hair? Second, he lived in Israel two thousand years ago. The first depictions of a white Messiah were created in Rome after Constantine invented Christianity in 312 CE. It is more likely that he had short black hair, and darker skin similar to most people currently living in the Middle East. Here's the earliest known depiction of him, found in Egypt, vs. the modern depictions of him. (Picture is shown of a dark-skinned icon of Jesus)

When you think of an angel, you probably think of a woman with long blonde hair or a fat baby with wings. However, this is not what they are at all. Angels, called in Hebrew Malakh, are spiritual messengers and servants of YHVH and Yahshua who are responsible for the delivering of important messages and visions to prophets and other people. They normally do not have an appearance, but when they come down to Earth, they take the form of men. Angels also do not marry or reproduce because they cannot die. There are different ranks and types of malakh, who may have different responsibilities. There are the four living beings, cheruvim, sarafim, the ophanim, and the archangel. The four living beings are four servants of YHVH who surround His throne. One has the face of a man, the others have faces of an ox, an eagle, and a lion. They have six wings covered in eyes. The sarafim are servants of YHVH with six wings who shine with bright fire and who fly around His throne singing 'Holy, holy, holy is YHVH of hosts, the whole Earth is full of His glory.'

Cheruvim are servants of YHVH who have the faces of a human, ox, lion, and eagle, with four wings. Before the Great Flood, a cheruv was also appointed to guard the Garden of Eden. The Ophanim are eye-covered beryl wheels within another wheel which moves alongside the cheruvs, contain their spirit, and are thought to be the wheels for the Throne of YHVH. It is not clear what the archangel Micha'el is exactly, but he may be the leader of the messengers who works both in the Kingdom of God and on Earth. Below him are the rest of the angels who deliver messages and prophecies to humans on Earth.

Ha-Satan, which means "The Adversary," is a name referring to the one who has caused the suffering and pain of the humans, more commonly called just Satan. He is also referred to as Abaddon (Destroyer) in the Book of Revelation. It is unknown who or what Satan is exactly, but

biblical clues point towards him being a rebellious and evil angel,
probably a saraf. Nobody knows the actual name of The Adversary, but
instead we are given titles. There are multiple misconceptions about
Satan. His name is not Lucifer, a Latin word which means morning star.
He has also not fallen from the heavens yet, but will remain there until
after the fifth trumpet is blown during the end times. Satan the Accuser
has been given power and authority by taking the title deed of this planet
from Adam. Once Yahshua strips away the seven seals, the title deed will
be taken from Satan and he will be cast down to the Earth, where he will
reign for 3 ½ years before he is locked away for one thousand years.
After the one thousand years, he will be defeated at The Battle of
Armageddon, then thrown into the Lake of Fire where he will be tortured
for eternity. He is the enemy who has caused suffering and death in this
world.

Although we have other planets, stars, and other celestial bodies, they are
for signs, seasons, and light. The Earth is the lowest, where us humans
live. Anything beyond us is considered the heavens. The space we can see
are part of the heavens. Beyond that are the very edges of the universe.
Beyond the visible heavens is the Kingdom of God Almighty, where
YHVH reigns with His son, the Lord Yahshua, who are served by the
angels. It is a spiritual realm beyond the confinement of the metaphysical
concepts of space, time, and matter. The Kingdom of God was created by
YHVH, who has always existed and who always will exist. Time, space,
and matter do not bind him like they do to us. Space is not important to
YHVH because His kingdom is infinite and because He does not need it
to exist. He created space. Time is not important because He has always
lived and always will live. He created time. Matter is not important
because He is the Holy Spirit who does not need physical, weighted,
atomic matter. He created matter. He created everything.

In about 4000 BCE, YHVH created the heavens and the Earth. On the
first day He created light and possibly the angels as well. On the second
day He separated the Earth from the heavens by creating the sky. On the
third day, He created ground, fungi, soil, vegetation, and trees. On the
fourth day He created the sun, the stars, and the moon. On the fifth day,
He created aquatic animals. On the sixth day, He created every land
animal as well as the first human, Ha-Adam (Adam). He rested on the

seventh day. Soon after, He created our soul with the breath of life, then placed Adam in the Garden of Eden. It is unknown where Eden was located, but by the descriptions given in The Bible, it was probably somewhere in the modern day Persian Gulf or the nation of Saudi Arabia. He then created the first woman, Chavah (Eve).

After the creation of man and woman, Satan, in the form a serpent, tricked Chavah into eating the fruit from the Tree of Knowledge, bringing death and knowledge of sin into the world. In order to keep the humans from becoming immortal, they were forced to leave Eden and began to cultivate crops. Soon after, the son of Adam, Qayin, killed his brother Hebel out of jealousy. YHVH forced Qayin to leave his family and wonder in the Land of Nod, where he built the great city of Hanokh. Throughout the next couple hundred years, evil angels who were followers of Satan created children with women, who then gave birth to abominable giants called the Nephilim. With a combination of the Nephilim and the wickedness of the humans, YHVH decided to wipe out what he had created However, a righteous man named Noach was instructed to build a boat, then to take his family on board. The Great Flood began in about 2350 BCE, killing everybody except for Noach, his wife, his sons Shem, Ham, and Yapeth, and their wives.

About 150 years after the Great Flood, the descendants of Noach lived only in the Middle East, specifically in modern day Armenia, Iran, Iraq, and Saudi Arabia. Nimrod, the son of Cush, son of Ham, began the first world empire in the land of Shinar. He ordered the building of a great tower, which he thought could reach up to heaven. Nimrod declared himself a god and began the systems of pagan worship, economy, and sorceries which are still used today. YHVH didn't approve of this, so He confused the languages of the people. They began to spread out and begin other civilizations such as Egypt, Harappa, China, and Greece. However, Nimrod continued his empire with the people who could understand him and expanded it into other parts of Mesopotamia, where he built the cities Uruk, Akkad, Calneh, Nineveh, Rehoboth-ir, Kalah, and Resen. Nimrod was eventually killed and his body parts scattered across the land. His wife lied to the people of the empire that Nimrod had ascended into heaven and become the sun god. Afterwards, when she gave birth to her son Tammuz, she claimed that he was the reincarnated

Nimrod. This is where all of the similar legends in all of the ancient mythologies come from. Fortunately, Avram, son of Terach was called away from Babylon by YHVH to the land of Israel, making Avram the first Hebrew. Hebrew means "To cross over."

After the confusion of languages, Noach's sixteen grandsons and their offspring began to spread across the world to different locations.
- *Elam - Elamites, Harappans, Dravidians*
- *Ashur - Assyrians*
- *Arpakhshad - Arabs, Israelites, Edomites, Ammonites, Moabites, Sabaeans, Amalekites*
- *Lud - Lydians, Luwians*
- *Aram - Aramaeans*
- *Cush - Ethiopians, Sumerians*
- *Mitzrayim - Egyptians*
- *Put - Libyans, Bantus, Berbers*
- *Canaan - Phoenicians, Hittites, Babylonians, Canaanites*
- *Gomer - Cimmerians, Turks, Armenians, Chinese, Japanese, South-Asian, Aryans, Native-Americans, Polynesians, Cappadocians, Magyars*
- *Magog - Germanics, Ugro-Finns*
- *Madai - Persians, Medes, Bactrians*
- *Yavan - Greeks, Illyrians, Macedonians*
- *Tubal - Iberians, Basques, Sardinians, Maltese*
- *Meshech - Slavs*
- *Tiras - Celts, Trojans, Thracians, Romans, Etruscans*

Yaakov (or Yisrael) was the father of the Israelites, the group of people who YHVH has chosen to be his prophets and priests. His ten sons and two grandsons founded the tribes of Israel, who were trapped in Egypt for 430 years. A Levite named Moses who was adopted by Egyptian parents left Egypt and wandered into the land of Midian, where he lived the next forty years of his life with his wife Zipporah and his father-in-law Yethro. When he was on Mt. Sinai, YHVH spoke to Moses and told him to lead the Israelites out of Egypt. After Moses returned, YHVH sent a series of plagues across the land to show His power over the Egyptians. After the firstborn son of the Pharaoh died, the Israelites were allowed to leave Egypt. They walked through the Sinai Peninsula until they reached the shore of the Reed Sea. The Egyptians followed them, ready to attack.

YHVH protected the Israelites and split apart the Reed Sea so they could cross. The sea then closed on the following Egyptians, killing the entire army, including the Pharaoh. Moses then led the Israelites to Mt. Sinai, where they rested. YHVH gave His commandments to the people and gave them their duties. The Israelites wandered in the desert for the next forty years before entering the Canaan under the leadership of Yehoshua.

The Tanakh is an acronym for the three major books of the Old Testament - The Torah (Instructions), the Nevi'im (Prophets), and the Ketuvim (Writings). The Torah was written in about 1300 BCE by Moses on Mt. Sinai and contains the first five books of The Bible - Genesis, Exodus, Leviticus, Numbers, and Deuteronomy. The Nevi'im is a collection of books written first by Shmuel, then by the other prophets of YHVH, from about 1080 BCE to 500 BCE. It contains Yehoshua, Judges, Shmuel, Kings, Yeshayahu, Yirmeyahu, Yezekiel, Hoshea, Yo'el, Amos, Ovadyah, Yonah, Mikhah, Nachum, Chabaquq, Tzefanyah, Haggai, Zekaryah, and Malakhi. The Ketuvim was written from about 900 BCE to 200 BCE and contains the books of Psalms, Proverbs, Iyov, Ruth, Lamentations, Ecclesiastes, Esther, Daniyyel, Ezra, Nehemyah, and Chronicles.

Israel became a kingdom in 1050 BCE with the reign of King Shaul and later King Da'ud (David). In about 930 BCE, Israel split into two kingdoms: Yehudah in the south, made up of the tribes of Yehudah and Binyamin, and Israel in the north. Because of the large amount of sin and unfaithfulness to YHVH in Israel, it was destroyed and the people of the nation were exiled by the Assyrians in 730 BCE. Yehudah, however, survived many empires. The first which took over the land of Israel was the Neo-Babylonian Empire, which exiled the people to their land in 608 BCE. After 70 years of captivity, the Persian king Cyrus defeated the Neo-Babylonian empire and allowed the Jews to return home. The Persians later conquered their territory and it became a state in their empire. Later, the Macedonian Empire led by Alexander the Great took the land in 332 BCE. The Yehudites gained independence in 140 BCE and founded the Hasmonean kingdom. The Romans captured the nation and made it a province in their empire in 63 BCE.

In about 3 BCE, a virgin woman named Miryam was given a vision by the angel Gavriel, who told her that she would conceive a child, who would be called Yahshua. At about the age of 30, Yahshua began to teach people all over Israel of the Torah and why the Pharisee's teachings are wrong. He performed miracles, including walking on water, turning water into wine, healing a blind man, and even raising Lazarus from the dead. In about 30 CE, he was betrayed by his disciple Judas Iscariot. Yahshua was captured by the Roman army, then taken to Yerushalayim to be crucified. Yahshua passed away on the cross, but rose three days and three nights later. Miryam found the tomb of Yahshua empty on the morning of the first day. Soon after, hundred of Yahshua's disciples saw him as he had risen from the dead. After giving his final words, Yahshua ascended into heavens.

I believe the end of the current Earth will happen as it's explained in the prophecies of Yezekiel, Daniyyel, Yeshayahu, Zekaryah, and Revelation. After the war chariots were released from the brass mountains, the world began to turn in an irreversible direction that will lead to thermonuclear war. The Messiah is currently breaking the seven seals. The first four have caused a large amount of conquest, war, famine, and death around the world. The fifth, which is probably where we are at right now, is the beginning of the end. The sixth seal will be the beginning of World War III, following the Pope proclaiming himself as God and uniting the Avrahamic religions under one world power. The seventh seal will be the beginning of the blowing of seven trumpets. The first four trumpets is the devastation of the nuclear war. The fifth trumpet is the beginning of Abaddon's reign on Earth, when the New World Order (Islam) will torture mankind as they try to rebuild society and to mimic the actions of Nimrod thousands of years ago. The 200 million man army of the NWO will kill the people of the Earth and cause extreme pain. Then the seventh trumpet will be blown, when Yahshua will return to Earth and guard the 144,000 innocent people from the tribes of Israel. The seven bowls of YHVH's great wrath will be poured upon the Earth, destroying the Whore of Babylon and the New Babylonian Empire. Yahshua will then lock up Satan for one thousand years while reigning on Earth. The survivors of YHVH's wrath will then form the nations of Gog and Magog, who will join Ha-Satan in the final battle in Israel. Ha-Satan will be defeated, and the final judgement will take place.

When we die, nothing special happens at all. Our body dies and our soul dies. We are asleep, or unconscious until the resurrection. When the Messiah returns, he will raise us from the dead by reuniting our soul with our body. Those who keep the commandments of YHVH and the faith of Yahshua will never die in spirit. If we do what we're told to do, then our spirit will remain, allowing our souls and bodies to be pure when entering the Kingdom of God. Those who are faithful to Yahshua, who do not accept the Mark of the Beast, who proclaim the word of YHVH, and who do not give in to Babylon will rise when the Messiah returns. After his one thousand year reign, everybody else will be resurrected and judged according to their actions.

If you are good and righteous in the sight of YHVH, you will be happy with what will happen next. The old earth and the old Kingdom of God will disappear, and YHVH will create a new one, a better one, without suffering, pain, death, or evil. The city of New Yerushalayim will come down from the Kingdom of God upon the new earth. The people who are saved will live in the Holy City with YHVH forever. They will live with Him, and He will make sure you are joyful and happy. The city wall will be very large, being 216 feet thick, with with a length and width of the city being 1400 miles. There are twelve gates to the city (three on each side), each guarded by twelve angels and named the names of the Israelite tribes. There are twelve foundation stones named after the apostles of Yahshua, made of jasper, sapphire, agate, emerald, onyx, carnelian, chrysolite, beryl, topaz, chrysoprase, jacinth, and amethyst. The gates are made of pearls and the city itself is made of pure gold. A great river will flow from the Throne of YHVH down into the city, and on each side will be a Tree of Life. People will finally see the face of YHVH. There is no sun, because YHVH gives light and warmth to the people of the city. There is no night or day, just eternity. If you follow YHVH's commandments, this is where you will be forever. If you think 120 years is a long time, imagine 120 billion years in a place hundreds of times better than Eden and millions of times better than Scotland!

Unfortunately, if you do not do what you're supposed to do, then you'll be apart of what's called the second death. If you stand before YHVH's throne and you are not found in the Book of Life, you will be thrown into a fiery magmatic lake of burning sulfur, where your body, soul, and spirit will be destroyed permanently.

The most important of YHVH's commandments are the first ten with an explanation. Do not have any other gods before YHVH. This means that you should only worship and pray to YHVH, and have no other gods in His face. Do not make any graven image or idol of anything on the earth, in the sea, or in the heavens above. This means you cannot make a statue of anything and call it your god, goddess, or idol. Do not use the name of God Almighty in vain. This means that you cannot let the name of YHVH become worthless by not using it or blaspheming it. Keep the Sabbath day holy and remember it. Do not do any work on the Sabbath. This means that you cannot do any work on the seventh day of the week, because it is the day when YHVH rested as well. Honor your father and mother. This means you cannot curse your parents, hit them, become rebellious, or hate them Do not murder. This means you cannot kill somebody unless YHVH allows it. Do not steal. This means you cannot take things that do not belong to you. Do not commit adultery. This means you can only have sexual intercourse with your spouse if they are the opposite gender of you and are a human being. Do not falsely testify against your neighbor. This means you cannot lie about somebody's actions. Do not covet your neighbor's possessions. This means you cannot look with greed towards something somebody else has, whether it's their house, car, clothing, spouse, pet, etc.

There are other commandments in the Torah which are important to follow. These include:

- *Do not kidnap people.*
- *You should accept equal punishment for what you have done to another. Eye for an eye, tooth for a tooth.*
- *Do not practice witchcraft. Witchcraft is the act of doing things and practices which go against YHVH, and saying you are doing it for God Almighty.*
- *Do not practice sorcery. Sorcery is doing, participating in, or taking anything that is unnatural. Drugs, occult, fortune-telling, and Babylonian medicine are examples of sorcery.*
- *Do not drink alcohol.*
- *Do not exploit widows, orphans, or people with disabilities.*
- *Do not practice usury.*
- *Do not eat animals that have been torn up by wild animals.*
- *Return borrowed items.*

- *Do not lie, gossip, or pass along rumors.*
- *Don't sentence an innocent person to death.*
- *Do not make bribes.*
- *Do not stand by if your neighbor's life is in danger.*
- *Do not eat or touch the carcass of animals who do not have both completely split hooves and who chew cud (pigs, camels, hyrax). Do not eat aquatic animals without both fins and scales (shrimp, crab, lobster). Do not eat flying animals (owls, bats, ravens). Do not eat winged insects. Do not eat any small animals which move across the ground or who have paws (lizards, rodents, dogs, cats).*
- *Do not drink blood or eat animal fat.*
- *Do not cheat or deceive people.*
- *Do not hold hate in your heart.*
- *Do not wear clothing made of both linen and wool.*
- *Do not mark your skin with tattoos.*
- *Do not trim your sideburns or beard.*
- *Respect your elders.*

I see that there are four main goals in life which should be accomplished to some extent by fulfilling your duty to the Earth and YHVH. To become a Hebrew, or "cross over," out of Babylon and back to the original way of life which is pure, To try and turn other people towards being a Hebrew, To teach the Torah and the Gospels accurately, To live a long and enjoyable life.

mNow I'm to the part where I explain why I've changed my religious beliefs away from the false doctrines of the Christian church. The Christian Church that exists today follows multiple practices and beliefs which began in the Catholic Church and spread to Protestantism and Orthodox Christianity. These practices, symbols, and doctrines include:

- *Saying the name of God Almighty is The Lord. It is not The Lord. The name of God is YHVH. Violation of the 3rd commandment.*
- *Saying the name of the Messiah is Jesus Christ. It is not Jesus Christ. The name of the Messiah is Yahshua.*
- *Trinity Doctrine. Originate in Babylon as the solar trinity of Nimrod (Father), Ishtar (Holy Spirit), and Tammuz (Son). Violation of the 1st commandment.*
- *Mary as the Queen of Heaven. Based off of the pagan worship of the mother of Tammuz, called Isis, Venus, Hera, Ishtar, Astarte,*

31

Eostre, Frigg, and Devaki. Violation of the 1st commandment.

- _The Eucharist._ This is a practice of sorcery, trying to turn wine and bread into the flesh and blood of their god. Violation of the sorcery commandment.
- _Baptism._ This is a pagan practice from Greece. Yahshua was not baptized by John the Baptist, he was mikvehed by Yochanan the Immerser. Violation of the heathen worship commandment.
- _Authority of the Pope._ The Bible says nothing of a pope. This practice was continued from the Roman tradition of Pontifex Maximus, the highest priest in ancient Rome. Violation of the 1st commandment.
- _Belief that priests can forgive sins and guarantee eternal life._ Only Yahshua can forgive. Violation of Yahshua's commandments.
- Gold monstrance, pine cone, all-seeing eye, statues of saints, Jesus, and Mary. Violation of 2nd commandment
- _Sunday as the day of rest and worship._ The Sabbath day is the seventh day, on from Friday night to Saturday night, not the day of sun worship continued from the Mithraic cult. Violation of 4th commandment.

The celebration of Christmas is a pagan practice which originated in Babylon to celebrate the birth of baby Tammuz on December 25th, not Yahshua. Yahshua was born some time during the fall, and has nothing to do with the story of Christmas. The list of pagan gods who were recorded as being born on December 25th, or after the winter solstice include: Horus, Osiris, Attis, Mithra, Heracles, Dionysus, Tammuz, Adonis, Shamash, Molech, Chemosh, Jupiter, Saturn, Zeus, Cronus, Krishna, Balder, Hermes, Ra, and Thor. The practice of putting up a Christmas tree began in Babylon and spread to Scandinavia, Egypt, and Persia. The way we do it now is based on the Norse festival of Yule, when they would put up an evergreen tree to honor their sun god Balder. A similar practice was done in Egypt, where they hung up trees upon walls to honor Ra (Nimrod), who was killed and cut up into pieces. They would then hang up gold and silver balls as an offering because they believed that his own were eaten by crocodiles and were not part of the reincarnated Horus. Persians did the same thing to honor Mithra. The Roman festival of Saturnalia, which is how the Roman Catholic church came up with the idea of Christmas, was a festival that honored Saturn *and Sol Invictus Mithra. An even more horrible practice is the concept of Santa Claus. The general gift-giving idea of Santa Claus came from St. Nicholas, who had nothing to do with the Messiah, but was instead an important man during the festival of Saturnalia. Santa Claus was modified a bit to resemble the ancient son of Nimrod, Tammuz, who wore the Phrygian cap that we see depictions of him wear today. Putting your child in the lap of Santa is a less violent but still very terrible practice mimicking how the ancient Canaanites and Babylonians would give their children to a large bearded man wearing a Phrygian cap sitting on his throne as a sacrifice to Tammuz, the baby who was born on December 25th and worshipped as the son of the Queen of Heaven and the sun god Nimrod. When you celebrate Christmas you're also celebrating Yule, Saturnalia, and the Egyptian, Babylonian, Hindu, Greek, Celtic, Canaanite, Turkic, and Slavic festivals worshipping the sun god.*

Easter and Lent are also pagan practices associated with Tammuz and Ishtar. The 40 days before Easter come from the Babylonian Weeping for Tammuz, a time when pagans would observe 40 days, one day for each day of Tammuz's life, in order to honor him after he was killed by a boar in a hunting accident. After the forty days were over, the people would celebrate Easter, named after Tammuz's mother Ishtar. It was on this day that she was said to return from heaven in a giant egg, which landed in the Euphrates River. Ishtar then exited the egg and turned a bird into an egg laying rabbit. They would celebrate this event by worshipping the sun, on Sunday (it's called that for a reason), and then have a feast eating the flesh of a wild boar. For further celebration of this event, the Babylonians would sacrifice their one month old babies to Tammuz, then dye an egg with the blood of their dead children. The name Easter has been seen in many ancient cultures, and they all are the origins of this event. Ishtar, Astarte, Astaroth, Eostre, Isis, etc. It was also celebrated in Scandinavia and Gaul as Ostara.

There are many pagan symbols in the Christian church. These include: the cross, the pine cone, halo, mitred hat, and the solar wheel. The symbol of the cross has nothing to do with the Messiah, but is instead a Babylonian symbol representing the diffraction of sunlight and the sun god. Yahshua was crucified on a cross because the Romans saw it as a sacrifice to Mithra. It was also used in Celtic religion and Egyptian religion, in the form of the ankh. The symbol of the pine cone was used by the Romans, Assyrians, and Egyptians to represent purification and the egg of Ishtar. The halo is the symbol of the sun behind the head of ancient pagan gods. It represented the sun god in nearly every ancient culture and is still used by the Catholics in depictions of the Messiah. The mitred hat is the hat worn by the Pope, which is based off the hats worn by Babylonian priest of the fish god Dagon, trying to imitate the fish on his head with a ridiculous hat. The solar wheel is found on Catholic clothing and in the center of the Vatican. It was also used by many ancient cultures to represent the sun god and even is still used in Buddhism today.

The calendar given in the Bible is very different from the Gregorian calendar invented by Pope Gregory XIII. The current year is 6016, 6016 years after creation. Months are 29-30 days long and begin the day after a new moon. A week is seven days long, the same as ours, but each day is just called "1st day, 2nd day, 3rd day...... A day is from night to night, sunset to sunset. This makes more sense than 6 hours of night, 12 hours of day, then 6 more hours of night. September 8th, 2016 on the Gregorian calendar is 06 - 05 - 6016 on the Hebrew or original calendar.

{There is a section here which deals with archaeology and scientific facts in the Bible which I choose to omit because of its lengthiness, and because it doesn't illustrate the point of what I believed}

To summarize my beliefs, I will say this: I believe and worship the one and only god, YHVH, Who created everything and Who is greater than anything else. I have faith that Yahshua will return to destroy suffering, pain, evil, sin, and sadness. I wish to follow all of the commandments of YHVH because it is the only way to live a great and wonderful life free of suffering. I believe what The Bible says and have no doubt in my mind that listening to the words of YHVH and Yahshua will give eternal reward. I hope to turn other people back to faithfulness of YHVH and away from the tyranny of Babylon. Amen."

If you read through all of that, congratulations. I apologize if you cringed, but know that you're not alone. I was deep within the Hebrew Roots movement at this point. I read this entire thing to my parents, and received very few questions, except for on minor details. By the end of this presentation to my

34

parents, I think I only created more confusion. Half of the people in the room didn't pay attention - it was mostly my mother and father who cared.

Afterwards, my father congratulated at me for having a belief. He told me directly that he didn't agree with a lot of what I said, but he was fine with the fact that I no longer considered myself a Lutheran, and promised he would support me. In addition, I also asked my mother if I could buy a Hebrew Roots bible, and she told me that I could if I used my own debit card. The following night, I planned on finding a Bible which used the sacred name.

CHAPTER 2: LIFE IN THE HEBREW ROOTS MOVEMENT

Daily Life and Activities

The Hebrew Roots movement definitely had an impact on my entire way of life. I was not the same person I was several months before, prior to discovering the doctrines of Michael Rood and other Torah teachers. After all, the Hebrew Roots movement places an emphasis on Hebrew culture - and that became my 'culture.' I started learning basic Hebrew words and phrases, including Hebrew prayers and blessings. One of these was the Aaronic Priestly Blessing in the book of Deuteronomy. Transliterated:

> *"Yevarekekha Yehovah veyishmerekha yahir Yehovah panav elekha vekunekah, yissa Yehovah panav elekha veyasim lekha shalom."*

Another one which I learned was the blessing over bread and wine, which I wouldn't actually use until the time of Passover the following year, but which I constantly repeated under my breath so that I could learn them. They are, transliterated:

> *"Baruch ata Yehovah eloheinu melekh ha'olam, ha'motzi lechem min ha'aretz."*

> *"Baruch ata Yehovah eloheinu melekh ha'olam, boreh peri ha'gaffen."*

These mean, "Blessed are you, Yehovah our God, king of the world, who brings forth bread from the earth" and "Blessed are you, Yehovah our God, king of the world, who creates the fruit of the vine." Among these blessings I would also say Hebrew prayers constantly, such as the Shema prayer found in Deuteronomy 6:4 -

> *"Shema Yisra'el, Yehovah eloheinu, Yehovah echad."*

In addition, as already stated in the previous chapter, I would use terms found in the Bible, but use Hebrew words for them instead. Just to go through a few: Instead of God, I said *Elohim.* Instead of Lord, I said *Adonai* or simply used the name *Yehovah.* Instead of Old Testament, I said *Tanakh.* Instead of law, I said *torah.* Instead of prophet, I said *nevi'im.* Instead of New Testament, I said *Brit Chadasha.* Instead of baptism, I said *mikveh.* Instead of Satan, I said *hasatan.* Instead of angel, I said messenger or *malakh.* Whenever I talked about eating restrictions, I talked about *kosher.*

I started using Hebrew names for days as well, instead of just counting the numbers of days. In this form, the Hebrew days of the weeks were *Yom rishon, Yom sheni, Yom shlishi, Yom rivi'i, Yom chamishi, Yom shishi, and Yom shabbat.* I was so insistent upon calling the days these names that whenever my brother mentioned the Gregorian days, I'd correct him. He used to make fun of me for it, and even purposefully pronounce the words wrong just to get on my nerves. In addition, whenever I used a word with the Hebrew letter *chet* (ח), which makes a 'kh' sound like in the word loch, he would mock me and exaggerate the harshness of the sound.

My focus on the Hebrew calendar grew sharper after I ordered a physical calendar off of Michael Rood's website. At about the same time, I decided to order a multitude of other books. The Bible I chose was from the ISR (Institute of Scriptural Research), a version translated from the Textus Receptus and which doesn't impose any pronunciation of the holy name of YHVH, but which instead writes both that and the name of Yeshua in Hebrew. In addition, it uses the Hebrew names for books, people, and places, so it was the perfect Bible for my Hebrew Roots background.

Other books which I bought at about the same time so that I could continue my studies included a book by a man named Todd Bennett, which was a lexicon of ancient Hebrew. The "Hebrew" which he wrote about in the book was not that which the Bible was written in, but instead used a script called Proto-Sinaitic which hasn't been used since the 12th century BCE. Another book was called "Patterns of Evidence: Exodus" by Tim Mahoney, which aimed to prove using archaeological evidence that the Exodus from Egypt was a historical event. There was also a book I purchased written by Michael Rood himself, called "The Mystery of Iniquity", which dealt with end times prophecy and the Great Tribulation. Upon reading this book, I became convinced that the idea of a pre-Tribulation rapture, which is something that I had previously believed just because of media exposure, was false.

I also bought several books on refuting evolution, including one which was way too complicated for my 14-year old brain to understand, which had complex scientific terminology and charts to posit a theory about the origin of the elements during the Genesis creation. The main book which I enjoyed, however, was the 1000-page "Evolution Handbook", which I often took with my new ISR Bible to school, and intentionally read it in my biology class.

School was a place where I grew angry, because of my new perception of the world. All the children I saw around me I assumed were heathens who had no knowledge of the Torah and the 'true religion' of YHVH. Whenever I finished my schoolwork, I would pull out my ISR Bible and read it in class. Some of my friends asked about it and were entirely confused when I started uttering Hebrew names and talking about 'Yeshua.' Most of them weren't Christians anyway, so that added to the confusion.

One of the days in late September 2016 I decided to open up to my friends about what I believed. I had recently found a name for my beliefs and what to call myself: Netzar. Or at least, that's what Michael Rood said. The idea goes that *netzar* is a Hebrew word which means "root", and we use it because it's related to the word used in the Old Testament to describe Jesus as the branch out of the root of Yishai (Jesse). In addition, the town of Nazareth apparently derived its name from such a word, and thus also the term Nazarene, which according to Acts 11:26, was a name for the early believers. I told two particular friends of mine (Timothy and Ryan) about this and explained all of my doctrines; repeating the same things about Yehovah and Yeshua and the Trinity doctrine, and about how Christian symbols and festivals originated in paganism. I got into a short argument with Ryan, who was a Mormon, about Christmas and the Bible, but I didn't know enough about his own beliefs to refute anything he said. I just insisted that I was right.

That was the attitude which I constantly had, the same attitude which Michael Rood and the other Torah teachers I watched had: the confidence that I was returning to the original beliefs of the followers of Christ, and that I was holier than those who called themselves Christians because of my obedience to the Torah. Thus, I started getting abundantly hostile toward Christianity. In my mind, all Christians were the same, all of it had originated from Constantine and the Roman church. That seemed to be my continual displeasure: that Constantine had brought the practices of Babylon which originated with Nimrod into true Christianity. These two names were stuck in my mind as the enemies of mankind.

I planned on writing about the Hebrew Roots movement myself. I loved writing, a hobby which especially rose in my life early in 2016 due to a growing obsession I had with literature. However, I decided to use my interest in writing, and my ability to stay focused, put my thoughts on a page, and to type fast to write books defending my new faith, similar to the books which I began to read in September. I started work on these books in October, and for the most part, all I did was outline them and write the first chapter. I wrote a whole chapter called "What is God? Who is God?" In this chapter, I explained that God is not a corporeal being which sits upon the clouds, but something which transcends our reality and our mind. I then attempted to prove God's existence through logic, using the basic arguments of Thomas Aquinas and other medieval philosophers.

In October were the "Feasts of the LORD" which appear in Leviticus 23, which I attempted to follow. However, since I didn't have a shophar for Yom Teruah (the Day of Trumpets), I could not keep this holy day, neither could I keep Sukkot because I did not have a booth. The only day which I kept according to the Biblical commandment was Yom Kippur, in which I did no work and fasted the whole day. I tried to deny myself even more, but my mother took my brother and I to see a movie, despite my attempts at resisting things which would be 'fun.'

And so went the first three months or so of being in the Hebrew Roots movement. My understanding and outlook of the world was that the world had forsaken the commandments of Almighty God. I believed that the only ones who truly understood the truth were me and the other Hebrew Roots people, such as Michael Rood, Zachary Bauer, Paul Nison, and the like. As a result of this, I separated myself from many previous friends and even just people in general. Often I would spend time alone at school reading my new Bible or contemplating about the doctrines I had learned, or writing out charts relating information about these things. My perception of a broken world which turned from God grew in the next few months as I began to learn some new things.

Conspiracies of Catholicism

Since beginning to watch Michael Rood, I had heard the claim that it was the fault of the Roman Catholic Church that "Churchianity" was corrupted with the doctrines of paganism. According to the narrative, which came from a 19th century minister named Alexander Hislop, there is an ancient legend of Nimrod, the ruler mentioned in Genesis 10 and 11 as being the founder of Babylon. After Nimrod established a world empire, he was killed, and his wife Semiramis exalted him and his son, Tammuz, as a god. This is supposedly where all pagan religions came from. The Babylonish practices filtered into

Rome, and then into Christianity through Constantine the Great. Constantine falsely converted to Christianity in 312 CE after allegedly seeing a vision of the cross in the sky, which Rood claims to have been from the difraction of sunlight, and thus subsequently brought sun worship into Christianity. This is where the symbol of the cross, the practice of going to church on Sunday, and the celebration of Christmas supposedly came from.

It sounded right, and it was repeated by virtually every person in the Hebrew Roots movement. At the time, I had no idea that these ideas had no basis in history but actually came mainly from the speculations of Alexander Hislop, who wrote at a time before much Mesopotamian archaeological excavation had taken place. However, Catholicism was still the biggest enemy of mankind, in my opinion. The other churches, particularly in Protestantism, although not as bad, still held on to some of Rome's lies, and therefore were not right with God either.

My hostility to Catholicism in particular rose on November 22nd. I remember this date because it was the anniversary of president John F. Kennedy's assassination, and after school, I was recommended a video on Youtube talking about conspiracy theories of JFK's death. This led me to watch a multitude of other videos on conspiracy theories, mostly well-known ones, such as the Vietnam War, 9/11, the concept of a 'new world order', etc. However, what particularly caught my eye were some videos I found on the Vatican and their riches, as well as videos about Catholic secret societies such as Opus Dei. From that I learned about the Society of Jesus, also known as the Jesuit Order, and decided to do more research.

I was amazed to find such a vast load of knowledge concerning the influence of the Jesuits upon modern history. One video I watched in particular was a three-hour documentary explaining that the rise of the New World Order has been brought about through the work of the Roman Catholics and the Jesuits, and that the Church is actually the whore of Babylon mentioned in the book of Revelation. This led me into a phase where I watched a myriad of videos by Seventh-Day Adventists (who are similar in beliefs to the Hebrew Roots in some respects), attempting to prove that the Pope is the Antichrist and the city of Rome is the Beast.

By the end of 2016, my new goal was not only to expose the Roman Catholics for changing the doctrines of the Bible, but also for subverting the entire world. I was convinced that the future Antichrist would be a Pope. Previously, I assumed that Islam was going to bring about the end times, but I heard a new theory, which came from a former Jesuit priest named Alberto Rivera, that Islam originated from the influence of the Roman Catholic Church in Arabia. The next step in getting deep into this theory was discovering a new Youtube channel, called "Southern Israelite."

The so-called Southern Israelite, named Drake Shelton, did not consider himself part of the Hebrew Roots because of minor differences in doctrines, but for the most part, I agreed with his beliefs. He rejected the Trinity, believed in soul-sleep, called God by the name Yahuwah and Jesus as Yeshua, while also emphasizing keeping the commandments, particularly the Sabbath day. There were some other doctrines which I found about later, but at this point in late 2016, what particularly interested me was his videos on the Jesuits. He seemed to have the largest treasure-trove of information on them, having made several hour-long videos talking about their influence on our culture.

At that point, I believed I needed to speak up. Not enough people were being reached.

"Biblical" Teachings on Youtube

I had a Youtube channel, called Mr. Tall23, which I hadn't used since the time in which I joined the Hebrew Roots movement, both because I didn't see any reason to continue to make my sketches and short films from before, but also because school distracted me from making videos. However, when we went on break in the winter, I decided to figure out what to do for my channel. I had previously considered making videos on observing the Torah, but the only time I ever got around to recording, I had decided to upload it on a new channel which quickly failed, as it only had about 3 subscribers, and my one video barely attracted 3 views in a month's time.

However, since Christmas was coming up, I had an idea of what to do. I did some brief research on Wikipedia and wrote it down on a document, then turned on the webcam on my computer and filmed a video. This was on December 22nd, 2016, when I uploaded a video called "Don't Celebrate Christmas Anymore." I never expected opposition, just people to respond to the truth and turn away from celebrating the supposedly pagan holiday.

However, I didn't get many views, and of those who did find the video, they disliked or left nasty comments.

I didn't stop, however. This was the beginning of a new project to make as many videos as possible on the subject of observing the Torah and returning to the "Hebrew Roots" of the Christian faith. After this, I recorded my own observance of Hanukkah, recording a video each day of lighting the candles on the menorah my mother had bought for me. This was followed by a video summarizing my beliefs and how I came to be a "Netzar."

I lost some followers at this point, but I didn't mind. I made so many videos at that time that for nearly two weeks straight in January there was a new upload every day on my channel. In particular, I made a new series called "The Problems with Christianity." There were eleven total episodes of this series before I had to stop it for running out of ideas. The topics and titles of these videos in order are: The name of Elohim, The name of the Messiah, the Trinity doctrine (and how it's false), Observing the Torah, the cross, heaven and hell, baptism, the celebration of pagan holidays, the pagan calendar, the pre-tribulation rapture, and Catholic sacraments.

A Summary of the Doctrines and Supposed Support for Them

Although I've already shared with you the powerpoint I shared with my parents, I suppose it necessary to explain in more complete detail that which I held to be true during this time of my life, especially as my understanding of these teachings developed around the turn of the year. Although during this whole period, the general ideas and concepts remained the same, I began to understand what I believed much more as time went on, explain it in different ways, and twist scriptures to support them (I say twist now, but at the time, I thought I was using them right). Keep in mind that the majority of what I'm about to say is simply factually inaccurate and contrary to the truths laid out in the Word of God - something I will prove in chapter 4 of this book.

The most important thing to me during my time in the Hebrew Roots movement was the Sacred Name. I believed that a believer in the Messiah should refer to him by his Hebrew name and to God by his name as revealed to Moses in Exodus 3. At first, I believed the sacred name to be Yahweh; that changed briefly to Yehovah, and by October 2016, I began to say Yahuwah. I thought that anybody not using this name was under the curse of God, and that anybody not praying using some form of the divine name was praying to a false God.

The first line of reasoning I had was that YHVH (in Hebrew, the letters yod hei vav hei) appeared 6800 times in the Old Testament. I thought, "surely there must be a reason for this." The word definitely does not mean LORD as it is translated into English in most Bibles, which seemed to me that the translators were hiding something. That something was the perfect name of God revealed to Moses in Exodus 3, where it says:

> Exodus 3:14-15 (ISR) - And Elohim said to Mosheh, "I am that which I am." And He said, "Thus you shall say to the children of Yisra'ĕl, 'I am has sent me to you.'" And Elohim said further to Mosheh, "Thus you are to say to the children of Yisra'ĕl, 'יהוה Elohim of your fathers, the Elohim of Aḇraham, the Elohim of Yitsḥaq, and the Elohim of Ya'aqoḇ, has sent me to you. This is My Name forever, and this is My remembrance to all generations.'

By the way, for the purposes of this section, I will be using the ISR version of the Bible which I used to demonstrate what the Bible I was reading said. The יהוה here is the Hebrew name of God (the Tetragrammaton, or 'four letters'), which is translated as LORD in modern English Bibles. Since this was what appeared in the original Hebrew manuscripts of the Bible, I assumed that this was the proper name we needed to use when referring to God. Another piece of evidence I used came from the story of Elijah the Prophet in the book of Kings, when he challenged the prophets of Baal. The ISR Bible says,

> 1 Kings 18:22 - And Ĕliyahu said to the people, "I alone am left a prophet of YHVH, but the prophets of Ba'al are four hundred and fifty men. "Now let them give us two bulls. And let them choose one bull for themselves, and cut it in pieces, and lay it on the wood, but set no fire. And I, I prepare the other bull, and shall lay it on the wood, but set no fire. "And you shall call on the name of your mighty one, and I, I call on the Name of YHVH. And the Elohim who answers by fire, He is Elohim." So all the people answered and said, "The word is good." And Eliyahu said to the prophets of Ba'al, "Choose one bull for yourselves and prepare it first, for you are many. And call on the name of your mighty one, but set no fire."

In this passage, Elijah challenges the prophets of Baal to call upon their God, while he calls upon the name of YHVH. My understanding of the word Baal was that a literal translation of it would be Lord. So, in my mind, when Elijah tells these false prophets to call on the name of their God, they called upon the name of the Lord. Therefore, it would be improper to translate the name YHVH as "The LORD." I believed that doing so, and refusing to use the name of God was disobeying the third commandment, which in the ISR says to "Not bring the name of Elohim to naught," or, to not make it worthless or nothing. In hiding the name of God and not using it, they made it worthless: this is what I thought Christians were doing. I would also use verses such as the following one to prove that believers should know the name of YHVH:

> Isaiah 52:6 (ISR) - "Therefore My people shall know My Name, in that day, for I am the One who is speaking. See, it is I."

The same thing happened with the name of Jesus. Besides the sacred name of God, I believed that the name of Jesus was also corrupted, and that the correct name to use was Yeshua. My claim was that Iesous was not found in the original Greek, but that it was actually Iesou, which came from Yeshu, the Aramaic form of Yeshua. As we shall see later, this was an absurdly incorrect belief. I claimed that saying Jesus was twisting his true name because of the fact that the letter "J" didn't exist in the English language at the time of the printing of the King James Bible. Rather, they used the Latin Iesus, coming from the Greek Iesous (pronounced Yee-soos). I had no scripture to back any of this up; it was all an assumption of how these languages worked.

The next doctrine which I entirely rejected was the Trinity. This was a big subject for me because it was the easiest for me to defend, based on the ambiguity of many Scriptures on the subject and the disagreements between later manuscripts on the doctrines. The subject of the Godhead has always been hotly debated throughout the history of the Christian church, so I used both Scriptural arguments and showed that many people in the "early church" also rejected the Trinity. Rather, the position I held was similar to that of Arianism; eventually it came to be Semi-Arianism after being influenced more by the so-called 'Southern Israelite.'

The doctrine I held was that the Father alone is God, and that Jesus Christ was a created being, begotten of the Father at the beginning of time. I believed that he is the Son of God and God's representative to mankind as well as the mediator between the Father and the world, but not in himself divine, just one who held divine authority which had been given to him by God. The Holy Spirit, or Ruach HaKodesh, as I called it, was not a person, but the divine mind and acting power of God which proceeds from him. This was the view of the Godhead which I held, and I ignorantly used many Scriptures as well as my own carnal logic to prove it. The main verses usually consisted of these:

> Revelation 3:14 - And to the messenger of the assembly in Laodikeia write, 'The Amĕn, the Trustworthy and True Witness, the Beginning of the creation of Elohim, says this:

> Colossians 1:15 - The Son is the likeness of the invisible Elohim, the first-born of all creation.

> 1 Timothy 2:5 - For there is one Elohim, and one Mediator between Elohim and men, the Man Messiah Yeshua.

> 1 Corinthians 8:5-6 - For even if there are so-called mighty ones, whether in heaven or on earth – as there are many mighty ones and many masters - for us there is one Elohim, the Father, from whom all came and for whom we live, and one Master Yeshua Messiah, through whom all came and through whom we live.

> Mark 12:29 - And Yeshua answered him, "The first of all the commands is, 'Hear, O Yisra'el, YHVH is our Elohim, YHVH is one.

In each of these verses, there was supposedly evidence that the Trinity was wrong. In Colossians 1:15 and Revelation 3:14 there are the statements that Jesus was "the beginning of the creation of Elohim" and the "first-born of all creation." This, to me, showed that Jesus was a created being and not that he has existed for all of eternity with God, as Trinitarianism teaches. In 1 Timothy 2:5, since it distinguishes the mediator from the one God and says that Yeshua is between God and men, I understood that to mean that Jesus was not God, but under God. In 1 Corinthians 8:6, it says "there is one Elohim, the Father...." This showed to me that the one God was only the Father and no other person. Finally, in Mark 12:29, Yeshua repeated the Shema prayer of Deuteronomy 6:4, which showed to me that even Jesus believed there was only one person in the Godhead.

There were other verses which seemed to reveal that Jesus was purely a man from God, that he was a servant of God, and that he considered the Father to be his God himself. Such verses included John 20:17, Acts 2:22 and 3:26. Since the Bible repeatedly mentions that there's only one God (Deut. 32:39, Isa. 43:10, 44:6, 45:5, Psalm 83:18, Joel 2:27, etc.), and since Jesus referred to his Father as "my God" (John 20:17), then Jesus is not God, but only the Father is, I claimed. I also used my own logic that a three-in-one God does not make any sense and is both literally impossible and contradictory to the Bible. I made the same accusations of polytheism that many other nontrinitarians do. There were other verses I used to support this doctrine, but for the most part, these were my main arguments.

I also brought up the accusation of paganism which I had done repeatedly with other beliefs and practices of Christianity. Since other religions have triads of gods, such as Hinduism (the Trimurti - Brahma, Vishnu, and Shiva), and Greek mythology (Zeus, Hades, and Poseidon), I concluded that the Trinity must have had pagan origins. I attempted to prove that the early Christians rejected the Trinity with cherry-picked quotes from 'Church Fathers' such as Ignatius of Antioch and Justin Martyr. I thought that the Trinity was invented in the 3rd century and set in stone at the Council of Nicaea, but developed into its modern doctrine only at the Council of Constantinople in 381 CE. I believed that Neoplatonists and Gnostics had infiltrated the church through people like Tertullian and Origen and had brought in this lie, but that the belief did not exist prior to the late-2nd century.

When people brought up Scripture to defend the Trinity, I usually had two reactions: to "go back to the Greek/Hebrew" or to lead them away with other Scriptures. I believed that the Bible didn't contradict itself, so when I came across the verses which appeared to teach against the Trinity, I decided to stick with those and explain away the other verses in a very roundabout way.

For example, the primary proof text of the Trinity, 1 John 5:7, I accused of being added to the King James Bible from the Textus Receptus, and decided to side with the Alexandrian text-type reading, which excluded the verse altogether. When it came to Colossians 2:9, I believed this verse was again often translated wrong, and that the word *theotes* which appears here, translated as "Godhead" in the KJV, should actually be "Mightiness" or "Divine Quality." So, my interpretation of Colossians 2:9 was that it meant that Yeshua had a divine quality in him (that he was like God), but not that he was actually God.

When it came to John 1:1, another important proof text for the deity of Jesus, I once again rejected this as being an improper translation, and resorted to the Jehovah's Witnesses rendering of the verse, which says in the last clause, "and the Word was a god." I thought there was proper linguistic support for this translation (despite my lack of knowledge in Greek). In 1 Timothy 3:16, I again rejected the Textus Receptus version of the verse and chose to believe the Alexandrian text, which says "he was manifested in the flesh." I even went as far as saying that Matthew 28:19 was not originally in the Bible, and thus the baptismal formula which contains the three persons of the Godhead should not be said. The Jesus-only baptism doctrine would come a bit later in my beliefs, though, even though I never accepted the Oneness doctrine.

Moving on to the next thing I believed - the inspiration of the Bible. Although I claimed it, I did not believe in the preservation, but considered that the word of God has been tampered with throughout history and that the only reliable source is the Masoretic Text of the Hebrew, and when it came to the Greek, any source which was the oldest I believed to be the most accurate. This is what fueled my desire to learn Hebrew words and phrases, and to continually look at Greek lexicons and dictionaries and interlinear texts, to "make sure" that the words were translated right. I had no actual Scriptural support for these beliefs, except using 2 Timothy 3:16 and claiming that the 'scriptures' mentioned here only referred to the Old Testament (since the New Testament wasn't written yet, for the most part), and thus also believed that the Tanakh was superior to the New Testament. In addition, I placed higher emphasis on the Gospels than the letters of Paul, believing that Paul was inspired by God, but in my concept of inspiration, this simply meant that God led him to write what he did, and not that the words are the very words of God themselves, and thus are mixed with opinions.

Because I viewed the Old Testament as being higher than the New, I also believed that the Torah was still in place and that we were supposed to obey all of the laws of Moses contained in the first five books; Genesis, Exodus, Leviticus, Numbers, and Deuteronomy. I disputed with the idea that the law was 'done away with', or as Christians would also say "we're not under the law." The main proof text for this was Jesus' statement in Matthew 5, in which he says in the ISR Bible;

> Matthew 5:17-19 - Do not think that I came to destroy the Torah or the Prophets. I did not come to destroy but to complete. "For truly, I say to you, till the heaven and the earth pass away, one jot or one tittle shall by no means pass from the Torah till all be done. "Whoever, then, breaks one of the least of these commands, and teaches men so, shall be called least in the reign of the heavens; but whoever does and teaches them, he shall be called great in the reign of the heavens."

Because in this passage he said "I did not come to destroy but to complete" and because he claimed that "one jot or one tittle shall by no means pass from the Torah till all be done," I came to the conclusion that this means that every precept in the Old Testament was still in place. The only laws which I didn't believe we needed to follow were the animal sacrifices, based on Hebrews 7, although I believed that this was only because it was useless and because there was no temple, but that in the future when Jesus reigns, animal sacrifices would continue.

Other verses which I used to support the notion that the Torah was still entirely in place included Romans 3:31, which says in the ISR, "Do we then nullify the Torah through the belief? Let it not be! On the contrary, we establish the Torah," and Romans 7:12, which says in the ISR, "So that the Torah truly is set-apart, and the command set-apart, and righteous, and good." I would also use verses which contrast righteousness to lawlessness (such as 2 Corinthians 6:14) to show that one was not considered righteous if they broke the laws of God. I also found specific examples of Paul mentioning keeping the feasts in the New Testament as evidence that the Old Testament laws were not done away with (such as in Acts 18:21 and 1 Corinthians 5:7-8, where Paul mentions keeping Passover).

During my time with the Hebrew Roots movement, I had little understanding of what salvation was and how to achieve it. My main concern was focused on entering into what the ISR calls the "reign of the heavens" a synonym for the kingdom of heaven. I believed that one who did not maintain good works would not be able to enter into the kingdom. The main verse I used to support this notion was Matthew 7:21-23, which says in the ISR biblbe,

> Matthew 7:21-23 - "Not everyone who says to Me, 'Master, Master,' shall enter into the reign of the heavens, but he who is doing the desire of My Father in the heavens. "Many shall say to Me in that day,

> 'Master, Master, have we not prophesied in Your Name, and cast out
> demons in Your Name, and done many mighty works in Your Name?'
> "And then I shall declare to them, 'I never knew you, depart from Me,
> you who work lawlessness!'

Because he specifically says in verse 23, "Depart from Me, you who work
lawlessness!" I assumed that this meant that those who did not follow the
Law of Moses would not be allowed into the kingdom of heaven. I also used
popular passages like James 2, which tells us that 'faith without works is
dead.' To me, that meant that if somebody claimed to believe but didn't obey
God, their faith didn't count for anything and was therefore, unreal. Because
of this emphasis on following the law, I also believed that following the law
was entirely possible and that true followers of Yeshua would be able, by the
help of God, to obey his every word. Verses I used to support this notion
included 1 John 5:3 which say of the commands that they "are not grievous,"
and Deuteronomy 30:9-16, where God says to the Israelites "For this
command which I am commanding you today, it is not too hard for you
(ISR)."

Many other scriptures, including Psalm 119:42, Matthew 19:17, John 14:15-
24, and Romans 2:12-16, 7:25 were all places I turned to to support this
Hebrew Roots doctrine. Thus, I had it fixed in my mind that one could only
enter the kingdom of heaven if they obeyed God's law, which to me, included
not only the Ten Commandments, but all of the laws in the Old Testament,
including the dietary laws, the feasts in Leviticus 23, and various other
ordinances. The Sabbath was one which I focused on the most, because it was
the 4th commandment, and yet was rejected by most Christians.

In order to support keeping the Sabbath, I used a combination of scripture
and history. Besides the verses already listed, I also used passages which
involved the use of logic to draw a deeper meaning out of them. For example,
in Acts 6, the ISR Bible says,

> Acts 6:11-14 - Then they instigated men to say, "We have heard him
> speak blasphemous words against Mosheh and Elohim." And they
> stirred up the people, and the elders, and the scribes, so they came
> upon him, seized him, and brought him to the council. And they set up
> false witnesses who said, "This man does not cease to speak
> blasphemous words against this set-apart place and the Torah, for we

49

have heard him saying that this Yeshua of Natsaret shall overthrow this place and change the institutes which Mosheh delivered unto us."

Because this passage says that those who accuse them of speaking blasphemously against the Torah are 'false witnesses' I assumed that this meant that they were in fact, keeping the Torah instead of abrogating it. This of course, included the Sabbath. The book of Acts also contains several references to the Sabbath and the practice of Paul preaching in synagogues on the Sabbath (Acts 13:42-43, 16:13, 18:4). Because he preached on the Sabbath instead of on Sunday, I believed this meant that meeting on the Sabbath was not only the practice of the apostles, but a requirement for believers.

Hebrews 4 was a passage I used to support my doctrine as well. This is because in the ISR version, verse 9 says "There remains a Sabbath-keeping for the people of Elohim" rather than "There remains a rest" as it says in the KJV. This was smoking-gun evidence that the Sabbath day wasn't done away with, but that even in the New Testament, we were required to rest one day of the week. The issue from that point was resolved, and switched from whether we should keep the Sabbath to whether it was on the seventh-day or the first-day of the week, Sunday. At the time I lumped most Christians in together as one, and thought that all denominations which met on Sunday did so because they thought this was the new Sabbath, as Rome taught.

To refute this idea, my primary verses I used were Matthew 12:8 and Mark 2:23-28, where Jesus reveals himself as the Lord of the Sabbath. In Revelation 1:10, John mentions the "Lord's Day." Since Jesus was the Lord of the Sabbath (in context, referring to the seventh-day Sabbath the Jews followed), the Sabbath must be the real Lord's Day, and not the Sunday which Christians observe. This was enough evidence from Scripture to settle the matter, but I also used historical records to support the idea that we needed to obey the seventh-day Sabbath.

In Acts 24:5, Paul is called "a ringleader of the sect of the Nazarenes." The church father Jerome mentioned in his commentary on Isaiah that the Nazarenes of the 5th century were a group which did not cease to follow the old law, including the Sabbath. These were the true believers, in my mind. In addition, the Smyrnean epistle describing Polycarp's martyrdom in the 2nd century mentioned the Sabbath. Then, the fact that this referred to the seventh day of the week and not the first was supported by history in that

50

Constatine I, the Roman emperor who 'converted' to Christianity established "the venerable day of the sun" as a day of rest by a decree in 321 AD. This and many other sources created an undeniable proof in my mind that the Sabbath was meant to be followed by believers in the Messiah, and that it had only been abolished or transferred to Sunday by the devilish Roman Catholics.

Another doctrine which was essential to my time in the Hebrew Roots movement was the doctrine of soul-sleep and annihilationism. My eschatological view was that there is no immediate heaven and hell upon death, but that every soul, regardless of their spiritual status, would remain in the grave, also known as *Sheol* in Hebrew, until the resurrection. Then, those who were faithful and obedient to the Messiah would be raised to live in the kingdom of heaven. At the second resurrection after the millenium, the remaining wicked people would be cast into the lake of fire, where they wouldn't burn for eternity, but would be destroyed immediately by fire.

The main support for this doctrine was the fact that the Bible constantly compares death to sleep, especially whenever a king of Israel and Judah died (1 Kings 2:10, 11:43, 14:20, 16:6, Psalm 13:3, 90:3-6, Matthew 9:24, Mark 5:39, Luke 8:52-53, John 11:11-14, Acts 7:60, 1 Corinthians 15:20). Since death was called sleep, I believed that death was simply a temporary unconscious state, with nobody burning in hell or living in the joy of heaven. The following scriptures further seemed to support the doctrine:

> Job 14:10-12 - But man dies and is powerless, and man expires, and where is he? Water disappears from the sea, and a river dries up and is parched, and man shall lie down and not rise. Till the heavens are no more, they awake not, nor are aroused from their sleep.

> Psalm 115:17 - The dead do not praise Yah, Nor any going down to silence.

> Ecclesiastes 9:5 - For the living know that they shall die, but the dead know naught, nor do they have any more reward, for their remembrance is forgotten. (ISR)

Because the dead are "powerless" and "do not praise Yah" and they "know naught," they must be in a state of soul-sleep. They did not exist in any afterlife, but were simply unconscious, waiting for the resurrection. To me,

51

the emphasis was not going to heaven but being resurrected. Those who obeyed the commands would only enter the kingdom if they were resurrected at the Second Coming. Until then, the spirit and the body were separated (Ecclesiastes 12:7), and since Genesis 2:7 describes a living soul as the union of spirit and body, my conclusion was that a person could not be conscious and living in any way without both.

Concerning hell, I couldn't fathom the idea that the wicked would be sent to burn for eternity in a fiery hell. To me, this concept was foreign to Scripture and was just based on a pagan conception of the underworld. The only fire the unbelievers would face is the temporary lake of fire. Most of my support for this doctrine was not based on clear scripture, but on linguistic gymnastics and "going back to the Hebrew or Greek." The word used most often when Jesus referred to hell in the New Testament is gehenna, which comes from the Hebrew term Gehinnom, meaning 'Valley of Hinnom.' This referred to a valley outside of Jerusalem where waste was burned and where pagans in the past often burned their children.

Another word used was Hades, which of course, came from the Greek common term for underworld. In Hebrew, the common word for hell was Sheol. However, because all of these terms were used interchangeably to mean both hell and the grave in modern Bibles, I assumed this was a purposeful tampering to hide the true nature of hell. Verses like Daniel 12:2, which talk about the resurrection, talk about the resurrection of some to "reproaches, and everlasting abhorrence (ISR)." Since they were described as "sleeping in the dust of the earth" and since they rose to damnation, this was proof to me that both the righteous and the wicked end up in the same place - sleep in the dust of the earth. In other words, the grave, or Sheol - not a fiery hell.

However, those who were sinners, although they did not go to hell, instead ended up in the lake of fire after the Great White Throne judgment, where they would be entirely destroyed by fire. Verses I used to support this include Matthew 5:29-30, where Jesus talks about the body perishing in hell (or Gehenna in the ISR Bible). In Matthew 10:28, Jesus also tells us to fear God, who can destroy both soul and body in Gehenna. To me, that was evidence that we do not burn for eternity, but are instead annihilated in the lake of fire.

The final piece of evidence I had for this eschatological interpretation is the fact that those who are thrown into the Lake of Fire are those who are not in the Book of Life, and that this punishment is called the 'second death' (Revelation 20:13-15). In addition, since Romans 6:23 tells us that the wages of sin is death, and because the Bible constantly talks about eternal life as the result of salvation, this showed me that those who ended up in the lake of fire could not possibly burn for eternity, because this would imply that they lived for eternity in hell. Thus, they must be annihilated in order for it to truly be the 'second death.'

The remaining doctrines I'm going to cover in this section were things I believed and defended heavily, but which were not essential to the faith and which I believed concerned the debate of whether we're obeying the truth or following traditions. A key verse for me during this time was one that Michael Rood, the man who led me into the Hebrew Roots movement, constantly repeated - Jeremiah 10:2, in which God commands Israel, "Learn not the way of the heathen." Thus, in the Hebrew Roots movement, there was a great purging of everything connected with paganism in any way. One of these things was the symbol of the cross.

I believed that the cross was a pagan symbol because of its connections to pre-Christian symbols like the Egyptian ankh and the hieroglyphic 'ndj.' In addition, various Sumerian and Babylonian gods were depicted wearing crosses. Alexander Hislop's book *The Two Babylons* also made a connection between the letter tau in the Phoenician and Greek alphabets with sun worship. The theory was that the symbol, which began in an 'x' shape, originated in Babylon to represent the god Tammuz, and later the Persian sun god Mithra, who was worshipped in the time of Jesus by a Roman 'mystery cult.' This same tau symbol was associated with the swastika or hakenkreuz of Indo-European paganism.

Also based on the psuedohistorical teachings of Michael Rood, which mainly drew from Alexander Hislop's work, the cross was only adopted by Christians several centuries after the death of Christ by Constantine, a worshipper of Sol Invictus, or "Invisible Sun," who used the symbol to represent the new faith of Catholicism. Even though I didn't know Greek, I once again, used the same tactics as the Jehovah's Witnesses in claiming that the Greek word *stauros*, which is translated a cross, actually meant 'upright stake.' Thus, I believed that Jesus was crucified on a stake, and that the idea of a cross came purely from paganism, and thus shouldn't be used to represent the faith of the Messiah.

Another thing associated with Christianity I rejected was the practice of baptism. Like with the Sunday-sabbath doctrine, I conflated all Christians as the same regarding baptism, and viewed the practice as a continuation of Greek washing rituals. Rather, the immersion practiced by John the Baptist (who I called Yohanan the Immerser, based on the ISR Bible), was the Jewish ritual washing known as *mikveh*. This *mikveh* is a bath of running water which is used to fulfill the commandments in the Old Testament to wash uncleanliness (such a in Leviticus 15:11-14). In my view, the New Testament immersions were simply a continuation of the mikveh, but this time, they washed away all sins. In the ISR Bible, John the Baptist says:

> Matthew 3:11 - I indeed immerse you in water unto repentance, but He who is coming after me is mightier than I, whose sandals I am not worthy to bear.

My understanding of 'repentance' was that it meant turning from sins. Thus, I believed that immersion in water was the beginning of a new life, to get rid of sins and to turn to obeying the Torah. This immersion was to be done in the name of Yeshua alone. This was based on the omission of "baptizing them in the name of the Father, Son, and Holy Ghost" in Matthew 28:19 in the ISR. Instead, the verse simply says to baptize "in my name." This translation decision was based on the Shem-Tov Hebrew text of Matthew, a 13th-century Hebrew translation of the Gospel of Matthew written by a Sephardic Jew. Several changes were made from the Greek text, one of them being the complete removal of references to the Trinity. Since I was in the "Hebrew Roots" movement, naturally, I was drawn more to this Hebrew version, believing it to be a copy of the 'original' Matthew. Thus, I believed that *mikvot* were to be performed in the name of the Master Yeshua.

Another doctrine I emphasized was the use of a Hebrew calendar over a pagan one. This Hebrew calendar was separate from the Orthodox Jewish calendar, but instead based on the Biblical months. The year began in the spring, in the month of Abib, which begins at the first new moon after the barley harvest in Israel was in the agricultural state known as *aviv*. Subsequent months were either 29 or 30 days long, and would begin when the first sliver of the 'renewed moon' was sighted. The weeks were seven days long, with each day being named in Hebrew. For example, the first day was *Yom rishon*, which simply means 'first day,' the second was *Yom sheni*, or 'second day,' and so on. Each day began and ended at sunset, and the most important day of the week was the seventh, *Yom shabbat,* or the Sabbath, which began on Friday evening. The one thing I disagreed on with Michael Rood was the year. Based on my own calculations of numbers in the Bible, I came the conclusion that the year was 5992, and not 6016. So, to me, March 28th, 2017 was Aviv 1, 5993.

The rejection of the Gregorian calendar for the Hebrew calendar was so important to me because of the presence of pagan names in the months and weekdays. For example, January is named after the Roman god Janus, and Thursday is named after the Germanic god of thunder, Thor. Thus, in my quest to eliminate all association with paganism, I revolved my life around the Hebrew calendar. Support for this was evident both in history and the Bible. Since the Gregorian calendar was simply a 1582 revision of the Julian Calendar, established by Julius Caesar in 46 BCE, it's a fact that the Israelites didn't use our modern reckoning of time. And since I believed that keeping the feasts of the LORD commanded in Leviticus 23 was necessary, figuring out the dates they fell on was important. After all, God told the Israelites to observe the Passover "in the first month, on the fourteenth day of the month (Leviticus 23:5)." If I didn't know when that was, I wouldn't be able to observe Passover.

The first month was called Abib. This was when the Israelites left the land of Egypt (Exodus 13:4) and when the Feast of Unleavened Bread and the Passover was celebrated (Exodus 23:14, 34:18, Deuteronomy 16:1). The namesake for the month is the Hebrew word *aviv*, which was a state the annual barley crop was in at the time of the Exodus. The ISR Bible tells us this about the plague of hail:

> Exodus 9:31 - And the flax and the barley were smitten, for the barley was in the aviv and the flax was in giv'ol. But the wheat and the spelt were not smitten, for they were afilot.

In the KJV, "the barley was in the aviv" is translated "the barley was in the ear." This is a stage of development in which barley is ripe to the point that it is brittle, so that the hail was able to destroy the barley crop in Egypt. The purpose of the Passover being in the month of Abib is that the barley needed to be ready for the wave offering given on the day of Firstfruits. According to Leviticus 23:9-11, the Israelites were to give a sheaf of the firstfruits of their harvest to the priest for an offering, the day after the Sabbath during the

Feast of Unleavened Bread. Thus, if the barley was not in the state of aviv by the time of a new moon, it was not ripe enough for harvest, and thus, not ready to give to the priests. In that case, an extra month would be added to the calendar for a total of 13 months. During my time in the Hebrew Roots movement, this never happened in the land of Israel, where other members of the movement kept watch and reported the state of the harvest online each year.

The months began at the time of the new moon, based on a few verses which reference blowing trumpets during the new moon (Psalm 81:3), which is connected with the command in Numbers 10:10 to blow trumpets in the beginnings of months. In addition, one of the Leviticus 23 appointed times, known as the Day of Trumpets or *Yom Teruah*, is "in the seventh month, on the first day of the month," and is a "remembrance of blowing of trumpets (Leviticus 23:24)." Therefore, the 'new moons' constantly mentioned throughout the Bible (1 Chronicles 23:31, 2 Chronicles 2:4, 8:13, Colossians 2:16) were the beginnings of the months in this Hebrew calendar I rigorously followed.

Similar to the rejection of the pagan calendar, I also rejected holidays which Christians observed that were apparently associated with paganism, again, to eliminate the 'way of the heathen (Jer. 10:2),' from the faith. The two which I celebrated in the past and which nearly all denominations observe today were Easter and Christmas. I believed that Easter was a corruption of the celebration of the Passover and Day of Firstfruits, and that it was in reality, a holiday associated again with Babylonian paganism. The evidence for this once again was based on a connection found in *The Two Babylons* between the name of Easter, the name of the Babylonian goddess of fertility Ishtar, and the name of the Germanic goddess Ostara. Simply because the names sounded similar, this was enough for me to say that Easter was pagan.

Instead, I focused on the importance of the resurrection on the Day of Firstfruits or *Yom Ha'Bikkurim*, when the firstfruits of the harvest were offered to God. Since the resurrection of Christ took place on the same day as the Day of Firstfruits, and since 1 Corinthians 15:20 calls him 'the firstfruits of them that slept,' his resurrection is the fulfillment of the Firstfruits. So, instead of observing Easter, I believed one should follow the Day of Firstfruits by obeying the command to abstain from work on that day.

Regarding Christmas, which is popular among Christians, my belief was based on Rood and Hislop's claims that everything associated with the holiday was based on sun-god worship. First of all, the date of Christmas on December 25th I denounced as entirely unbiblical. Instead, as Hebrew Roots movement teachers taught, December 25th was the birthday of several pagan gods, such as Zeus, Horus, Mithra, Apollo, and Sol Invictus, but not Jesus. The reason behind their birth on this day was because it was close to the Winter Solstice, after which the days would get progressively longer. I believed that this date was chosen by Constantine for the celebration of Christmas so that the pagan Catholics could continue their worship of Sol Invictus. Other pagan festivals around Christmastime included Saturnalia, a 7-day wild party festival of Rome based on the worship of Saturn, and the Germanic Yule festival which celebrated the 'Wild Hunt' of Odin.

The Christmas tree, another symbol associated with Christmas, I rejected as pagan based on Jeremiah 10, which says,

> Jeremiah 10:3-4 - For the customs of the people are vain: for one cutteth a tree out of the forest, the work of the hands of the workman, with the axe. They deck it with silver and with gold; they fasten it with nails and with hammers, that it move not.

This seemed suspiciously like a Christmas tree. It mentions people cutting down trees and then decking it with silver and gold. This apparently revealed that this was a pagan practice dating back to Babylon and Egypt. According to Rood, decorating Christmas trees is a representation of the Egyptian myth of Osiris, who was cut up by his brother Set into several pieces. His genitals were never found, but were remade by Isis to produce the god Horus, who was supposedly born on December 25th. Thus, the practice of hanging gold and silver spherical ornaments on a tree supposedly represented the artifical genitals of Osiris.

Thus, as a result of many of the Christmastime practices originating in paganism, and the day itself supposedly having been chosen by the Roman pagans as a continuation of *Dies Natalis Sol Invictus* (Birthday of the Unconquerable Sun) and Saturnalia, I refused to celebrate Christmas in both 2016 and 2017. Instead, I celebrated Hanukkah. Even though it's not commanded in the Bible, a single reference to its celebration in the New Testament (John 10:22) and its background in the defeat of Antiochus

Epiphanes (who I viewed as a shadow of the Antichrist) was enough to convince me it was acceptable.

The last thing I viewed as part of the 'way of the heathen' which was to be rejected were the various terms used among Christians which I didn't believe were biblical. Instead, my 'biblical' substitute for these terms were Hebrew words and phrases which Messianic teachers like Michael Rood used. An example is the term Christ. I believed that Christ, although it had the same meaning as Messiah, should not be used to refer to our Saviour. The reasoning behind this was that supposedly Greek gods such as Serapis and Apollo also were called 'Christ,' which is the English form of the word *christos.* A literal translation means 'anointed one.'

Another term was Holy Ghost or Spirit. To me, the word spirit was also pagan because of its association with supernatural undead beings. So, instead of saying this, I said *Ruach Ha'Kodesh,* which literally translated would mean "Set-Apart Breath." Since this term or variants of it are used in the Old Testament, I didn't see anything wrong with referring to the Holy Ghost by this term.

Besides these and examples already given such as mikveh, I did use a lot of Hebrew names. Every Bible character was referred to by me by their Hebrew name, or at least, the way a modern person who spoke Hebrew would say the names. For this, I didn't have any Biblical support for this practice. Rather, I perceived using the English form of the names as "changing" what their names actually were, and giving them a "pagan" nickname. After all, this was the Hebrew Roots movement. Everything was based on the concept that the religion founded by Jesus had roots in Hebrew culture. So, because Peter was called 'Shimon Kefa' by his Aramaic-speaking counterparts, I saw no reason to use the modern English renderings.

The final doctrine I want to cover is the heavy belief in Zionism and an emphasis on the Jewish people and modern-day state of Israel. I believed the Jews, or at least, the sects who obeyed the Torah without the manmade traditions, such as the Karaites, were able to also enter into the kingdom. I also believed that all of Bible-prophecy focused on the modern-day state of Israel and supported movements for the 'Greater Israel,' a theoretical state which owned all of the land between the Nile and the Euphrates River, based on the promise given to Abraham in Genesis 15:18.

This was one of the doctrines that I didn't write about or make videos about, and had little Biblical support for the notion. Most of it was based on the promises given to Abraham, such as in Genesis 12:2-3 when God says to Abraham, "And I will bless them that bless thee, and curse him that curseth thee: and in thee shall all families of the earth be blessed (v. 3)." In addition, God said to the Israelites, "For thou art an holy people unto the Lord thy God: the Lord thy God hath chosen thee to be a special people unto himself, above all people that are upon the face of the earth (Deuteronomy 7:6)." With multiple Old Testament references to Israel being the chosen nation of God and promises of land being given to the children of Israel, I concluded that this meant the Jews, regardless of their spiritual state, were still able to come to God without Jesus Christ.

Focus on Israel

During my time in the Hebrew Roots movement, I had very little interest in the New Testament and the concept of 'church.' Rather, my main focus was on Israel and the promises God gave to the Israelites. In 2017, especially in the spring as it moved towards the summer, I was especially on-edge based on world events and ideas about what would happen in the future. Even though I had no physical connection to Israel, I knew that I did have a Jewish great-grandmother, which was enough for me to consider myself Jewish by ethnicity. And because of my religious beliefs, I felt a nationalism towards Israel. All of my political beliefs and interpretation of modern events were based on the state of Israel.

The Hebrew new year began on March 28th, and to celebrate, I made a special video. The intro for the video included several clips of Israeli military technology and battles in various wars against the Arabs - who I believed to have no right to any of the land in the Levant or northern Arabian desert. Thus, I was very militaristic in mind - believing that it was the right of the Jews to invade the lands of the Palestinians and expand their land to establish a state in preparation for the "Greater Exodus," the term used to describe the promise to bring the other tribes back into the land of Israel, as found in Ezekiel 36 and Isaiah 49.

My belief in this Zionist doctrine meant that the politically confusing time of early 2017 would be one in which I watched and read the news with anticipation of new events concerning Israel. Even at school, when I was done with my work or even just sitting around at lunch, I would read articles on Breitbart Jerusalem, the Jerusalem Post, Infowars, and other websites talking about the various wars in the Middle East, nationalist movements around the world, and elections of political leaders. Particularly concerning was Donald Trump. I initially supported Trump, but I didn't like his cabinet, which I perceived to be a bunch of Jesuit pawns. One of these, H.R. McMaster, who was the National Security Advisor at the time, had tried to send troops into Syria as a reaction to the supposed gas attacks by Assad. This angered me particularly because I assumed this would create another power struggle similar to Iraq and soon launch a third world war.

Michael Rood made several predictions concerning the end times, including his 'Prophecy of Balaam's Ass' in which he interpreted the beating of Balaam's ass as being a code for the agreements made between Israel and Palestine through the years and their breaking by the Muslims. For example, after the 1993 Oslo Accords, seven years later, the Second Intifada began in Palestine. Seven years after that was another peace accord, in 2007. This and other streams and videos were all intricate and convincing enough to make me believe that the final 70th week of Daniel's prophecy would begin on the Day of Trumpets in 2017. Therefore, any possibility of a war in the Middle East, or any signs of the establishment of a New World Order, made me believe that Israel would soon prevail over the nations, and that when such an event happened, the Greater Exodus would begin, and I would be able to join my Messianic brothers to worship God among his people.

My support of Zionism was bolstered when I made a new friendship in April 2017, a man named Nathanael Kuechenberg. Kuechenberg had also been in the Hebrew Roots movement, since 2009, when he was converted after attending a conference by Michael Rood as a child with his parents. Initially, Kuechenberg only left a few comments on my channel, but he spoke with authority (obviously having much more of a background in the religion than I did) about the pronunciation of the name of God and various other doctrines. At the time, I said "Yahuwah" but he insisted it was Yehovah, and offered to explain the Hebrew behind it to prove it.

I watched a few videos on his channel and soon learned that Nathanael knew how to read and speak both Greek and Hebrew, and that he had even worked on his own translation of the New Testament. He had been to Israel on many occasions and personally walked on the Temple Mount, observed the ruins of

Sodom and Gomorrah, and gone to other biblical sites. For the next few months, we would occasionally email each other about various topics, and leave comments on each others channels. One of these topics was the subject of the end times. He too believed, based on calculation of the Hebrew year, that the end times were approaching quickly. Our theory was a common one held by even many Christians: that Jesus would return in the "Sabbath Millenium" which began in the year 6000. Thus, since I believed the year was 5993, and he came to the same conclusion on his own, we both believed the final seven years would begin soon.

Another thing I should mention, just to show how deep into this Israel-loving Zionism I was, is that I learned songs in Hebrew, especially the Israel national anthem, *Hatikvah*. I would sing these songs in the shower, and as mentioned before, even pray sometimes in Hebrew. I wanted to learn Hebrew eventually and take any opportunity to go to Israel (as long as it wasn't during the thermonuclear war I believed would come soon).

Phase II: Nazarene

Beginning around the summer of 2017, I would say that I entered into a new phase in my following of the Hebrew Roots movement, which included a slight change in my beliefs and a decision to intensely research the doctrines of my faith. There are many characteristics of this phase, so some of it might be out of order, but most of the information regards how I lived the rest of 2017.

First, I finally found a name for myself and for my beliefs. Previously, I had heard the term 'netsar' from Michael Rood's broadcasts, and unable to understand the meaning behind it, used it very sparingly. However, beginning around the summer of 2017, I learned that the term 'natsar,' meaning 'to guard' in Hebrew, is the root word for the town Nazareth, where Jesus was raised. I also learned that in Acts 24:5, Paul is accused of being a "ringleader of the sect of the Nazarenes," and that church fathers such as Jerome and Epiphanius referred to a group called the Nazarenes in the 4th century who continued to follow the Law of Moses, especially the Sabbath. Thus, I applied the name Nazarene to my faith, as one who guarded the commandments.

The Southern Israelite, whose videos I watched more and more around this time, also used that name to refer to himself. Thus, I considered myself not just as a Torah-keeper, but as a Nazarene from this point on. My life soon became consumed by attempting to grow in my beliefs. This was particularly influenced by the Southern Israelite himself and several others with similar beliefs, who presented themselves as experts in the matters they presented.

One of these other people is Rob Skiba, a Youtuber who was friends with Messianics like Paul Nison and Zachary Bauer. In the summer, I watched a whole video series by Rob Skiba about Nimrod and his theories about the Antichrist. Many of these seminars promoted extra-biblical texts like the Book of Jubilees and Enoch, and used Gnostic terms like 'archon' to demonstrate a mystical cosmic struggle between the "Nephilim" and God. This peaked my interest in the subject of the nature of the Antichrist as well as the apocrypha.

As I studied the subject of the Antichrist and began to gain an interest in the seed-serpent doctrine, my beliefs faced a constant evolution as I searched for the truth about various issues. No longer was my main concern obedience to the Torah, the Sacred name, and the issue of heaven and hell; now, I was concerned mainly about prophecy and its effects on the people of Israel. In addition, as I went back to Rob Skiba videos for research, I was sucked into another movement for a few weeks which I believed was essential to getting rid of the traditions of false Christianity.

Rob Skiba, as well as Drake Shelton (Southern Israelite) both taught that the earth is flat, and did so in such a dogmatic way that it made it seem like this was an important part of a Christian's faith. The argument was, since so many unbelievers question the Bible, the goal was to show both that the Bible teaches that the earth is flat, and to prove it with science. Skiba performed countless experiments on his channel, such as sending a camera on a balloon 100,000 feet in the air to find the curvature of the earth, all to try to prove that the earth was flat.

At first, I was skeptical, but after a bit of looking into the idea, I gradually accepted it more and more. This was especially thanks to Drake Shelton, who had published a book called "225 Reasons Why I Believe the Earth is Flat" and who regularly held debates on his channel in which he demolished his uneducated opponents using philosophy, history, and science. I believed from that point that this was a doctrine of the Bible, and that any attempt to attack it was just an attempt to attack the Bible. This got me into a few arguments with my brother and some friends, since every new doctrine I learned I attempted to teach to others. Even though I abandoned the belief about two months later, it was definitely an important part of my time in this Hebrew Roots movement.

However, I shouldn't depart from talking about Drake Shelton just yet. From July onwards, this man became in many ways a mentor to me, and although I still considered other Messianic teachers as authoritative and knowledgable, my focus was mainly on what the Southern Israelite taught in his books, articles, and videos. Strangely, Shelton did not consider himself a member of the Hebrew Roots movement based on his adherence to Calvinism and covenant theology, which he believed the Hebrew Roots attacked. However, he was a nontrinitarian, Torah-keeper, soul-sleep believer, and Jesuit hater, which was enough for me to consider him as one who knew what he's talking about, even though I disagreed on some minor things.

Shelton, who subscribed to my channel around this time, and who I would occasionally talk with in the comments of his or my own channel, influenced me in several ways. One of these ways was by greatly bolstering my nationalism. However, this time, it was less focused on Israel and the Jewish people, but on Gentiles who were under Yeshua as well, particularly my own ethnicity. Shelton, who was a Southern nationalist (hence the name Southern Israelite), believed in a doctrine that each individual nation, even those who followed Christ, were meant to be separate and thus should advocate for secession. He especially supported the idea of the Confederate States of America and a separate nation for the WASPs (White Anglo-Saxon Protestants) in the south.

With my Swedish, Irish, Scottish, Irish, and Polish heritage, I started to embrace the culture of my ancestors without departing from my belief in Zionism, and believed that doing so was an important part of being a believer. Thanks to Drake Shelton, for most of the remainder of my time in the Hebrew Roots movement, I believed that the solution to the problem of sin in our world was to create these Christian, segregated nations, which based their laws and principles upon the foundation of the Torah. Part of this nationalist doctrine was now the attempt at resisting against movements which I believed endangered my own nationality, such as the Black Hebrew Israelites, who teach that African-Americans are the true Jews, and that Caucasians and the Jews of our day were impostors descended from Edom. I made a video against the Hebrew Israelites in July, and after receiving several response videos from one of the preachers in GMS (Great Millstone, one of the HI organizations), I made several additional videos, which were each an hour in length, to refute their claims.

Another way that Drake Shelton influenced me during this time was by inspiring me to write about the Bible. I had always loved writing, and back in autumn 2016, I had begun several failed attempts to write books about my faith and defend what I considered to be 'the faith once delivered to the saints.' Now, since the Southern Israelite shared a link to the Google Drive containing all of his books, I was inspired again to create my own works upon reading them. I began my first project in early August, which I called "The Great Conspiracy." This title was chosen because of the perception that the truth had been hidden from man, and the goal of the book was to address doctrines in the Bible, to show what 'the truth' was, and to expose the Catholic and Jesuit attempts at defeating the truth.

For the next few weeks, I worked diligently on this book, using every chance I got to add to the information within. The book was laid out in chapters which addressed specific doctrines. The first chapter talked about God, and taught the Sacred Name and Arianism while attempting to refute the Trinity. The second chapter focused on creationism and the idea of a Flat Earth (I removed this section about a week after writing it after I began to question these beliefs a bit). The third chapter focused on the concept of sin and the afterlife. At this point, in about September, I went on a hiatus, although I didn't plan to completely stop work on the book. For the time being, I had a new project to work on.

The Southern Israelite had his own blog, which he wrote using the Wordpress website which allowed one to create their own website. As soon as I learned about this, I caught on to the idea, and made my own website, which I titled "Mr. Tall23 the Nazarene" on September 5th, 2017. My writings were now directed there, where I could publish my ideas and beliefs in short articles instead of writing an entire book. For the first few weeks, my articles covered various topics, including Bible prophecy, an article attacking the position that the KJV is the word of God, the feasts of the LORD, and an article which explained alleged Bible contradictions.

I also wrote an article called "23 Reasons I Am Not a Mormon." This had roots in arguments I had with Mormons at my school, people who I knew and who I questioned. Of course, my contention with their religious beliefs was based on the Hebrew Roots position, which I tried unsuccessfully to push on these Mormons, even though I believed that I was able to defend my beliefs quite adequately. I definitely had a prideful attitude.

Over a break I had from school for two weeks, I worked hard on writing articles for my blog website. One of these articles was inspired by Drake Shelton and Rob Skiba's talks about extra-biblical texts. I focused on the apocrypha of the New Testament and wrote an article determining which texts were to be considered inspired by God. Over several days, I read through the various extra gospels and epistles dating from the 2nd to the 4th centuries, and wrote about why they shouldn't be considered God's word. However, by the end of the article, I came to the conclusion that the epistles of Polycarp and Clement should be considered inspired scripture, while the book of Jude should not. This was because Jude supposedly quoted from Enoch and the "Assumption of Moses", two non-canonical Old Testament texts. So, I refrained from reading or quoting the book of Jude for the rest of my time in the Hebrew Roots movement.

Obeying the Torah in New Ways

In this period as a Nazarene, I was able to fully understand more of my doctrines by actually practicing what I believed. Because of the sudden nature of my conversion in 2016, and the lack of any background in anything related to Hebrew Roots from my family, it was difficult for me to keep many of the laws I believed were important to serving God. The fact that I was only 15 years old at the time contributed to this as well. However, as my parents became more and more accepting of my new religion, it became easier for me to gain access to objects which would allow me to obey the Torah.

One of these was the wearing of *tzitzit*, or white and blue tassels worn on the corners of a garment, as commanded in Numbers 15:38 and Deuteronomy 22:12. I asked my mother for tzitzit as a gift for my birthday in May, and although they arrived late, I was happy to finally receive them in June. These tzitzit were not on a prayer shawl as Jews traditionally wore them, but attached to a leather snap which could be clipped to belts. As soon as they came in the mail, I immediately tried them on and wore them for the remainder of the day.

After receiving these tzitzit, I wore them every day that I went into public. After I got back from summer break I wore them to school as well, and let them hang down proudly, as to identify myself as a Torah-keeper. I received several inquiries from friends and teachers about what I was wearing. Several people thought I was a Jew, but I explained to them I was not, but that I wore these tassels because I believed it was commanded by Yeshua. In my freshman year of high school, not many people knew about my association with these Hebrew Roots doctrines. However, by the end of my sophomore year, it was well-known among all of my friends and acquiantances (although many of them just considered me to be a Jew).

Another way in which I was able to begin obeying the Torah was by buying a ram-horn shofar in September just in time for Yom Teruah, or the Day of Trumpets. My mother purchased the shofar for me and I began practicing blowing the horn in the weeks leading up to the holiday. When it finally came on September 21st of that year, I went onto a balcony at my house and blew the horn as hard as I could to announce the feast day (while wearing my tzitzit). I believed I was obeying God's commandments by doing this.

Ten days later was Yom Kippur, or the Day of Atonement, in which the Torah commands us to afflict our souls. This is commonly taken to mean that we are to remove any pleasures in our life, including food. So, I fasted the entirety of Yom Kippur, although I made sure to eat as much food as possible the day before so I wasn't hungry. Nonetheless, I was famished at the end of the fast, and I was glad to have gotten through the day by the time the sun set.

The next Feast of the LORD, Sukkot, or the Feast of Tabernacles, in which the Bible commands to build a booth to dwell in for a length of seven days, I was unable to celebrate because of the inaccessibility to a booth. I supposed using a tent would be a reasonable alternative, and asked my mother to buy one, but she didn't understand the nature of the holiday, and when the first day came, I was without a booth. So, the best I could do was abstain from work on the first and seventh days. I made a video about this disappointment, in which I sounded discouraged because of my lack of ability to obey the Torah's commandments.

However, Nathanael Kuechenberg messaged me after I uploaded this video and suggested that I come to Indiana the next year to celebrate Sukkot with his congregation and family, or suggested that I could visit Israel for the same purpose. At this point in early October, I began to talk more and more to Nathanael over Youtube, even though we had never spoken face to face. It was at this point that Nathanael finally convinced me, using evidence from the Hebrew *niqqud*, or vowels markings, that the Tetragrammaton is pronounced as "YeHoVaH" and not "YaHUwAh" as I assumed. So, from thence, I called upon the name of Yehovah, believing that this distinction was important.

Overall, my life in the Hebrew Roots movement was chaotic and involved a constant fear and worry of disobeying God's commands, assuming that if I intentionally broke them, I would end up in the lake of fire and not partake in the resurrection. I was earnestly deceived into believing that this was how a Bible-believing man who claimed Yeshua as their Messiah should live life. Every week, I would abstain from work on the Sabbath. Every few days, I would say some Hebrew prayer or blessing, and I would try to read passages of the ISR Bible and study them. However, in retrospect, I didn't practice much of what I taught on Youtube, and was quite weak in my knowledge of the Bible.

CHAPTER 3: SALVATION - CHANGING INTO A FUNDAMENTAL BAPTIST

The Error of Calvinism

At the end of the year 2017, there began a gradual change in my beliefs which would ultimately take me out of the Hebrew Roots movement. In context, this began during the celebration of Hanukkah in December of that year. Since I believed that Christmas was a pagan holiday but didn't believe there was anything wrong with Hanukkah, this would be the second time I lit a menorah. My parents, who still celebrated Christmas with the rest of our family, continued to give gifts for the holiday season, but delivered them during Hanukkah instead.

I had asked for several particular books which I hoped to read to expand my knowledge of the faith and the Bible. Among these publications were books by Drake Shelton, which I had never actually purchased before. However, I wanted to not only support his ministry, but be able to read his works without having to access the Google Drive link he had set up. The two books I bought were "The Noahic Roots of Pagan Idolatry" and "A Defense of the South Against the Jesuit Counter-Reformation," both of which did not necessarily focus on doctrinal issues, but on historical ones.

Two other books I received were books by Ron Rhodes as part of his "Reasoning from the Scriptures" series, which used logical and scriptural arguments to show the falsehood of several religions and denominations. The two I received attacked Mormons and Jehovah's Witnesses. I read both, unsure of what to find inside. I already had some arguments against the Mormons, and although I agreed with some of the doctrinal points of the JWs, rejected them because of the cultic nature of the Watchtower Society. One thing which irked me in these books was the defense of the Trinity, a doctrine I rejected. I subsequently made a series on my Youtube channel attempting to refute the claims of Ron Rhodes, which compared the attributes of God in the Old Testament with Jesus.

The main thing which intrigued me were the chapters focusing on the subject of salvation within these two books. Both books mentioned the gift of everlasting life and the concept of being saved from sins. I realized that terms like this were used in the Bible, but had never considered other views of what salvation might mean. In fact, I realized by the turn of the year that I didn't even really know what others believed. My belief had always been, just do good and obey God's commandments, and I'll partake in the resurrection.

My questions about salvation grew heavier when I read about Calvinism in the books by Shelton. Many of his political beliefs and ideas of establishing a nation based on God's laws came from the attempt at instituting a theocratic representative state in Scotland under the Solemn League and Covenant in 1643, which protected the Reformed faith in England. Most of Drake Shelton's heroes were Presbyterians or from other Calvinist groups. I learned that he himself had studied to be a Presbyterian minister in college before leaving Christianity to become a 'Nazarene.' Soon after, I found videos on his channel trying to defend Calvinism and explain what the Calvinist doctrine was.

However, I had no idea what any of this meant. He threw around terms like "justification" and "sanctification" and "salvation." I realized that in my year and a half in the Hebrew Roots movement, all of the people I listened to, such as Michael Rood and Paul Nison, focused only on the so-called 'Gospel of the kingdom' and the issues of the Torah, but rarely ever mentioned words like salvation. In addition, besides some rudimentary knowledge on the concept of predestination, I had no idea what Calvinism taught.

I researched it, and soon came across a video in mid-January called "5 Points of Calvinism Refuted," made by the Baptist preacher Steven Anderson. I had heard of this man before and even watched a video by him once before on Bible prophecy nearly a year prior, but I didn't know anything about him or support him. Nonetheless, I listened to the entire hour-long sermon. By the end, not only was I convinced that Calvinism was a false doctrine, but I was surprised by the number of verses he quoted from to support his views, and even intrigued by the use of soteriological terms and phrases I still did not grasp.

Salvation Research

At the time, this understanding of salvation was not something which I sought for in order to get saved. I believed that all I had to do was have an understanding of what it was. Since I earnestly believed that the doctrine I already held to was the truth, I believed that I would be able to reconcile the verses given in these particular sermons with my own belief. I decided that the best way to look into these doctrines was to take as many verses as possible which focused on the different aspects of salvation and different views of it (such as faith, baptism, commandments, obedience, universality, atonement, grace, Calvinism, etc.) and organized the verses I found into these categories, before comparing them with each other to figure out what they meant.

By February or March, I had come to the conclusion that salvation was the promise of one day receiving eternal life at the resurrection, and that one needed to have faith, be baptized, and maintain their faith and repentance from sin until the end. This is what I believed the Gospel was, and I earnestly attacked the doctrines of faith alone and eternal security. Since watching the sermon about Calvinism, however, I couldn't stop myself from going back to similar sermons by Baptist pastors. Throughout spring of that year, I listened to what these Baptists had to say, mainly because of their heavy use of scripture.

I would often try to dispute these sermons, especially those which taught eternal security or the Trinity, both doctrines I completely denied. I believed that I had them duped when angry Baptists would reply to me and try to refute my arguments. However, I was confident that my arguments and the verses I gave were undefeatable. Another thing that irked me was the independent Baptist tendency to attack the Hebrew Roots movement as well. I stayed away from any videos which attacked the Sabbath or soul-sleep. Most of the time, these videos were directed towards the Seventh-Day Adventists.

Since I adhered to believer's baptism by immersion, I began to consider myself a Baptist in that sense, although I still referred to myself as a Nazarene in public or on my channel. The Baptist sermons I listened to only affected my thinking slightly. I heard more and more scriptures which I began to think about and ponder on, since I had never heard them before. Upon research in my own Bible, the ISR, I found that within was written almost the exact same words. This made me begin to reconsider who I was and what I believed.

I began researching different sects of Christianity and theological opinions. Since being introduced to the wide-world of Christian sects and movements which I had never even considered back in January, I had spent most of my time listening to Baptist sermons, particularly those by Steven Anderson and his pastor friends, such as Roger Jimenez, but had dialed back with listening to Messianic and Hebrew roots teachers and preachers. However, my opinion on these churches is that they still corrupted the truth because they didn't preach the Torah and taught the Trinity doctrine, although I believed that they were saved, according to my definition of salvation.

Gradual Change to Faith Alone

As I listened to more and more sermons and the Biblical evidences given in them, I couldn't but gradually change my beliefs, although I still stubbornly held onto some of the ideas from the Hebrew Roots movement. In spring of 2018, I believed that salvation was only by faith, but that those who had the opportunity to be baptized needed to be baptized. I also believed that one could lose their salvation by making the decision to abandon their faith in Christ, but that sin did not determine their standing in salvation.

I decided to make a video series on the Book of Romans in March, in which I managed to get through 6 chapters. Most of what I learned about the chapter was from sermons by people like Steven Anderson, who often quoted from Romans to support the doctrines of the Gospel. I found from reading the Book of Romans that much of what I saw in there I had rarely heard from my time in the Hebrew Roots movement. I had only attempted to read the book once or twice, back in early 2017, and since I didn't understand much of it, I decided to put it off for later. My interpretations given for these videos were very surface-level, but I began to defend the doctrine that one did not need to obey the Torah in order to have eternal life.

However, I still rejected many key components of the Gospel as I formed my own theology which began to look more like the theology of several Adventist groups such as the Church of God (7th-Day). Even though this was a time of my beliefs rapidly changing, I still wanted to align myself with a particular group. In addition, I didn't abandon my association with any of the Hebrew Roots people I knew. I still listened to Drake Shelton, although less often, because of my disagreement with his Calvinist doctrines. In fact, I received two books by him for my 16th birthday that May, one refuting feminism and one refuting libertarianism. Both were important subjects, in my opinion, but neither focused on theology.

Nathanael Kuechenberg was another friend of mine who I actually grew closer to by this point. For the first time ever, in April, Nathanael and I talked face-to-face over Google Hangouts, and did a livestream together. I came to find out that Nathanael himself did have similar beliefs about salvation, acknowledging that one simply needed to have faith in Christ and call upon the name of the Lord in order to be saved. He said that he felt that keeping the Torah was more of an effort to get closer to God, and that he didn't feel like many Christians who didn't obey the dietary laws, Sabbath, and holydays were necessarily evil.

Nathanael and I did several livestreams together for the next few months, talking about a range of topics. One topic which I stepped up my interest in was the Godhead. I still completely rejected the Trinity, although I did acknowledge the Semi-Arian position which puts Christ of a similar substance to the Father. So, essentially, my problem with the Trinity was the assertion that he was equal with the Father, which I assumed meant that the Son was equal in rank and not subordinate to the Father. I would talk about these distinctions in several livestreams, including one on Nathanael's channel. Another topic we seemed to focus on was mocking the attempts at dating the end of the world, which was especially a common trend in 2018.

Another change in my belief came regarding the name of Jesus. At one point I exclusively used the name of Yeshua, believing that "Jesus" came from paganism and was not related to the true name of God at all. By the beginning of 2018, I realized that Jesus was simply the English rendering of Yeshua, and that the word Iesous in Greek was the same name as Yeshua, although I never referred to Christ by the name of Jesus. However, beginning around May and June, I began to use the name of Jesus in videos on my channel. I realized the absurdity of speaking English and claiming that Jesus was an acceptable name of Yeshua while never referring to him as Jesus.

I also began to use the King James Version of the Bible around this time, and would occasionally quote from it in my videos, although the primary Bible I read was still the ISR. This is because I found out that the New Testament portion of the ISR was also based on the Textus Receptus, and thus, the King James Version was not as different from the ISR as I initially assumed. The Independent Baptists I watched on Youtube convinced me that the King James Version was a good translation, using the historical facts about its translation and the text from which it drew to support the notion (although I did not yet believe it was perfect).

By this time in the summer, I had dropped the belief that baptism saves us. I still disagreed with the Independent Baptists on the subject of eternal security, but I believed that faith alone is what saves a person. I considered myself an 'Arminian', the soteriological view which opposes itself to Calvinism. Essentially, I believed that mankind had the free will to come to God through faith, but that they also had the ability to stop believing, and would thus lose their salvation. This view strangely came from a combination of my own study of the Bible and the constant preaching of the Gospel in sermons by the independent, fundamental Baptists I listened to. The overwhelming Biblical evidence made it hard for me to doubt what the Bible said about salvation. However, I was still trusting in myself at this point and not fully in Christ to save me.

Eternal Security (Getting Saved)

Although being stubborn, it wouldn't be long until I finally made the decision to trust Christ as my personal saviour. For some reason, perhaps because of the power of the preaching of God's word from the King James Bible, I was drawn in more and more to sermons by Independent Fundamental Baptists. However, wanting to plant my feet in the false doctrine I had believed for nearly two years, I focused on sermons about sin and social topics and not sermons on the core doctrines of the faith, such as the Gospel and the Trinity.

My life changed in late June. One day, as I was lying in my bed listening to a sermon by Steven Anderson, he mentioned the doctrine of eternal security. I still didn't agree with him on it, but I didn't believe that it was a dangerous doctrine. However, suddenly, a thought struck into my head: what if I was wrong? I was betting my entire salvation on the assumption that I interpreted verses like 2 Peter 2:20 and Hebrews 6:4-6 correctly. However, since I had never read the entire Bible, I knew that I might be missing something.

So, curiously, I searched for a sermon on the subject. The video was called "Eternal Security of the Believer" and was an hour in length. I sat in place and watched the entire thing, listening very carefully. In this sermon alone, several dozen undeniable scriptures were laid out to teach the Gospel. As I listened, I felt a fear growing in my heart. The pastor preached the whole Gospel, including that if we do not trust in Christ to get us to heaven, we will die in our sins. I suddenly realized the reality of my condition, looking back on my life in the last two years. In all my time in the Hebrew Roots movement, I believed that I needed to obey the Torah in all of its precepts. I learned the hard way that this is simply impossible.

I realized that no matter how hard I tried, I could not free myself from the power of temptation. Even further, I realized that I did not truly believe in Christ. I believed that it was still up to me, that I had the power to turn from Christ by sinning willfully or by choosing to stop believing. My full faith was not on him and his death, burial, and resurrection. By the end of the sermon, through the endless Scripture given and the countless evidences of the eternity of salvation, it was as if a lightbulb clicked on in my head. I finally understood the Gospel, and I realized the importance of getting saved. Instead of being stubborn and rejecting it, I decided to respond to the conviction in my heart. I believed, and I called upon the name of the Lord, asking God to save me and to forgive me of my sins. I do not remember the exact date, but the best guess from looking at old documents is that I was saved on June 25th, 2018.

Abandoning Hebrew Roots

Not long after I was saved, I was immediately drawn by the Lord to fulfill his will. I felt refreshed, like a burden had been lifted off of my back, and I was ready to serve the Lord as a new child of God. The Lord's change in my heart was manifest in several ways. One of these ways was by an intense zeal to soulwin and share the message of the Gospel with somebody else. Although I was still too young, both physically and spiritually, to go out on my own, I planned to begin door-to-door soulwinning as soon as I was able to drive and started going to church. I listened to even more sermons teaching the principles of what and how to preach, and I gained motivation through even more videos about soul-winning events from Baptist pastors.

My ardent yearning for sharing the Gospel was further realized by my creation of my own soulwinning maps in local neighborhoods to plan out which streets I could go to and how many houses I could knock in a certain time. Although at the time they were useless for me, I didn't expect to give up hope, and to find a local church to join to carry out evangelism for. I knew of three Baptist churches in my area: Fairhaven Baptist Church, First Baptist Church of Florence, and Florence Baptist Church, none of which I knew anything about. When I got back to school in July, I tried preaching to a few of my friends. Most of them didn't want to listen because of the unexpectedness that I would suddenly try to convert them to Christianity, especially since for so long I took part in the Hebrew Roots movement (which they viewed as Judaism).

Another way in which God changed my life was through revealing the nature of false doctrine. I had believed many things while in the Hebrew Roots movement, and since getting saved, the Spirit has taught me many things from clear Scripture. One thing I tended to do was ignore certain scriptures, especially the Book of Jude, which I thought shouldn't be in the canon. However, upon getting saved, I realized that the entire KJV Bible was God's perfect inspired and preserved word. I also abandoned my strange belief in Jesus-only baptism and accepted the fact that one should be baptized in the name of the Father, Son, and Holy Ghost.

I began to read the Bible on July 4th, having made a schedule for which passages to read every day so that I could read the entire KJV from cover to cover in 7 months. I did not own an actual Bible yet, so I downloaded an app that I could read from, and made sure to focus on each of the passages I picked every day. As I read, God opened up my eyes to several doctrines which weren't entirely clear to me yet. I began to understand the place of Christians as God's people and the Biblical doctrine that the Gentiles had been graffed into Israel. I thus rejected the heavy Zionism and Jewish nationalism which I got from the Hebrew Roots movement.

Bible prophecy also became clearer to me as well, as I began to study the book of Revelation and Daniel and see how the events would play out in the end times without having somebody teach me what these books said. The only doctrine I had trouble understanding at first was the Trinity. I recognized Jesus Christ's place as the Son of God, and of his Godhead, but I didn't understand the relationship of the Father, Son, and Holy Ghost, and rejected the name "Trinity" because I still mistakenly believed that this position held that the three persons were equal in rank, power, and will, and not just in substance.

However, by the end of 2018, after beginning to read the New Testament and listening to sermons about the Trinity, it became clear to me what the Scriptures say about the Godhead. By this time, I had also dropped the use of the name Yeshua completely and use of any other Bible, and considered myself to be a full, independent Baptist.

The following year was great in my walk with the Lord. Early in the year, I started attending a local Baptist church in my area. On January 27th, I was baptized and became a member of the church. Since then, I've attended every Sunday service and nearly every Wednesday service. God has done great things in my life, including giving opportunities to preach the Gospel to unbelievers, including some of my old friends who were in need of a saviour. By summer of 2019, all ties with the Hebrew Roots movement had disappeared, as I realized what the Scriptures say about the ceremonial laws, including dietary laws, holy days, and Sabbaths, in the New Testament, and how they're done away with. I thank God for taking me out of that wicked movement which corrupts the truth of God's word.

CHAPTER 4: THE ERRORS OF THE HEBREW ROOTS MOVEMENT

The Premise: Jewish Supremacy

In this chapter, I will labour to refute the doctrine of the Hebrew Roots movement by going in depth into each of the main characteristics and doctrines of this religion. Keep in mind, this will not be comprehensive. Not everybody who considers themselves to be a "Messianic Jew" or a member of the Hebrew Roots movement believes all of these doctrines, and some may even hold to doctrines which are not covered. The main doctrines addressed in this chapter are those which I believed, which mainly came from 'Torah' teachers like Michael Rood, my biggest influence in falling into this trap.

The first doctrines which should be addressed is that basis of the Hebrew Roots movement itself: the assumption that things which are Hebraic and Jewish are inherently rooted in true worship of God. It is presumed that since the Israelites were God's chosen people in the Old Testament, the apostles and disciples of Jesus adhered to a religion which was much closer in its roots to Judaism, and that the religion which Christ established continued to maintain the practices of the Jews. Thus, Hebrew names are used, the laws of Moses are followed, and Zionism is supported.

Many in the Hebrew Roots movement even embrace non-Messianic Jews, based on the belief that they are still God's chosen people. Thus, those in the movement have typically a negative attitude towards Gentiles and Gentile culture, while simultaneously supporting the nation of Israel and the modern-day Jews in the land regardless of their faith in Christ. As I said in the biography of my time in the Hebrew Roots movement, I loved the land of Israel and believed that these people deserved more land and more power in the Middle East.

However, the idea that the Jews are God's chosen people in the New Testament, that they are under God's will, that they worship the same God as us, and that the religious practices of the Jews have anything to do with the religion of the New Testament is all entirely foreign to Scripture. So, I want to first focus on tearing down the lies of the Hebrew Roots surrounding the Jews, Judaism, and Israel.

First of all, salvation is not limited or concentrated on one physical nation. The New Testament constantly makes it clear that Christ's gift comes to all nations. No emphasis is placed on the Jews.

> Acts 10:34-35 - Then Peter opened his mouth, and said, Of a truth I perceive that God is no respecter of persons: <u>But in every nation he that feareth him, and worketh righteousness, is accepted with him.</u>

> Romans 16:25-26 - Now to him that is of power to stablish you according to my gospel, and the preaching of Jesus Christ, according to the revelation of the mystery, which was kept secret since the world began, But now is made manifest, and by the scriptures of the prophets, according to the commandment of the everlasting God, <u>made known to all nations for the obedience of faith:</u>

> Revelation 5:9 - And they sung a new song, saying, Thou art worthy to take the book, and to open the seals thereof: for thou wast slain, and hast redeemed us to God <u>by thy blood out of every kindred, and tongue, and people, and nation;</u>

The Bible makes it clear that salvation is a gift which is offered to all nations; that God does not care which nation a person is from. He is not a respecter of persons. If somebody is a Gentile, yet they fear him and believe on him, then they are "accepted with him," meaning, they are counted among God's people with the Jews. We see in the book of Revelation also that those who are in heaven come from every kindred, and tongue, and people, and nation. It is not limited to the Israelites only. In fact, the New Testament even says:

> Romans 2:8-11 - But unto them that are contentious, and do not obey the truth, but obey unrighteousness, indignation and wrath, Tribulation and anguish<u>, upon every soul of man that doeth evil, of the Jew first, and also of the Gentile</u>; But glory, honour, and peace, to every man that worketh good, <u>to the Jew first, and also to the Gentile: For there is no respect of persons with God.</u>

This passage once again shows to us a simple truth: that there is no distinction between the Jews and the Gentiles in God's mind. Their place as the chosen people in the Old Testament means nothing, because God places tribulation and anguish to every soul of man that doeth evil. It doesn't matter if they're of the Jews, God regardless will place his wrath upon those who do not obey the truth.

The mindset that the Jews are special is thus foreign to Scripture. Those of the Hebrew Roots movement, who claim to believe the New Testament, reject most of its teachings, on the basis of the belief that the Tanakh is more important. However, even in the Old Testament, God makes it clear that God does not make a distinction between the nations, but that even those of the Gentiles can serve God and be his people. The scriptures say,

> 1 Kings 8:43 - Hear thou in heaven thy dwelling place, and do according to all that the stranger calleth to thee for: that all people of the earth may know thy name, to fear thee, as do thy people Israel; and that they may know that this house, which I have builded, is called by thy name.

> Psalm 22:27 - All the ends of the world shall remember and turn unto the Lord: and all the kindreds of the nations shall worship before thee.

Both of these passages talk about people from every nation, and from all over the earth knowing God and turning to him. Psalm 22 is a prophesy of Jesus' death. In context, then, verse 27 is about how Christ' death on the cross, which was the basis of the new covenant (Luke 22:20), draws all men unto God (John 12:32). In the new testament, then, all the nations have a chance to worship before God. The gates have been opened up to all peoples, not limited to Israel.

It should be noted that in these scriptures it talks about the Gentiles worshipping God and fearing him. In the Hebrew Roots movement, I recognized that Gentiles were still able to be saved, but my mindset was that the physical nation, particularly the Jews, were more important, and that they were still God's chosen people who God fought for above all others. However, the truth we see in the New Testament is far from this unfounded claim. Instead, the Bible shows us that the Jews as a nation have rejected the Lord, that they worship God in vain, that they do not even believe the Scriptures, and that they are contrary to the truth of the Gospel. Jesus said,

> Matthew 15:3-9 - But he answered and said unto them, <u>Why do ye also transgress the commandment of God by your tradition?</u> For God commanded, saying, Honour thy father and mother: and, He that curseth father or mother, let him die the death. But ye say, Whosoever

shall say to his father or his mother, It is a gift, by whatsoever thou mightest be profited by me; And honour not his father or his mother, he shall be free. Thus have ye made the commandment of God of none effect by your tradition. Ye hypocrites, well did Esaias prophesy of you, saying, This people draweth nigh unto me with their mouth, and honoureth me with their lips; <u>but their heart is far from me</u>. 9 <u>But in vain they do worship me, teaching for doctrines the commandments of men</u>.

In the Hebrew Roots movement, I acknowledged that the Pharisees had corrupted the truth and that they were thus against God. However, what I failed to realize is that the Jews today as a whole continue to do this. The Jews in Israel, which do not believe on Christ, teach and practice for doctrines the commandments of men. Their Talmud, which they claim to be based on the "Oral Torah" is the opinion of rabbis during antiquity, and is not inspired of God. However, even considering the Jews who claimed to depart from Talmudic teachings, such as the Karaites, Jesus says,

> John 5:46-47 - Do not think that I will accuse you to the Father: there is one that accuseth you, even Moses, in whom ye trust. For had ye believed Moses, ye would have believed me: for he wrote of me. But if ye believe not his writings, how shall ye believe my words?

Jesus tells the Jews that if they had believed Moses, they would have believed him. Karaites such as Nehemia Gordon, a friend of Michael Rood's who regularly appears in his programs, do not truly believe Moses. If they did, they would not reject Christ. The fact that they continue to obey the Torah yet do not trust in Christ shows that they are trusting in the works of the law and not in the faith of Christ. Galatians 5:4 says of those who are justified by the law that "ye are fallen from grace."

If Jews were truly God's people, and if they still worshipped the same God which we worshipped, then they would follow after God. However, the Scriptures constantly show that they do not believe Moses or any of the words of God. Jesus also said,

> John 8:47 - He that is of God heareth God's words: ye therefore hear them not, because ye are not of God.

Of course, the context shows that the people Jesus is preaching to were the

Jews. In verses 39 and 41, they claim that Abraham is their father, and that God is their Father, but Jesus replies simply by saying "Ye are of your father the devil" in verse 44. The Jews thus refused to hear the preaching of God's word through his Son, and rejected Jesus and refused to love him (see verse 42), and are therefore of the devil. They are not of God. Using the reasoning Jesus gave in this chapter, this would apply to any Jew which rejects Christ, no matter their stance on the Torah or how deep they are in their Pharasaic traditions. Another passage which shows that the Jews hate the word of God is this:

> Galatians 6:13-16 - For neither they themselves who are circumcised keep the law; but desire to have you circumcised, that they may glory in your flesh. But God forbid that I should glory, save in the cross of our Lord Jesus Christ, by whom the world is crucified unto me, and I unto the world. For in Christ Jesus neither circumcision availeth any thing, nor uncircumcision, but a new creature. And as many as walk according to this rule, peace be on them, and mercy, and upon the Israel of God.

Concerning those who are of the fleshly circumcision, the Jews; they do not even keep the law. These people who the Hebrew Roots recognize as God's chosen people, and who view as a righteous nation; The Bible says of them that they only are circumcised to glory in the flesh. The Bible teaches us that "For we are the circumcision, who worship God in the Spirit, rejoice in Christ Jesus, and have no confidence in the flesh (Phil. 3:3)," a passage of course written to Gentile believers in Philippi. On the contrary, Jews reject Christ and put their confidence instead in the flesh, believing that they can be saved by the works of the law, despite breaking the commandments constantly.

> Romans 9:30-33 - What shall we say then? That the Gentiles, <u>which followed not after righteousness, have attained to righteousness, even the righteousness which is of faith</u>. But Israel, which followed after the law of righteousness, <u>hath not attained to the law of righteousness. Wherefore? Because they sought it not by faith, but as it were by the works of the law</u>. For they stumbled at that stumblingstone; As it is written, Behold, I lay in Sion a stumblingstone and rock of offence: and whosoever believeth on him shall not be ashamed.

Here a difference is put between the Gentiles who have faith and the Jews who seek righteousness by the works of the law. This passage shows us clearly that the Jews have not obtained righteousness, while the Gentiles have. How can Israel be special in God's eyes if they aren't even righteous to God? Instead, the Gentiles who have faith have attained to righteousness. It's because of their faith in Christ that they have righteousness imputed to them (2 Cor. 5:21). The physical nation of Israel stumbled at the stumblingstone, Jesus Christ. They have fallen from serving the living God.

Before moving on to explain what the Scriptures say about who Israel is, and about who the chosen people of God are, I want to first show that the Jews rejected Christ also in the sense that they put him to death and crucified him. In my absurd nationalistic attitude towards Israel and the Jews, I was offended at any claim that the Jews had killed Christ. Rather, my response was that the Romans had put Jesus to death. I believed that claiming otherwise was an anti-Semitic attack on God's chosen people. However, this can't be further from the truth. The Bible says:

John 1:11 - He came unto his own, and his own received him not.

'His own' refers to his people, Israel, which did not receive him, but instead rejected him. This rejection is shown at the crucifixion in vivid detail:

Matthew 27:20-25 - But the chief priests and elders persuaded the multitude that they should ask Barabbas, and destroy Jesus. The governor answered and said unto them, Whether of the twain will ye that I release unto you? They said, Barabbas. Pilate saith unto them, What shall I do then with Jesus which is called Christ? They all say unto him, Let him be crucified. And the governor said, Why, what evil hath he done? But they cried out the more, saying, Let him be crucified. When Pilate saw that he could prevail nothing, but that rather a tumult was made, he took water, and washed his hands before the multitude, saying, I am innocent of the blood of this just person: see ye to it. Then answered all the people, and said, His blood be on us, and on our children.

This scripture portraying the trial of Jesus and his condemnation to death outlines what really happened, and who is responsible for his death. This gospel record shows us that it is the multitude of the Jewish people who cried out for Jesus to be crucified. Pontius Pilate, the Roman governor, was the one who tried to plead for Jesus and reason with the Jews, asking them, "Why, what evil hath he done?" Yet the Jews continued to cry out for Jesus to be put to death. Finally, Pilate washes away the bloodguiltiness, and the Jews take upon themselves the guilt for his death, saying "His blood be on us, and on our children." If that isn't clear enough, here's a passage which explicitly says the Jews killed Jesus:

> 1 Thessalonians 2:14-16 - For ye, brethren, became followers of the churches of God which in Judaea are in Christ Jesus: for ye also have suffered like things of your own countrymen, even as they have of the Jews: Who both killed the Lord Jesus, and their own prophets, and have persecuted us; and they please not God, and are contrary to all men: Forbidding us to speak to the Gentiles that they might be saved, to fill up their sins alway: for the wrath is come upon them to the uttermost.

Verse 15 says that the Jews both killed the Lord Jesus and their own prophets. To deny the bloodguiltiness of the Jews is to deny direct scripture. They didn't believe in Jesus, they rejected the word of God, and thus, they wanted to put him to death for what they perceived to be blasphemy. This is a recurring theme in the book of John (John 5:18, 7:1, 8:37, 40, 10:31). The Jews didn't like what Jesus was saying, so they continuously sought opportunities to kill him, and this was finally fulfilled when they put him to death at the cross.

This is a controversial subject, but what 1 Thessalonians 2:15 says is undeniable. Many, including myself at one point, label this as an anti-Semitic lie. Yet, if we are to believe what the Bible says, we cannot deny the clear testimonies concerning the crucifixion of Christ and who was behind it. However, the information does not stop there. Not only did they kill "the Lord Jesus, and their prophets, and have persecuted us," but the passage says also that they "please not God, and are contrary to all men," and that they try to stop the spread of the Gospel. Because of this, "the wrath is come upon them to the uttermost."

This is a harsh statement. 1 Thessalonians 5:9 tells us that "God hath not appointed us to wrath, but to obtain salvation by our Lord Jesus Christ." The Jews, however, because of their wickedness and refusal to accept the truth, are not saved, but under the wrath of God. As it is written, "He that believeth not the Son shall not see life, but the wrath of God abideth on him (John 3:36)." If Israel as we know it today, including the inhabitants of the land of Israel and the Jewish people, were the 'chosen people of God' as many claim, then why does the Bible speak so powerfully against them, persistently emphasizing that they are unrighteous, wicked, opposed to and unbelieving in God's word, and that God's wrath is upon them? The only way they can escape from this wrath is to repent from their unbelief to Christ.

> Acts 2:22-36 - Ye men of Israel, hear these words; Jesus of Nazareth, a man approved of God among you by miracles and wonders and signs, which God did by him in the midst of you, as ye yourselves also know: Him, being delivered by the determinate counsel and foreknowledge of God, <u>ye have taken, and by wicked hands have crucified and slain</u>: Whom God hath raised up, having loosed the pains of death: because it was not possible that he should be holden of it. For David speaketh concerning him, I foresaw the Lord always before my face, for he is on my right hand, that I should not be moved: Therefore did my heart rejoice, and my tongue was glad; moreover also my flesh shall rest in hope: Because thou wilt not leave my soul in hell, neither wilt thou suffer thine Holy One to see corruption. Thou hast made known to me the ways of life; thou shalt make me full of joy with thy countenance. Men and brethren, let me freely speak unto you of the patriarch David, that he is both dead and buried, and his sepulchre is with us unto this day. Therefore being a prophet, and knowing that God had sworn with an oath to him, that of the fruit of his loins, according to the flesh, he would raise up Christ to sit on his throne; He seeing this before spake of the resurrection of Christ, that his soul was not left in hell, neither his flesh did see corruption. This Jesus hath God raised up, whereof we all are witnesses. Therefore being by the right hand of God exalted, and having received of the Father the promise of the Holy Ghost, he hath shed forth this, which ye now see and hear. For David is not ascended into the heavens: but he saith himself, The Lord said unto my Lord, Sit thou on my right hand, Until I make thy foes thy footstool. <u>Therefore let all the house of Israel know assuredly, that God hath made the same Jesus, whom ye have crucified, both Lord and Christ.</u>

In this passage, Peter preaches to those at Jerusalem and directly acknowledges that they have taken and crucified Jesus Christ. It's undeniable that the Jews are responsible for the death of Christ, and this is even recognized by the apostles, who are speaking with the leading of the Holy Ghost and testifying the Gospel.

Some may say that the Jews did not kill him because he laid down his life for us (1 John 3:16). However, not only is this denying several clear passages, but it's just nonsense. If a gunman comes into my house and I take a bullet for a family member, I not only did so willingly, but I did so to save that person. This does not mean that the gunman didn't kill me. A willingness to lay down your life does not mean you are the one killing yourself.

After Peter testifies the Gospel, and shows the Jews that Christ was raised from the dead after they crucified him, they were "pricked to the heart" and they asked "Men and brethren, what shall we do?" Peter replied to this by saying "Repent, and be baptized every one of you in the name of Jesus Christ for the remission of sins, and ye shall receive the gift of the Holy Ghost (Acts 2:38)." The Jews had crucified Christ because they had rejected him. The only way to be reconciled to God was to repent, meaning *to turn* to Christ in faith.

What I didn't understand during my time in the Hebrew Roots movement is that under the new covenant, God makes no distinction between the different peoples under the new testament. The Jews and the Gentiles are one by faith in Christ Jesus (Galatians 3:28), and "there is no difference (Romans 10:12)." The only distinction made is between those who are unbelievers and those who are believers. The unbelieving Jews, which constitutes the majority of the Jewish people, are thus not counted to be the same as the believers. He is no respecter of persons.

I want to make clear that this is not "replacement theology." This teaching, also known as supersessionism, relies on the assumption that there is a universal church separate from the nation of Israel. Groups such as the Roman Catholics hold to this replacement theology teaching, which is that the church has replaced or superseded Israel in the New Testament. The Bible does not teach this. Rather, the Bible teaches that the collective body of believers, regardless of their flesh-and-blood nationality, is Israel, while the church is a local congregation of saved and baptized believers. The unbelieving Jews who reject God, although they may be physically descended from Jacob, are not part of what the Bible calls the "Israel of God." Thus, it is not a replacement, but a casting out of the unbelievers. Let's see what the Bible has to say:

> 1 Peter 2:9-10 - But ye are a chosen generation, a royal priesthood, an holy nation, a peculiar people; that ye should shew forth the praises of him who hath called you out of darkness into his marvellous light; Which in time past were not a people, but are now the people of God: which had not obtained mercy, but now have obtained mercy.

It should be noted that the book of 1 Peter was not written to Jews, but to Gentile converts:

> 1 Peter 1:1 - Peter, an apostle of Jesus Christ, to the strangers scattered throughout Pontus, Galatia, Cappadocia, Asia, and Bithynia,

Peter specifically addresses the recepients of the letter as "strangers" and directed it to regions in Anatolia. Yet, he writes that they are "an holy nation, a peculiar people." Thus, even though these people are Gentiles and not of the physical nation of Israel, Peter recognizes that they are a holy nation. This is the same promise that God makes to the Israelites in Exodus 19:6, that they would be "a kingdom of priests, and an holy nation." Notice that Peter recognizes in these verses that in time past, these Gentiles were not the people of God, but that they are now, collectively, despite even coming from different geographical regions and ethnic backgrounds. Notice the use of similar language in this following passage as well:

> Romans 9:25-26 - As he saith also in Osee, I will call them my people, which were not my people; and her beloved, which was not beloved. And it shall come to pass, that in the place where it was said unto them, Ye are not my people; there shall they be called the children of the living God.

We as Gentiles were not considered the people of God in the Old Testament. However, now, even though in time past we were not his people, now we are both his people, but also the children of God as well. This passage is quoting from the following verse in the book of Hosea:

> Hosea 2:23 - And I will sow her unto me in the earth; and I will have mercy upon her that had not obtained mercy; and I will say to them which were not my people, Thou art my people; and they shall say,

Thou art my God.

So, answer this question. Were the Israelites considered the people of God in the Old Testament? Absolutely - God told Moses to say to the Israelites "And I will take you to me for a people, and I will be to you a God" in Exodus 6:7. Hundreds of years later, Hosea prophesies that there will come a day when a people which were not God's people will be called his people. The New Testament reveals that this was spoken to the Gentile believers in Christ. Thus, it is evident that God's people Israel is not a separate nation of the physical descendants of Jacob, but includes believing Gentiles as well. Let's see what else the Bible says on this matter:

> Ephesians 2:11-19 - Wherefore remember, that ye being in time past Gentiles in the flesh, who are called Uncircumcision by that which is called the Circumcision in the flesh made by hands; 12 That at that time ye were without Christ, being aliens from the commonwealth of Israel, and strangers from the covenants of promise, having no hope, and without God in the world: 13 But now in Christ Jesus ye who sometimes were far off are made nigh by the blood of Christ. 14 For he is our peace, who hath made both one, and hath broken down the middle wall of partition between us; 15 Having abolished in his flesh the enmity, even the law of commandments contained in ordinances; for to make in himself of twain one new man, so making peace; 16 And that he might reconcile both unto God in one body by the cross, having slain the enmity thereby: 17 And came and preached peace to you which were afar off, and to them that were nigh. 18 For through him we both have access by one Spirit unto the Father. 19 Now therefore ye are no more strangers and foreigners, but fellowcitizens with the saints, and of the household of God.

This passage teaches this truth as well. Breaking these verses down, we first see in verse 11 that the people Paul is addressing, the Ephesians (from Ephesus, an Anatolian city of Greek nationality) were Gentiles in the flesh in the past, and were considered to be the uncircumcision. These two, the Uncircumcision and Circumcision, are thus compared: the Uncircumcision (Gentiles) were considered aliens (meaning, foreigners) from Israel, and from the covenants of promise. The passage thus starts out by laying down the fundamental truth which 1 Peter 2 and Romans 9 tells us as well: that this is being addressed to Gentiles and not flesh-and-blood Israelites, and thus were not considered the people of God in time past.

However, "in Christ Jesus ye who sometimes were far off are made nigh by the blood of Christ." We can't take this out of context. If the context is talking about how we were Gentiles in the past and were strangers to the commonwealth of Israel, then what were we made nigh to? To the commonwealth of Israel. It thus explains this in the following verses, that he has made both one. The only thing he could possibly be referring to when using the word 'both' are the only two antecedents referred to in the preceding verses: the Uncircumcision and the Circumcision. Therefore, we as the Gentiles who are uncircumcised in the flesh are made one with those who are the circumcised in the flesh, the Jews. Verse 16 tells us also that we're made of one body.

Moving down to verse 19, it concludes by telling us that we are no longer strangers and foreigners (remember, in context, aliens to the commonwealth of Israel and strangers to the covenant of promise), but are now made fellowcitizens of the saints. Thus, we can conclude from Ephesian 2 that the Gentiles, through Christ, have become of Israel, and partake also of the covenant of promise. The attitude therefore that the Jews are the 'chosen people' and should be designated as special in comparison with other nations is thus foreign to the scriptures. Let's see what else the Bible has to say about this subject:

> Galatians 3:7-9 - Know ye therefore that they which are of faith, the same are the children of Abraham. And the scripture, foreseeing that God would justify the heathen through faith, preached before the gospel unto Abraham, saying, In thee shall all nations be blessed. So then they which be of faith are blessed with faithful Abraham.

This passage shows us again that it is through faith in Christ Jesus that the people of God are reckoned. In the passage in Ephesians, the blood of Christ makes the Gentiles nigh to the commonwealth of Israel. In this passage, we see that those who are of faith are considered the children of Abraham, and are blessed with faithful Abraham. Those who support the Zionist doctrine, especially Michael Rood, continuously claim that God promised Abraham and his descendants (the physical nation of Israel) inheritance in the land of Canaan and the gift of being the people of God. Yet, in Galatians 3, we are informed that all nations are blessed in Abraham, not just one particular nation.

Do the Jews have faith in Christ? No, predominantly they reject Christ and as we have seen, have not attained unto righteousness because they seek it by the works of the law and not by faith (Romans 9:30-33). So are they the children of Abraham? According to Galatians 3:7-9, the answer is no. Yet the Zionist will still object, "but didn't God give the promises to Abraham and to his seed?" Let's see what the Old Testament says:

> Genesis 12:7 - And the Lord appeared unto Abram, and said, <u>Unto thy seed will I give this land</u>: and there builded he an altar unto the Lord, who appeared unto him.

> Genesis 13:14-16 - And the Lord said unto Abram, after that Lot was separated from him, Lift up now thine eyes, and look from the place where thou art northward, and southward, and eastward, and westward: <u>For all the land which thou seest, to thee will I give it, and to thy seed for ever.</u> And I will <u>make thy seed as the dust of the earth</u>: so that if a man can number the dust of the earth, then shall thy seed also be numbered.

> Genesis 17:4-10 - As for me, behold, my covenant is with thee, and thou shalt be a father of many nations. Neither shall thy name any more be called Abram, but thy name shall be Abraham; for a father of many nations have I made thee. And I will make thee exceeding fruitful, and I will make nations of thee, and kings shall come out of thee. <u>And I will establish my covenant between me and thee and thy seed after thee in their generations for an everlasting covenant,</u> to be a God unto thee, and to thy seed after thee. <u>And I will give unto thee, and to thy seed after thee, the land wherein thou art a stranger, all the land of Canaan, for an everlasting possession;</u> and I will be their God. And God said unto Abraham, Thou shalt keep my covenant therefore, thou, and thy seed after thee in their generations. <u>This is my covenant, which ye shall keep, between me and you and thy seed after thee;</u> Every man child among you shall be circumcised.

Everytime a promise is made in the book of Genesis, God does not just give the promise to Abraham himself, but also to 'thy seed.' However, we cannot simply conclude that the meaning behind this is that all the physical descendants of Abraham have been given the promises of God. This is what the Zionists claim. Since God promised the land, the covenant, the status as God's people, and to be as the dust of the earth to the seed of Abraham, then the Jews have been given all of these things by God. Is this true? Let's see what the Bible says:

> Galatians 3:16 - Now to Abraham and his seed were the promises made. He saith not, And to seeds, as of many; but as of one, And to thy seed, which is Christ.

We are explicity told that the promises made to Abraham and his seed refers to Abraham and Christ. "Thy seed" is not Israel or the Jews, but Christ. Reading on in the chapter, we find out also that those who are in Christ are counted for the seed as well:

> Galatians 3:27-29 - For as many of you as have been baptized into Christ have put on Christ. There is neither Jew nor Greek, there is neither bond nor free, there is neither male nor female: for ye are all one in Christ Jesus. And if ye be Christ's, then are ye Abraham's seed, and heirs according to the promise.

He says clearly: There is neither Jew nor Greek. Our ethnic background and blood does not determine our standing with God. Rather, if we are of Christ, then are we reckoned as Abraham's seed, and heirs according to the promise. Therefore, the promises made in Genesis of the land, the covenant, the status as God's people, and the innumerable number were made to Abraham, to Christ, and all those who are of Christ, regardless of whether they're a Jew or a Gentile. These promises were made to the seed of Abraham, which is not the physical nation today. Rather, the Bible teaches us instead that the Jews who reject Christ Jesus are not considered to be of Israel.

> Romans 9:3-8 - For I could wish that myself were accursed from Christ for my brethren, <u>my kinsmen according to the flesh: Who are Israelites</u>; to whom pertaineth the adoption, and the glory, and the covenants, and the giving of the law, and the service of God, and the promises; Whose are the fathers, and of whom as concerning the flesh Christ came, who is over all, God blessed for ever. Amen. Not as though the word of God hath taken none effect. For <u>they are not all Israel, which are of Israel</u>: Neither, because they are the seed of Abraham, are

90

they all children: but, In Isaac shall thy seed be called. That is, <u>They which are the children of the flesh, these are not the children of God: but the children of the promise are counted for the seed</u>.

Paul starts off by identifying who he's talking about in this passage: Israelites according to the flesh. This would be equivalent to the modern Jews who live in the state of Israel and elsewhere. Paul tells us that "they are not all Israel which are of Israel." Simply put, just because they are physical Israelites, just because they are descended from Jacob/Israel, does not mean they are considered Israel, or the 'Israel of God' mentioned in Galatians 6. These are the children of the flesh, or Israel according to the flesh, but not the children of promise. Instead, those who are the children of the promise are counted to be the seed of Abraham, through Isaac. Galatians 3 has already shown us that this refers to believers in Christ, who are counted for the seed. However, the next chapter goes on to say this as well:

> Galatians 4:21-31 - Tell me, ye that desire to be under the law, do ye not hear the law? 22 For it is written, that Abraham had two sons, the one by a bondmaid, the other by a freewoman. 23 But he who was of the <u>bondwoman was born after the flesh; but he of the freewoman was by promise</u>. 24 Which things are an allegory: for these are the two covenants; <u>the one from the mount Sinai, which gendereth to bondage, which is Agar</u>. 25 For this Agar is mount Sinai in Arabia, and answereth to Jerusalem which now is, and is in bondage with her children. 26 But Jerusalem which is above is free, which is the mother of us all. 27 For it is written, Rejoice, thou barren that bearest not; break forth and cry, thou that travailest not: for the desolate hath many more children than she which hath an husband. 28 Now we, brethren, <u>as Isaac was, are the children of promise.</u>29 But as then he that was born after the flesh persecuted him that was born after the Spirit, even so it is now. 30 Nevertheless what saith the scripture? <u>Cast out the bondwoman and her son: for the son of the bondwoman shall not be heir with the son of the freewoman</u>. 31 So then, brethren, we are not children of the bondwoman, but of the free.

Notice the similarity of terms to that which is used in Romans 9, mainly that there is a comparison between those which are the children of the flesh and those who are the children of the promise. The Bible already told us in the previous chapter that even the Gentiles which have faith are counted for the seed, and heirs according the promise. In this chapter, we are presented with the story of the two sons of Abraham: Ishmael, born to Hagar, and Isaac, born to Sarah. Hagar was the bondwoman of Abraham, and thus represents the bondage of the law. In the story of Genesis, Ishmael is born first, and is born not according to the promise of God, but rather by the will of Sarai, who wished to have a son for Abram (Genesis 16:1-4).

However, Isaac, the son of the freewoman Sarah, was born according to the promise of God (Genesis 17:15-21). God said "But my covenant will I establish with Isaac." Galatians 4 thus uses this difference to show the difference between the children of the flesh and the children of the promise. In verse 24, Paul writes that the two women are a picture of the two covenants which God would make. The bondwoman represents the covenant established at Sinai, or the Mosaic law, and says also that she "answereth to Jerusalem which now is." Thus, considering the Jewish people, who as a nation have rejected Christ and thus are still 'under the law;' they are the children of the bondwoman.

There then switches to a comparison with the children of promise, who is represented by the "Jerusalem which is above" and those who are under the new covenant. In verse 28, Paul addresses these Gentiles as the children of promise, as Isaac was. Because we have been redeemed from being under the law (Galatians 4:5) we are no longer in the bondage of the covenant at Sinai, like the Jews are. Verse 29 identifies these same people as being 'born after the Spirit.' This again refers to believers in Christ, those who have been born again. Jesus said "That which is born of the Spirit is spirit. Marvel not that I said unto thee, ye must be born again (John 3:6-7)."

Finally, the clarity of Galatians 4 concludes by quoting from what Sarah said in Genesis 21 after the birth of Isaac: "Cast out the bondwoman and her son, for the son of the bondwoman shall not be heir with the son of the freewoman." Based on the information we've already seen, we can thus conclude that those Israelites who are descended from Abraham according to the flesh, because they are the children of the flesh (of the bondwoman), they have not only been cast out, but are not heirs of the promise. Only we, who have been called in Isaac, by the promise of faith, are blessed with faithful Abraham. John the Baptist said:

Matthew 3:9 - And think not to say within yourselves, We have

Abraham to our father: for I say unto you, that God is able of these stones to raise up children unto Abraham.

It doesn't matter that the Jews are children of Abraham according to the flesh. The Jews boast in this, claiming that this makes them special among the nations of the earth. Unfortunately, many Christians have been led astray into this same racist and unbiblical doctrine. They may be the children of the flesh, but they are not considered the seed of Abraham. Those who are in Christ Jesus, regardless of their fleshly nationality, are the true seed of Abraham. The Bible additionally says:

Romans 2:28-29 - For he is not a Jew, which is one outwardly; neither is that circumcision, which is outward in the flesh: But he is a Jew, which is one inwardly; and circumcision is that of the heart, in the spirit, and not in the letter; whose praise is not of men, but of God.

So, not only are they not of Israel, they're not even truly 'Jews' in God's eyes. The nation of Judah, under the New Testament, are not those who are circumcised in the flesh. The Jew is the one who is circumcised inwardly, in the heart. This verse agrees with every passage we have looked at in scripture so far. However, the most important passage by far to show this simple doctrine is Romans 11. The chapter is long, so let's first look at what the passage says together, and then break it down:

Romans 11:1-32 - I say then, Hath God cast away his people? God forbid. For I also am an Israelite, of the seed of Abraham, of the tribe of Benjamin. God hath not cast away his people which he foreknew. Wot ye not what the scripture saith of Elias? how he maketh intercession to God against Israel saying, Lord, they have killed thy prophets, and digged down thine altars; and I am left alone, and they seek my life. But what saith the answer of God unto him? I have reserved to myself seven thousand men, who have not bowed the knee to the image of Baal. Even so then at this present time also there is a remnant according to the election of grace. And if by grace, then is it no more of works: otherwise grace is no more grace. But if it be of works, then it is no more grace: otherwise work is no more work. What then? Israel hath not obtained that which he seeketh for; but the election hath obtained it, and the rest were blinded. (According as it is written, God hath given them the spirit of slumber, eyes that they should not see, and ears that they should not hear;) unto this day. And David saith, Let their table be made a snare, and a trap, and a stumblingblock, and a recompence unto them: Let their eyes be darkened, that they may not see, and bow down their back alway. I say then, Have they stumbled that they should fall? God forbid: but rather through their fall salvation is come unto the Gentiles, for to provoke them to jealousy. Now if the fall of them be the riches of the world, and the diminishing of them the riches of the Gentiles; how much more their fulness? For I speak to you Gentiles, inasmuch as I am the apostle of the Gentiles, I magnify mine office: If by any means I may provoke to emulation them which are my flesh, and might save some of them. For if the casting away of them be the reconciling of the world, what shall the receiving of them be, but life from the dead? For if the firstfruit be holy, the lump is also holy: and if the root be holy, so are the branches. And if some of the branches be broken off, and thou, being a wild olive tree, wert grafted in among them, and with them partakest of the root and fatness of the olive tree; Boast not against the branches. But if thou boast, thou bearest not the root, but the root thee. Thou wilt say then, The branches were broken off, that I might be grafted in. Well; because of unbelief they were broken off, and thou standest by faith. Be not highminded, but fear: For if God spared not the natural branches, take heed lest he also spare not thee. Behold therefore the goodness and severity of God: on them which fell, severity; but toward thee, goodness, if thou continue in his goodness: otherwise thou also shalt be cut off. And they also, if they abide not still in unbelief, shall be grafted in: for God is able to graft them in again. For if thou wert cut out of the olive tree which is wild by nature, and wert grafted contrary to nature into a good olive tree: how much more shall these, which be the natural branches, be grafted into their own olive tree? For I would not, brethren, that ye should be ignorant of this mystery, lest ye should be wise in your own conceits; that blindness in part is happened to Israel, until the fulness of the Gentiles be come in. And so all Israel shall be saved: as it is written, There shall come out of Sion the Deliverer, and shall turn away ungodliness from Jacob: For this is my covenant unto them, when I shall take away their sins. As concerning the gospel, they are enemies for your sakes: but as touching the election, they are beloved for the father's sakes. For the gifts and calling of God are without repentance. For as ye in times past have not believed God, yet have now obtained mercy through their unbelief: Even so have these also now not believed, that through your mercy they also may obtain mercy. For God hath concluded them all in unbelief, that he might have mercy upon all.

Reading the chapter, we can already see a basic synopsis: that Israel, God's chosen people, includes both the Gentiles and the Jews who believe, but the unbelievers who have rejected Christ have been cast out of Israel. This summary aligns with the writings of Ephesians 2 and Galatians 4. Let's break down the text:

> Romans 11:1-6 - I say then, <u>Hath God cast away his people? God forbid</u>. For <u>I also am an Israelite, of the seed of Abraham, of the tribe of Benjamin</u>. God hath not cast away his people which he foreknew. Wot ye not what the scripture saith of Elias? how he maketh intercession to God against Israel saying, Lord, they have killed thy prophets, and digged down thine altars; and I am left alone, and they seek my life. But what saith the answer of God unto him? I have reserved to myself <u>seven thousand men, who have not bowed the knee to the image of Baal</u>. Even so then at this present time also there is <u>a remnant according to the election of grace</u>. And if <u>by grace, then is it no more of works: otherwise grace is no more grace. But if it be of works, then it is no more grace: otherwise work is no more work</u>.

Every detail in these first few verses is important to understanding the text. Paul starts off with a thesis, that God has not cast away his people. He gives himself as an example. He was a Benjaminite, and thus of the physical nation of Israel, and yet was not cast away from God. However, does this mean that everybody who was considered an Israelite in the Old Testament was still considered to be so? This does not seem to be the case, because Paul uses the example of Elijah in 1 Kings 19. The answer of God, according to verse 4, was that God had left seven thousand men which had not bowed to Baal (quoted from 1 Kings 19:18).

What does this show us, then? That although the majority of the nation had gone astray from God, there still remained a remnant of 7000 in the land which still served the true God. Paul thus uses this to say "Even so then at this present time also there is a remnant." Comparing the two stories, Elijah assumed that he was the only person still serving God (v. 14). God tells him about the 7000 men to show that there still remained a remnant of Israel. That's what remnant means; a small number of things or people which remain. There is thus a remnant of Israel even under the New Covenant, only a small quantity of people who remain serving God, who have not gone astray like the worshippers of Baal.

Paul makes it clear who this remnant is in verse 5 and 6, that they are "according to the election of grace." He then defines grace, that grace cannot be by works, because the two do not allow each other. Grace by definition is mercy and kindness, not something which is earned by working (I'll go more into this later). The Jews believe that they are saved by the works of the law (Romans 9:30-33), and since they do not have faith in Christ, they do not have the grace of God either, since "ye are saved by grace, through faith (Ephesians 2:8)." Thus, the remnant which is left, and which God has not cast away, are the Jews who believe (such as Paul himself, or the other apostles). Let's move on:

> Romans 11:7 - What then? Israel hath not obtained that which he seeketh for; but the election hath obtained it, and the rest were blinded.

Using the information from the preceding verses, we see that Israel (the physical nation) has not obtained what it seeks for. The election, which would be those elected by grace, the remnant, has obtained it. The rest (the Jews who have not been elected according to grace) have been blinded. We know that the Jews seek for the promises of God, especially an inheritance in the land and a special place as the people of God. Yet, this desire has been unfullfilled because they refused to believe God, and therefore, have been blinded. This concept of being 'blinded' is elaborated on in the following verses:

> Romans 11:8-10 - (According as it is written, God hath given them the spirit of slumber, eyes that they should not see, and ears that they should not hear;) unto this day. And David saith, Let their table be made a snare, and a trap, and a stumblingblock, and a recompence unto them: Let their eyes be darkened, that they may not see, and bow down their back alway.

The blindness is thus shown to be from God, who gave them eyes and ears that shouldn't see or hear. Because they rejected Christ, they were given the eyes of blindness. This shouldn't be taken lightly; for God darkened their eyes "that they may not see, and bown down their back alway." In other words, it's forbidden for them to see. They are 'alway' (meaning, perpetually, forever) going to bow down their back to God.

The severity of this blindness is demonstrated when Jesus preached to the Jews and did many miracles before them. Instead of accepting him as the Christ, they rejected him and refused to believe. Immediately after prophesying his death, when the Jews failed to understand what he spoke of, John writes this:

> John 12:38-40 - That the saying of Esaias the prophet might be fulfilled, which he spake, Lord, who hath believed our report? and to whom hath the arm of the Lord been revealed? <u>Therefore they could not believe</u>, because that Esaias said again, <u>He hath blinded their eyes, and hardened their heart</u>; that they <u>should not see </u>with their eyes, nor understand with their heart, and be converted, and I should heal them.

This blindness by God is not a description of the unbelief itself, but the result of their unbelief. They rejected Christ as their Messiah, so God blinded their eyes and hardened their heart, so that they could not believe, and should not see or understand. "Could not" is not a difficult phrase to understand. It means, in other words, that it was impossible for the Jews to believe, that they were not able to. The Bible refers to those who have been blinded by God in this manner as 'reprobates.'

In Romans 1, for example, we see a description of these reprobates. Verses 18-21 establish that these are those who "hold the truth in unrighteousness," have "that which may be known of God" manifest in them, and who "knew God." However, "when they knew God, they glorified him not as God, neither were thankful; but became vain in their imaginations, and their foolish heart was darkened (Romans 1:21)." Verse 24 goes on to tell us that 'God gave them up to uncleanness', verse 26 tells us that 'God gave them up to vile affections', and verse 28 tell us that 'God gave them over to a reprobate mind.' The word reprobate means "rejected" (see Jer. 6:30). They rejected God, so God gave them up and rejected them.

In 2 Timothy 3:7-8, which speaks of these same reprobates, we learn that they are "never able to come to the knowledge of the truth." This is very similar to the wording of John 12 concerning the Jews who didn't believe on Christ. It has the same use of absolutes to show that these people are hardened by God himself and thus can never be saved because they will never believe. If you would like more detail about the reprobate doctrine, I have written another book, *Exposing the Wickedness of the Sodomites and Defending the Reprobate Doctrine from the Holy Bible* which focuses on the issue. For now, let's move on with Romans 11:

> Romans 11:11-15 - I say then, Have they stumbled <u>that they should fall? God forbid: but rather through their fall salvation is come unto the Gentiles, for to provoke them to jealousy</u>. Now if the fall of them be the riches of the world, and the diminishing of them the riches of the Gentiles; how much more their fulness? For I speak to you Gentiles, inasmuch as I am the apostle of the Gentiles, I magnify mine office: If by any means <u>I may provoke to emulation them which are my flesh, and might save some of them</u>. For if the casting away of them be the reconciling of the world, what shall the receiving of them be, but life from the dead?

Here, Paul tells us that the stumbling of the physical Jews (that they believed not on Christ, the stumblingstone and rock of offence in Sion, Romans 9:32-33) was not for the purpose of the falling of Israel. God did not blind them simply to destroy his people. He did so to bring salvation to the Gentiles also, according to verse 11. Paul therefore, as the apostle to the Gentiles, magnifies his office (meaning, makes it of greater importance). The purpose of this is to 'provoke them to jealousy" and to "provoke to emulation them which are my flesh, and might save some of them." You see, not all of the Jews who do not believe right now will never believe. Only those who have rejected Christ completely and refuse to believe are those who are in permanent blindness.

Therefore, the new covenant under Christ has expanded the nation of Israel to include the Gentiles as well, and salvation has come to them, because the Jews of the flesh had stumbled at the stumblingstone of Sion, which is Jesus Christ. One of the purposes of this is to bring back some of the Jews, to make them envious of this new covenant in Christ. Let's see what the following passage says:

> Romans 11:16-24 - For if the firstfruit be holy, the lump is also holy:

and if the root be holy, so are the branches. And if some of the branches be broken off, <u>and thou, being a wild olive tree, wert grafted in among them, and with them partakest of the root and fatness of the olive tree</u>; Boast not against the branches. But if thou boast, thou bearest not the root, but the root thee. Thou wilt say then, The branches were broken off, that I might be grafted in. Well; <u>because of unbelief they were broken off, and thou standest by faith</u>. Be not highminded, but fear: For if God spared not the natural branches, take heed lest he also spare not thee. Behold therefore the goodness and severity of God: on them which fell, severity; <u>but toward thee, goodness, if thou continue in his goodness: otherwise thou also shalt be cut off</u>. And they also, <u>if they abide not still in unbelief, shall be grafted in</u>: for God is able to graft them in again. For if thou wert cut out of the olive tree which is wild by nature, and wert grafted contrary to nature into a good olive tree: how much more shall these, which be the natural branches, be grafted into their own olive tree?

Here we see a parable which shows us who Israel is, which agrees with what we already saw in Ephesians 2 and Galatians 3-4. Paul identifies the Gentile Romans he is writing to as representing the wild olive tree in verse 17. Since we have been grafted in among the natural olive tree, we "partake of the root and fatness of the olive tree." Comparing with Galatians 3:29, it is evident that this refers to the promises of God. The Gentiles have become part of Israel, and therefore, partake of the same things which the physical seed partakes of.

However, there are other branches which were from the natural tree (the Jews) which were broken off from the tree. We see in verse 20 that the reason they were broken off is "because of unbelief." Therefore, the unbelieving Jews have been cut off from the original tree, Israel. This is the same truth we are told in Galatians 4; that the children of the flesh, of the bondwoman, because they are under the bondage of the law, have been cast out, while those who were children of the freewoman were brought in.

Verses 22 reveals to us that God's severity is shown towards those who were broken off (again, those who do not believe), but goodness to the Gentile believers. Is there then anything about the Jews which makes them inherently special? No, God has cast out those who have not believed from Israel. The only way in which they can be grafted back into the natural tree is "if they abide not still in unbelief." Notice that this is a conditional statement. The Jews can only return and be grafted back in if they believe. The Jews who do not believe on Christ are therefore not of Israel. Here's what the next section of Romans 11 says:

> Romans 11:25-27 - For I would not, brethren, that ye should be ignorant of this mystery, lest ye should be wise in your own conceits; that blindness in part is happened to Israel, until the fulness of the Gentiles be come in. And so all Israel shall be saved: as it is written, There shall come out of Sion the Deliverer, and shall turn away ungodliness from Jacob: For this is my covenant unto them, when I shall take away their sins.

Despite the multitude of preceding verses which teach that the Jews have fallen out of Israel and are rejected because they have not believed, those who support Zionism will take this particular section out of context, particularly verse 26 - "all Israel shall be saved." To them, whether they're a dispensationalist or a Hebrew Roots, this means that the Jews will be saved even though they've rejected Christ. There are many theories about how this will happen, the most prominent being that the Jews will one day as a nation turn to Christ. According to Rood's chronology of the end times, this will happen at the beginning of Daniel's 70th year, when the Israelites will collectively return to the land of Israel and return to God with all of their hearts.

However, this is not what Paul is saying. First of all, it has already been noted that "they are not all Israel, which are of Israel (Romans 9:6)." In telling us that all Israel shall be saved, we therefore cannot immediately conclude that this means that all of the physical descendants of Israel shall be saved. This is an absurd interpretation anyway, because anybody who knows anything about probability and genetics is aware that the possibility that there's somebody on Earth who isn't descended from Abraham is astronomically low or impossible. Abraham and his grandson Jacob lived near 4,000 years ago. Since then, through the movement of the nations, especially the Jewish diaspora, the blood of the Israelites has spread to all nations. If we are talking about the physical descendants of Jacob, then nearly everybody would be saved.

Another reason why this interpretation is nonsense is because millions of

100

Israelites in the past have already died, being unsaved. If Paul said in the 1st century that "all Israel shall be saved", yet this is fulfilled in the end times, then it would make no sense. Every Jew who has died in their sins in the last 2000 years, even though they'd be part of "Israel" according to the Hebrew Roots position, was still unsaved. The Hebrew Roots followers may then alter their position to that of people like John Hagee, who teaches that the Jews have always been saved. This would still contradict the Scriptures, because the Bible says "For by grace ye are saved, through faith," and "if ye believe not that I am he, ye shall die in your sins (John 8:24)," which Jesus said to the Jews. The Jews who do not believe that Jesus is the Christ or the Son of God have therefore died in their sins.

So, does that make Romans 11:26 false? Absolutely not. As Paul has been teaching, the Gentiles were grafted in among Israel while those who didn't believe were cut off. All Israel shall be saved because those in Israel are only those who believe. In other words, Paul is also saying "All those who believe shall be saved" as he does the chapter before (Romans 10:9). It's not difficult to understand when you take the verse in context.

Returning back to the above passage, we see again that "blindness in part is happened to Israel, until the fulness of the Gentiles come in." This shows us the physical nation of Israel, which was blinded in part (those who aren't elected through grace are blinded, v. 6-7), will remain that way until the fulness of the Gentiles come in. The term 'fulness of the Gentiles' is another twisted term. For those who hold to the faulty belief that the Jews collectively will be saved in the 70th week, this fulness begins at the start of the tribulation.

However, the phrase "fulness of the Gentiles come in" should not be difficult to understand. The context shows us that the Jews fell that salvation might come to the Gentiles. The fulness of the Gentiles, therefore, refers to when all of the Gentiles who will believe enter into Israel and are accepted into the kingdom. The Old Testament prophesies that people from all nations of the earth will come and worship before God, saying "All nations whom thou hast made shall come and worship before thee, O Lord; and shall glorify thy name (Psalm 86:9)." Even in the Book of Revelation we are told: "for all nations shall come and worship before thee; for thy judgments are made manifest." This is in Revelation 15:4, right before the wrath of God is poured out upon the earth, and after the rapture has already taken place, yet they still say "all nations shall come and worship before thee," implying that this is a future event.

When Jesus speaks on the Mount of Olives about the signs of his coming, he specifically mentions that the times of the Gentiles are fulfilled after the tribulation and after the abomination of desolation have taken place, saying:

> Luke 21:20-24 - And when ye shall see Jerusalem compassed with armies, then know that the desolation thereof is nigh. Then let them which are in Judaea flee to the mountains; and let them which are in the midst of it depart out; and let not them that are in the countries enter thereinto. For these be the days of vengeance, that all things which are written may be fulfilled. But woe unto them that are with child, and to them that give suck, in those days! for there shall be great distress in the land, and wrath upon this people. And they shall fall by the edge of the sword, and shall be led away captive into all nations: and Jerusalem shall be trodden down of the Gentiles, until the times of the Gentiles be fulfilled.

We know from Revelation 11 that the Gentiles tread the holy city underfoot for the period of 42 months, while the Beast is in power (v. 2). Thus, the time of the Gentiles are not fulfilled until after the Beast's power is taken away and Christ's kingdom is set up in the world. At this point, after the rapture comes and God's wrath is poured upon the earth, (Matt. 24:29-31, 1 Cor. 15:51-53, 1 Thess. 4:14-17), then is "all Israel saved." The blindness which had happened to Israel is thus removed because all of those who reject Christ, who are of the physical seed of Israel, are destroyed by God's wrath (Rev. 15-16). Moving to the final portion of Romans 11:

> Romans 11:28-32 - As concerning the gospel, they are enemies for your sakes: but as touching the election, they are beloved for the father's sakes. For the gifts and calling of God are without repentance. For as ye in times past have not believed God, yet have now obtained mercy through their unbelief: Even so have these also now not believed, that through your mercy they also may obtain mercy. For God hath concluded them all in unbelief, that he might have mercy upon all.

This last portion shows again what Paul has already revealed throughout the entirety of Romans 11, that because the Jews did not believe, mercy has come

102

to the Gentiles. We therefore, as Gentile believers, are grafted into the natural tree and become of Israel. If the whole chapter is taken in context, it's not difficult to understand what is being said. Israel consists only of those who believe, whether they're Gentiles who were grafted in or Jews who have not been kicked out because they received Jesus as their Messiah.

To say that the Jews have a special place in the sight of God, and to say that they somehow shall inherit the promises of God is contrary to clear scripture. Jesus said "Except ye repent, ye shall all likewise perish (Luke 13:3)." The Jews who have not turned to Christ die in their sins because of their unbelief. John the Baptist said, "He that believeth not the Son shall not see life, but the wrath of God abideth on him." If the unbelievers shall not see life, then the unbelievers of the past, including the Jews who have died in their sins, will never be part of God's kingdom, but will be cast into the lake of fire, as we are told in the Book of Revelation. That includes Michael Rood's buddy Nehemia Gordon. Jesus said,

> Matthew 21:42-44 - Jesus saith unto them, Did ye never read in the scriptures, The stone which the builders rejected, the same is become the head of the corner: this is the Lord's doing, and it is marvellous in our eyes? Therefore say I unto you, The kingdom of God shall be taken from you, and given to a nation bringing forth the fruits thereof. And whosoever shall fall on this stone shall be broken: but on whomsoever it shall fall, it will grind him to powder.

The kingdom of God was taken from the physical seed and given to the spiritual seed, the true Israel, the Israel of God (Galatians 6:15-16). What the Hebrew Roots people do not understand, and what I failed to understand, is that the status of the physical nation as God's people was never an absolute promise; it was conditional:

> Exodus 19:5-6 - Now therefore, if ye will obey my voice indeed, and keep my covenant, then ye shall be a peculiar treasure unto me above all people: for all the earth is mine: And ye shall be unto me a kingdom of priests, and an holy nation. These are the words which thou shalt speak unto the children of Israel.

The condition is that the nation was to obey the voice of God and keep his covenant. Yet we see throughout the Old Testament that the Jews refused to listen and were constantly disobedient, to the point that God cast them out of his sight and did not fulfill what he had promised Israel (the 'then' portion of the conditional statement).

> 2 Kings 17:7-20 - For so it was, <u>that the children of Israel had sinned against the Lord their God,</u> which had brought them up out of the land of Egypt, from under the hand of Pharaoh king of Egypt, and had feared other gods, 8 And walked in the statutes of the heathen, whom the Lord cast out from before the children of Israel, and of the kings of Israel, which they had made. 9 <u>And the children of Israel did secretly those things that were not right against the Lord their God,</u> and they built them high places in all their cities, from the tower of the watchmen to the fenced city. 10 And they set them up images and groves in every high hill, and under every green tree: 11 And there they burnt incense in all the high places, as did the heathen whom the Lord carried away before them; and wrought wicked things to provoke the Lord to anger: 12 For they served idols, whereof the Lord had said unto them, Ye shall not do this thing. 13 Yet the Lord testified against Israel, and against Judah, by all the prophets, and by all the seers, saying, Turn ye from your evil ways, and keep my commandments and my statutes, according to all the law which I commanded your fathers, and which I sent to you by my servants the prophets. 14 <u>Notwithstanding they would not hear, but hardened their necks, like to the neck of their fathers, that did not believe in the Lord their God. 15 And they rejected his statutes, and his covenant that he made with their fathers, and his testimonies which he testified against them; and they followed vanity, and became vain, and went after the heathen that were round about them,</u> concerning whom the Lord had charged them, that they should not do like them. 16 <u>And they left all the commandments of the Lord their God,</u> and made them molten images, even two calves, and made a grove, and worshipped all the host of heaven, and served Baal. 17 And they caused their sons and their daughters to pass through the fire, and used divination and enchantments, and sold themselves to do evil in the sight of the Lord, to provoke him to anger. 18 Therefore the Lord was very angry with Israel, <u>and removed them out of his sight:</u> there was none left but the tribe of Judah only. <u>19 Also Judah kept not the commandments of the Lord their God, but walked in the statutes of Israel which they made.</u>

20 And the <u>Lord rejected all the seed of Israel, and afflicted them, and delivered them into the hand of spoilers, until he had cast them out of his sight</u>**.**

This is perhaps one of the harshest passages in the Old Testament which show us the reality of how sinful Israel really was. God promised the children of Israel that they would be a kingdom of priests and a holy nation only if they obeyed his voice; yet here, we are told plainly that "they left all the commandments of the LORD their God." The ultimate result of this is that LORD rejected them, afflicted them, and cast them out of his sight. This doesn't sound like God dealt with their sin lightly. In contrast to the disobedience of Israel, we are told in 1 Peter:

> 1 Peter 2:9-10 - But ye are a chosen generation, a royal priesthood, an holy nation, a peculiar people; that ye should shew forth the praises of him who hath called you out of darkness into his marvellous light; Which in time past were not a people, but are now the people of God: which had not obtained mercy, but now have obtained mercy.

The Jews disobeyed God and refused to believe him. The Gentiles who are in Christ therefore have become a royal priesthood and an holy nation; the same conditional promises offered to the physical nation of Israel in Exodus 19 at Mount Sinai. The Bible says:

> Philippians 3:3 - For we are the circumcision, which worship God in the spirit, and rejoice in Christ Jesus, and have no confidence in the flesh.

They are NOT the true Jews, they are NOT Israel, they are NOT the seed of Abraham, and they are NOT the circumcision. All of these things which the modern Pharasaic Jews claim the Bible explicitly denies, and tells us that those who are of Christ are truly the people of God. It's not difficult to understand. Do not be deceived by the lies of the Zionists. In the new covenant, the believers, the Christians, are Israel. God is done with the physical seed unless they repent from their unbelief.

According to this principle, the scriptures tell us about the "them which say they are Jews, and are not, but are the synagogue of Satan (Revelation 2:9)." Remember, Romans 2:28 tells us "He is not a Jew which is one outwardly; neither is that circumcision which is outward in the flesh." The physical Jews call themselves Jews (meaning, of Judah) and consider themselves to be the seed of Abraham, yet God denies this. Their synagogue is not a synagogue which worships God, but the devil. Jesus told the Pharisees that their father was the devil (John 8:44), and we read that "Whosoever denieth the Son, the same hath not the Father (1 John 2:23)."

How is it then that the nation of Israel, which, except for the small remnant which has believed, who follow the traditions of the Pharisees, and who deny the Son, are the people of God? They are no better than the ancient nation which God cast out of his sight. If he did so in the Old Testament, there is no reason to conclude that he won't do so in the New Testament.

I have therefore rejected this Zionist doctrine which I rightfully call "Jew Worship." The Hebrew Roots cultists focus so much on Israel that there is little or no talk about the Gospel. To many Messianic preachers, the main goal is to support the murderous, Christ-hating Rothschild regime which falsely bears the title of 'Israel.' To them, the Bible is not about the sacrifice of Christ to bring us salvation from sins, but about the Jews inheriting the land and triumphing over the nations. To them, the Jews and the nation of Israel is the center of prophecy and God's plan for humanity. To them, everything in the Bible is about the Hebrews.

This is why the whole movement is called "Hebrew Roots." The idea is that Christianity has strayed too far from its mother religion. To them, the only difference between Judaism and Christianity is that Judaism doesn't believe in Jesus, and has a few minor additions to the Torah which are found in their Mishnah. However, this couldn't be further from the truth. I will thus show why it is entirely unfounded to claim that the religion of the apostles had 'Hebraic Roots' and that Christianity has strayed from the truth.

The "Hebraic Roots" of the Scriptures?

Besides debunking the Zionist doctrine, it's also important to show that the Hebrew Roots are wrong also about the Bible, the very foundation of our beliefs and practice. The Hebrew Roots movement takes a very strange position on the Bible. In accordance with their belief that Christianity is rooted in everything Hebrew; they believe that this was the language that the New Testament was written in. Thus, they often look for Hebrew texts of the New Testament and use these, claiming that they're the 'originals.'

Hebrew Rootists also use the same tactics as critical pseudo-scholars who attack the Bible, by constantly doubting English translations and looking for new manuscripts and texts which they think will unlock hidden mysteries of the Bible. This has led many to also accept non-canonical texts such as Maccabees, Enoch, and Jubilees, claiming that these "used to be" in the Bible but were taken out by the pagan Christians. They thus doubt the preservation of God's word. Further problems are caused by the fact that Hebrew Roots people, although often not knowing how to speak Hebrew, 'go back to the Hebrew' to try to find the 'true meaning' of certain verses.

Both what the Bible says itself and history is against these practices and beliefs. First of all, the only evidence which exists for a book written in Hebrew in the New Testament is that of Matthew. Papias of Hierapolis, a disciple of John (c. 60 - c. 160 CE) wrote about the origins of two of the Gospels in his work *Exposition of the Sayings of the Lord*, written about 100 CE, which tells us that Mark wrote down his Gospel using information he got from Peter, and that Matthew wrote his Gospel originally in Hebrew. This is testified also by Irenaues of Lyons, who in *Against Heresies* (c. 180), issued his Gospel among Hebrew-speaking people.

However, the problem with claiming that we should thus look for a Hebrew gospel is that no such thing exists. Matthew, although written in Hebrew, was soon after translated into Greek, as this was the *lingua franca* of the Roman Empire at the time; these Greek manuscripts are all which have been passed down to us. Even with this fact, Hebrew Roots people, such as Michael Rood, will promote the "Shem Tov" text, which appears to be a Hebrew text of Matthew.

What they don't often mention is that this manuscript dates from the 14th century, and was written by a Sephardic rabbi, Shem-Tov ben Isaac ben Shaprut. The text itself is part of a larger text, called The Touchstone, which was written by ben Shaprut for the purpose of arguing that Jesus isn't the Messiah or God. However, there exist no other Hebrew copies from which this text could have derived from. The assumption is made that since Matthew was written in Hebrew, and that this is a version of Matthew in Hebrew, this must be the original.

However, only a few centuries after Matthew's Gospel was written, many had testified that Gnostics and other heretical Christians had corrupted

Matthew's gospel in Hebrew to serve their own purposes. Epiphanius of Salamis (310 CE - 403 CE) wrote of one of these corruptions, saying:

> "They too accept the Gospel according to Matthew. Like the Cerinthians and Merinthians, they too use it alone. They call it, 'According to the Hebrews,' and it is true to say that only Matthew put the setting forth and the preaching of the Gospel into the New Testament in the Hebrew language and alphabet." (*Panarion*, 30.3.7)

> "In the Gospel that is in general use amongst them [Ebionites], which is called according to Matthew, which however is not whole (and) complete but forged and mutilated - they call it the Hebrew Gospel - it is reported… (*Panarion*, 30.13.2)"

Epiphanius identified the fact that Matthew originally wrote his Gospel in Hebrew, but acknowledges also that it existed only in his time as a corrupted version used by the sect known as the Ebionites. The Ebionites were a group which rejected the pre-existence of Jesus Christ, believing that he was only a man and a prophet of God, and believed that obeying the Law of Moses is necessary for salvation. The Latin writer Tertullian's *Against All Heresies* claims that Ebion was the disciple to Cerinthus, a gnostic heretic in the 1st century, who, according to Irenaeus, taught the same heresies as the Ebionites, used the same corrupted version of Matthew, and who was thoroughly refuted by John the Apostle using the Gospel of John.

Considering that all historical sources show that Matthew's Hebrew Gospel was corrupted even by the time of the 2nd century, and that the Shem-Tov writing contains the same errors of the Ebionites, including removing all references to Jesus' divine origins; it's more than likely that the 14th-century published version is simply a copy of the "Gospel According to the Hebrews" and not Matthew's original text. Therefore, it should not be considered reliable by any means.

Concerning the other Gospels; there exists no other manuscripts of them in Hebrew, neither is there a written testimony by the church 'fathers' of the other Gospel writers writing in Hebrew. This makes sense; Greek was the common language in the Mediterranean at the time, and the majority of Christians were Gentile converts who spoke and read in Koine Greek. Luke likely never knew Hebrew at all; he was a Greek from Antioch. It thus makes sense that the Gospel of Luke was written in Greek.

The same goes for the Epistles and the Book of Revelation - with the exception of the Epistle to the Hebrews, the audiences are all Greek-speakers. Just think, why would a letter to Romans be in Hebrew, or a letter to people from Corinth (in Greece), Galatia (in Anatolia), in Ephesus (Anatolia), Philippi (Macedonia), Colosse (Anatolia), or Thessalonica (Macedonia)? Why would a letter to Greek-speakers such as Timothy, Titus, and Philemon be in Hebrew? Why would a letter to "strangers scattered throughout Pontus, Galatia, Cappadocia, Asia, and Bithynia" be in Hebrew? Why would Revelation, which was originally delivered to the churches in Ephesus, Smyrna, Pergamos, Thyatira, Sardis, Philadelphia, and Laodicea (all in the Greek-speaking region of Asia Minor) be in Hebrew?

Furthermore, why, if the New Testament was primarily written in Hebrew, are there no manuscripts to prove this? Shem-Tov's Matthew is the only text which even claims to be an original, and as already shown, there are numerous problems with its reliability. All other Hebrew texts of the New Testament are modern, and are not copies, but translations. On the contrary, there exist over 5,000 Greek manuscripts of the NT.

Another problem with the claim that the New Testament was written in Hebrew is that the Gospels explain both Jewish customs and Aramaic terms. If the audience were in fact Hebrew-speakers, this would be entirely unnecessary. For example, the Passover and other appointed times are referred to by the title of 'feast of the Jews' several times in the Book of John (John 2:13, 5:1, 6:4, 7:2, 11:55). If the audience was a Hebrew-speaking people, surely they would be familiar with these feasts which the Jews celebrated. Why then, does John refer to them as if the recipients of the Gospel had no knowledge of these feasts?

We also see the defining of Aramaic and Hebrew phrases used by Jesus. Here are some examples:

> Matthew 27:46 - And about the ninth hour Jesus cried with a loud voice, saying, <u>Eli, Eli, lama sabachthani? that is to say, My God, my God, why hast thou forsaken me?</u>

> Mark 5:41 - And he took the damsel by the hand, and said unto her, <u>Talitha cumi; which is, being interpreted, Damsel, I say unto thee,</u>

arise.

Mark 7:34 - And looking up to heaven, he sighed, and saith unto him, Ephphatha, that is, Be opened.

Mark 14:36 - And he said, Abba, Father, all things are possible unto thee; take away this cup from me: nevertheless not what I will, but what thou wilt.

John 1:38 - Then Jesus turned, and saw them following, and saith unto them, What seek ye? They said unto him, Rabbi, (which is to say, being interpreted, Master,) where dwellest thou?

John 1:41-42 - He first findeth his own brother Simon, and saith unto him, We have found the Messias, which is, being interpreted, the Christ. And he brought him to Jesus. And when Jesus beheld him, he said, Thou art Simon the son of Jona: thou shalt be called Cephas, which is by interpretation, A stone.

John 20:16 - Jesus saith unto her, Mary. She turned herself, and saith unto him, Rabboni; which is to say, Master.

All four Gospels give the clear indication that they were not written in Hebrew or Aramaic by the presence of these words. If these texts were simply translations of the original text, then why were these words left untranslated? Why didn't the translators write "She turned herself, and saith unto him, Master" instead of leaving the word 'rabboni' as well as its interpretation? The answer is, because this was the original, unaltered text of God's word.

Those in the Hebrew Roots movement attack the fundamental belief in the inspiration and preservation of God's word, however. Like many secular scholars who have no faith in the Bible, they seek to change what Scriptures say, and will do anything to twist what the words say to support their doctrine. In order to accomplish such a wicked task, they need to rest their faith on the idea that "it says something different in the Hebrew." The vast majority of Hebrew Roots people do not even speak Hebrew, and ignore the fact that all of the King James translators were fluent in Hebrew and Greek, and based their translation on the thousands of manuscripts available at the time, instead of obscure texts which would be found in the dirt after being buried for thousands of years.

Everything surrounding the Bible is very core to our beliefs and practice. Our doctrines are based on what the Scriptures say alone, so we need to be sure that what we're reading in English is truly God's word. We can be sure of this based on God's promises of both inspiration and preservation.

> 2 Timothy 3:16 - All scripture is given by inspiration of God, and is profitable for doctrine, for reproof, for correction, for instruction in righteousness:

> 2 Peter 1:19-21 - We have also a more sure word of prophecy; whereunto ye do well that ye take heed, as unto a light that shineth in a dark place, until the day dawn, and the day star arise in your hearts: Knowing this first, that no prophecy of the scripture is of any private interpretation. For the prophecy came not in old time by the will of man: but holy men of God spake as they were moved by the Holy Ghost.

All Scripture is given by inspiration. The word inspiration literally means "breathed-out." The words which we read in the Bible are the very words of God, which he spake to the holy men of God through the Holy Ghost. This is where we get the Bible from, from the very inspiration of God. While there are many in the Hebrew Roots movement who accept this without controversy, there are some who object that the New Testament does not fall into the category of 'scriptures' which these passages refer to, and are therefore, not entirely inspired. However, looking again at 2 Peter, we see this:

> 2 Peter 3:15-16 - And account that the longsuffering of our Lord is salvation; even as our beloved brother Paul also according to the wisdom given unto him hath written unto you; As also in all his epistles, speaking in them of these things; in which are some things hard to be understood, which they that are unlearned and unstable wrest, as they do also the other scriptures, unto their own destruction.

Here Peter mentions the epistles of Paul, and discusses how there are people who twist his words for their own purpose. The key here is the end of verse 16 which says "as they do also the other scriptures." In saying this, it's implied that the epistles of Paul are to be considered part of the 'scriptures,' which are of equal value to the rest of the Bible. This is not a problem for many Hebrew Rootists, who will accept the New Testament without question as well.

However, their idea of the inspiration of the Bible often stops at the so-called "originals." Since the Old Testament was originally written in Hebrew (and the NT, according to them), only the Hebrew was inspired, but our English translations are not the same.

The same myth of things being 'lost in translation' which perpetuates among liberal Christians exists among the Hebrew Roots as well. Their belief is that the King James Bible is not the inspired word of God because it's not in Hebrew. Hence, we go back to the central concept of this movement: the idea that everything about God and the Bible revolves around Hebrew culture and language. There are several problems with this conclusion.

First of all, there are no existing "originals." If only the originals are inspired, then all Hebrew and Greek manuscripts we have are not inspired. The Masoretic Text's oldest copies, known as the Ben Asher manuscripts, all date from the 9th and 10th centuries CE. The Dead Sea Scrolls date back no further than the 3rd century BCE. The oldest Hebrew text ever discovered are the silver scrolls found at Ketef Hinnom which contain the priestly blessing, dating from the 7th century BCE. None of these are the original. They are copies.

Second, God promised to preserve his word as well. Our faith in the Bible as God's word does not stop at inspiration, but at preservation. The originals were preserved in copies which have been passed down in generations, not just in the original languages, but in foreign languages as well. Here's what the Bible says about the preservation of God's word:

> Psalm 12:6-7 - The words of the Lord are pure words: as silver tried in a furnace of earth, purified seven times. Thou shalt keep them, O Lord, thou shalt preserve them from this generation for ever.
>
> Isaiah 40:8 - The grass withereth, the flower fadeth: but the word of our God shall stand for ever.
>
> Matthew 24:35 - Heaven and earth shall pass away, but my words shall not pass away.

God promises that his words will never pass away, but that he would preserve them forever. Therefore, not only was the word inspired, but that which was inspired was preserved, so that even in this generation (Psalm 12:7) we continue to have the words of God. We as English-speaking people who serve the LORD have a preservation of God's word, perfectly translated into the English language, the King James Bible. English is the most widely-spoken language in the world, with over 1.5 billion speakers (400 million native speakers, 1.1 billion as a second language). Historically, English-speaking people have been the most active in the spread of God's word. Most missionaries have been sent from the English-speaking world (Britain, the US, Australia, Canada, New Zealand) than any other.

Meanwhile, the two languages the Bible was originally written in, Hebrew and Greek, have a different story. Hebrew was a dead language for over a millenium, spoken by nobody and read only by rabbis of the Judaic religion. Greek was and still is a language spoken by practicers primarily of the Eastern Orthodox religion, a pagan corruption of Biblical Christiantiy similar to Roman Catholicism. It's absurd to suggest that true believers, who overwhelmingly have no knowledge of the original languages, are without the word of God. 2 Timothy 3:17 tells us that the scriptures were inspired "that the man of God may be perfect, thoroughly furnished unto all good works." The word of God is for US, to reveal to US as believers God's plan for our lives.

Although I don't want to go too much in the textual debate, a quick summary for why we should rely on the King James Bible as the preserved word of God in the English language is this: this Bible was translated by a team of 54 scholars, all fluent in Hebrew, Greek, and other classical languages the Bible had been translated into. The KJV translators used the Masoretic Text, or the preserved Hebrew text, for the Old Testament, and the Textus Receptus for the New Testament. This is the only Bible which does such. All the modern versions, whether it's the NIV, the NASB, the ESV, or any others, base their translation upon two manuscripts known as the "Alexandrian Text."

The Alexandrian Text is the text-type which consists primarily of the Codex Sinaiticus and the Codex Vaticanus. The former was found in the 19th century by Constantin von Tischendorf at a monastery in the Sinai Peninsula, where it was ready to be burned by the priests there because it was viewed as 'junk.' And indeed, it is junk. The Sinaiticus text contains numerous examples of places where text was rewritten, contradictions, grammatical mistakes, and inconsistencies with the other Alexandrian text, the Codex Vaticanus. The Codex Vaticanus is named such because it has historically been stored in the

Vatican Library. This Alexandrian text-type is missing many verses, including Matthew 12:47, 16:3, 17:21, 18:11, Mark 9:44, 11:26, 15:28, 16:9-20, Luke 17:36, John 5:4, 7:53-8:11, Acts 8:37, 15:34, 24:7, 28:29, and countless other missing phrases. Note that the final 11 verses of Mark are missing. In these manuscripts, there is even a space for where the text *should* have been, indicating that this was a mistake and that these manuscripts are indeed corrupt.

By comparison, the Textus Receptus (Received Text) is based on the Byzantine-text-type, which consists of over 5,000 Greek manuscripts, which all agree with each other and with the earliest papyri from the 2nd to 4th centuries. The verses remain intact and the text remains consistent, and was used for over a thousand years before Desiderius Erasmus began to compile them into a single volume of the New Testament in 1516. This was revised several times to correct minor mistakes, until the production of Stephanus' Textus Receptus in 1550, which is what the King James Version is based on. The fact that this Received Text is what was preserved shows it to be God's word. The Alexandrian-texts were buried away for a millenium and a half, surviving only because of their lack of use. Are we to believe that believers were without the word of God for that long, despite God's promise to preserve his word? Which do you believe, the modern "scholars" (most of who don't even believe in God or the Bible), or the promises of the LORD in the Old Testament?

Thus, we can be confident, without vain Hebrew studies, that we can pick up the Bible in the English language and read it, knowing that the words which we have today are the same words which God revealed to his holy prophets thousands of years ago. The Hebrew Roots movement's tendency to question God's word is the same tactic Satan used when he said to Eve, "Yea, hath God said?" Satan's strategy has always been to cast doubts about the Word in the mind of believers. However, just as Peter said "we have also a more sure word of prophecy."

Sacred Name

Now that we've dealt with the subject of the Hebrew Bible, there's another subject which relates to the Hebrew Roots' emphasis on the Hebrew language: the Hebrew names, particularly the Sacred Name. Although some differ on this doctrine, many in the Hebrew Roots movement believe that the name of God in Hebrew, known as the Tetragrammaton (four letters, YHWH) should be how we address God, and that the name of Jesus is actually Yeshua (or Yahusha, or Yahushua, or some other variation). Some in the movement believe that these names are preferable, but that there's nothing wrong with saying LORD or Jesus, while others, such as myself, believed that the latter two are pagan corruptions of the 'true name.'

Like the Jehovah's Witnesses, this has grown to become a big issue in this movement. I recall from my experience in the Hebrew Roots that this was usually the first thing I talked about whenever somebody asked about my religion. I always wanted to make sure that they understood I don't believe in "Jesus" or "the LORD" but in "Yeshua" and "YHVH." The pronunciation of these titles changed as my faith developed. At first, I said *Yahshua* and *Yahweh*. Then, I said *Yeshua* and *Yehovah*. Then, I changed shortly after to *Yahushua* and *Yahuwah*. About a year later, I went back to *Yeshua* and *Yehovah*.

As if the world depended upon it, many Hebrew Roots' followers will be dogmatic about their way of pronouncing the sacred name (some go as far as accusing others of being deceptive for saying it slightly differently). Concerning the Tetragrammaton, names include *Yehovah, Yehoah, Yehuah, Yahuah, Yahweh, Yehweh, Yahawah* and many others. Concerning the name of Christ, names include *Yeshua, Yahshua, Yahushua, and Yahusha*. So, which one is right? Does it even matter?

Those in the Hebrew Roots movement are assertive on their way of pronunciation. Remember, the backbone of this ideology is that we should be as Hebrew as possible. Despite the vast majority of believers speaking other languages and having no knowledge of Hebrew, it's almost guaranteed to these people. Before discussing these names in particular, I want to give a lesson in language itself.

First of all, we should understand that all languages are created by God.

> Genesis 11:1-9 - And the whole earth <u>was of one language, and of one speech</u>. And it came to pass, as they journeyed from the east, that they found a plain in the land of Shinar; and they dwelt there. And they said one to another, Go to, let us make brick, and burn them thoroughly. And they had brick for stone, and slime had they for morter. And they

said, Go to, let us build us a city and a tower, whose top may reach unto heaven; and let us make us a name, lest we be scattered abroad upon the face of the whole earth. And the Lord came down to see the city and the tower, which the children of men builded. And the Lord said, Behold, the people is one, and they have all one language; and this they begin to do: and now nothing will be restrained from them, which they have imagined to do. <u>Go to, let us go down, and there confound their language, that they may not understand one another's speech</u>. So the Lord scattered them abroad from thence upon the face of all the earth: and they left off to build the city. Therefore is the name of it called Babel; <u>because the Lord did there confound the language of all the earth: and from thence did the Lord scatter them abroad upon the face of all the earth</u>.

The confusion of the languages was the LORD's doing. It was God who created a separation in the languages of the earth. The reason why we speak a Germanic language today and not a Semitic one was because of this event at the Tower of Babel. Second, we need to understand that there's no special language which God communicates to us or anybody else in. This is already illustrated by the fact that the New Testament was written in Greek. Greek was the *lingua franca*, or common language, of the Roman Empire, due to the influence of Hellenic culture spread by Greek colonies and the Macedonian Empire. Greek was to antiquity what English is to the world today. Even then, the Greek language was not special beyond the fact that it was the most commonly-spoken language. We see in the Book of Acts,

> Acts 2:1-11 - And when the day of Pentecost was fully come, they were all with one accord in one place. And suddenly there came a sound from heaven as of a rushing mighty wind, and it filled all the house where they were sitting. And there appeared unto them cloven tongues like as of fire, and it sat upon each of them. And they were all filled with the Holy Ghost, and began to speak with other tongues, as the Spirit gave them utterance. And there were dwelling at Jerusalem Jews, devout men, out of every nation under heaven. Now when this was noised abroad, the multitude came together, and were confounded, because that <u>every man heard them speak in his own language</u>. And they were all amazed and marvelled, saying one to another, Behold, are not all these which speak Galilaeans? And how hear we every man in

our own tongue, wherein we were born? Parthians, and Medes, and Elamites, and the dwellers in Mesopotamia, and in Judaea, and Cappadocia, in Pontus, and Asia, Phrygia, and Pamphylia, in Egypt, and in the parts of Libya about Cyrene, and strangers of Rome, Jews and proselytes, Cretes and Arabians, <u>we do hear them speak in our tongues the wonderful works of God</u>.

Even when the ministry of the New Testament had just begun, we already have the proclamation of the word of God in dozens of other languages. This shows us that God does not hold one language above another. We read in the scriptures that God is not a respecter of persons (Acts 10:34). It makes no sense to assume that God would prefer one language over another, especially in the New Testament, which is opened to people of every kindred, nation, people, and tongue (Revelation 7:9).

Another thing which needs to be understood is that every language is *different*. This is something which people in the Hebrew Roots movement apparently have a hard time comprehending. All languages have their own sets of phonemes, or sounds made in the language. For example, the English language does not have the Hebrew *chet* sound, although it exists in other languages, like German and Greek. Since each language has their own independent set of sounds, when names are transliterated into other languages, they will sound slightly different.

For example, my name Alexander (pronounced in English as al-ıks-an-dər) is Alejandro (ɑl-eɪ-hɑn-droʊ) in Spanish, Alexandros (ɑl-eɪks-ɑn-droʊs) in Greek, and Alistair (al.i.stə) in Scottish Gaelic. Etymologically, they're the same name and come from the same root, but because languages develop independently, the names are changed slightly to adapt to the languages' phonemes. Another example is Michael, which could also be *Michel* in French, *Mikhail* in Slavic languages, and *Mikha'el* in its original language, Hebrew.

This also applies to the name of Jesus. Those in the Hebrew Roots movement want to attack the name of Jesus as if it's not the name of the Messiah, with no evidence whatsoever. Again, the intensity of this argument varies depending on who you talk to. There exist some radical Hebrew Roots followers who believe that Jesus has nothing to do with the Messiah, but that it's a pagan word which means "Hail Zeus." The only evidence of this is that the ending of Jesus sounds similar to how we say Zeus.

This simply demonstrates the Hebrew Roots' ignorance of the Greek language. First of all, the name of the pagan god Zeus is not pronounced as "zoos" like we say. In Greek, it's spelled Ζεύς (which is pronounced as zevs). By contrast, the name of Jesus, which comes from the Greek Iesous, is written as (Ἰησοῦς, pronounced as Yi-sus). Not only is the ending of Iesous spelled differently, but it's said entirely differently. There's no evidence Iesous has anything to do with the name of Zeus.

So, where does the name of Iesous come from? This isn't difficult to figure out either. The Hebrew Roots movement claims that the original name of Jesus is 'Yeshua' in Hebrew. This is correct. However, since Greek has different phonemes and rules than Hebrew, the name had to be written different. The *shin* was changed to a *sigma* because there is no 'sh' sound in Greek. Another *sigma* was added onto the end because in Greek, masculine names do not end with vowels, but with *sigma* (such as Cephas, Iakobos, Andreas, Ioudas, Ioannes, Philippos, Bartolomaios, etc.). Many names which have Hebrew origins are changed with a *sigma* on the end because of this rule of the Greek language.

So, simply put, the name of Iesous is not a 'pagan' corruption, but simply the Greek form of the name Yeshua. It's no less the same name as Alexander is to Alexandros. And remember, the New Testament was written in Greek, not Hebrew. Therefore, when the Ephesians read the epistle written to them, they saw the name Ἰησοῦς. That's what Paul wrote down on the papyrus. Likewise, as the Greek was translated into English and the English language developed, Iesous became Jesus. It's not a different name, but the same name, in the English language.

As English speakers, this is the name we should call Christ by. Denying that name and claiming it's from paganism is not only ignorant but deceptive and dangerous. The New Testament lifts up the name of Jesus above all others. We see in the Bible,

> Acts 4:10-12 - Be it known unto you all, and to all the people of Israel, that by the name of <u>Jesus Christ of Nazareth</u>, whom ye crucified, whom God raised from the dead, even by him doth this man stand here before you whole. This is the stone which was set at nought of you

builders, which is become the head of the corner. Neither is there salvation in any other: for there is none other name under heaven given among men, whereby we must be saved.

Those who deny the name of Jesus Christ are not saved. Without this name, we cannot come to salvation, for salvation is only in the name of Jesus, according to the word of God. Although this includes the different forms of the name in different languages, it does NOT include the strange manmade forms like *Yahusha* which have no basis in any existing language.

Furthermore, what we can learn from the above passage is that we are saved through Jesus Christ. The Hebrew Roots movement makes the same mistake that the Jehovah's Witnesses make, in lifting up the name of Yahweh or Yehovah above the name of Jesus. This is why they will not only adamantly defend their pronounciation of the Messiah's name, but also of the Tetragrammaton. Many emphasize YHWH more than Yeshua. However, looking at the above passage, we see that there is salvation in none other name that Jesus Christ of Nazareth.

The Hebrew Roots heretics lift up another name above that of Jesus, claiming that we Christians are doing wrong for not using the name of YHVH and exalting his name. However, when they stand before the throne of God, they will not confess the name of YHVH, they will confess the name of Jesus!

> Philippians 2:9-11 - Wherefore God also hath highly exalted him, and given him a name which is above every name: That at the name of Jesus every knee should bow, of things in heaven, and things in earth, and things under the earth; And that every tongue should confess that Jesus Christ is Lord, to the glory of God the Father.

The Scriptures show us that the name of Jesus Christ is above every name. YHVH is a name. Therefore, the name of Jesus Christ is above YHVH, and every person who has ever lived will bow to the name of Jesus and confess that he is Lord. There is NO mention of the name of Yehovah in the New Testament. The name Jesus appears nearly 1000 times, but the name Yehovah never appears.

The New Testament, being written in Greek, does not transliterate the Tetragrammaton into Greek letters, but rather, when it quotes the Old Testament, substitutes the word κύριος (kyrios) over 700 times. Kyrios means

Lord. In the King James Bible, there is therefore no error when the name of God is rendered as LORD. This is what the apostles wrote under the guidance of the Holy Ghost, and the reason was simple: because the name of Jesus was to be exalted, and not the Old Testament name of YHVH. The latter is what men called upon for salvation in the Old Testament, but under the new covenant, the name of Jesus has been revealed as the only way to salvation.

Different names have been revealed throughout history for men to call on God by. Prior to Moses, the name of the YHVH was not even known, but rather, the name God Almighty was used:

> Exodus 6:2-3 - And God spake unto Moses, and said unto him, I am the Lord: And I appeared unto Abraham, unto Isaac, and unto Jacob, by the name of God Almighty, but by my name Jehovah was I not known to them.

Therefore, it is no surprise that in the New Testament, we are saved by the name of Jesus (Acts 4:12) and not by the name of Jehovah. The Hebrew Roots falsely exalts this name and brings down the name of Jesus, then further complicates things by arguing over how to pronounce each name correctly. None of this is Biblical. Jesus is God Almighty, and is Jehovah. Even this doctrine, called the Trinity, is denied by many in the Hebrew Roots movement. This will be addressed later. However, for now, I want to move onto the main heresy of the Hebrew Roots movement.

Justification and Salvation: Faith or Torah?

Since the focus is on the supposed roots of the New Testament in Hebrew culture, there exists a desire to hold onto the Old Testament laws as well. Although at first, many Hebrew Roots deceivers simply promote their views as returning to obedience to God as a believer, it's evident that many go much further than that. The majority of the Hebrew Roots movement believes that the Old Testament Law of Moses, or the "Torah" is how we are to be justified and saved.

They thus fall into an error which many false religions fall into, by teaching the extremely unbiblical false Gospel of salvation by the works of the law. When I was in the Hebrew Roots movement, I learned from the various 'Torah teachers' of the Internet that God demands obedience to his Ten Commandments as well as his other commandments, and that wilfull disobedience to his laws will result in the fate of one ending up in the lake of fire. These Messianics falsely claim that Christians' attitudes towards the laws are negative and teach that because we believe they're not necessary for salvation, that somehow means we're promoting a license to sin.

None of this is true, however, and demonstrates that the Hebrew Roots understanding of both the Bible and Christian theology is just as ignorant as total unbelievers. Salvation is a very important doctrine, in fact, the primary message of the Bible. The scriptures tell us that "The Father sent the Son to be the Saviour of the world (1 John 4:14)." Hebrew Roots teachers such as Michael Rood have this false belief that Christ only came to return Israel back to following the laws and not be their saviour. They have no understanding of the Gospel or its message.

So, in a detailed explanation, I will show what the Gospel is, how a person is saved, and how the Hebrew Roots' adherence to the Torah for salvation is unbiblical and dangerous. We ARE NOT saved by the law, or by our desire to repent from sins, or by any of our own righteousness, but entirely by the righteousness of Jesus Christ.

First, the Scriptures teach us that all of mankind is inherently wicked and sinful in God's eyes. This is a basic truth of the Bible and the first thing we need to acknowledge before believing the Gospel. Without knowing what we need saving from, we cannot believe that Christ is our saviour. Those in the Hebrew Roots movement have a self-righteous, holier-than-thou attitude in which they present themselves as followers of God's laws. However, this contradicts myriads of scripture. The Bible says,

> Romans 3:10-18 - As it is written, There is none righteous, no, not one: There is none that understandeth, there is none that seeketh after God. They are all gone out of the way, they are together become unprofitable; there is none that doeth good, no, not one. Their throat is an open sepulchre; with their tongues they have used deceit; the poison of asps is under their lips: Whose mouth is full of cursing and bitterness: Their feet are swift to shed blood: Destruction and misery are in their ways: And the way of peace have they not known: There is no fear of God before their eyes.

> Romans 3:23 - For all have sinned, and come short of the glory of God.

The point is clearly made, especially by quoting from the Old Testament, that mankind is completely wicked. The Scriptures say simply "there is none righteous, no not one," "There is none that doeth good, no, not one," and "All have sinned, and come short of the glory of God." These are all absolutes. All means all. Every human being is guilty of sinning against our holy God. This is shown not only here, where Paul quotes from Psalm 5:9, 10:7, 14:1, 36:1, 53:2-3, 140:3, and Isaiah 59:7, but also in the following passages:

> 1 Samuel 8:46 - If they sin against thee, (for there is no man that sinneth not,) and thou be angry with them, and deliver them to the enemy, so that they carry them away captives unto the land of the enemy, far or near

> Ecclesiastes 7:20 - For there is not a just man upon earth, that doeth good, and sinneth not.

This universality of sin, that everybody has disobeyed God's commands (for sin is a trangression of the law, 1 John 3:4) is not only declared throughout the Bible, but shown in several examples. Even the Israelites, to whom God gave the commandments, were unable to follow them:

> 2 Kings 17:13-20 - Yet the Lord testified against Israel, and against Judah, by all the prophets, and by all the seers, saying, Turn ye from your evil ways, and keep my commandments and my statutes, according to all the law which I commanded your fathers, and which I sent to you by my servants the prophets. Notwithstanding they would not hear, but hardened their necks, like to the neck of their fathers, that did not believe in the Lord their God. And they rejected his statutes, and his covenant that he made with their fathers, and his testimonies which he testified against them; and they followed vanity, and became vain, and went after the heathen that were round about them, concerning whom the Lord had charged them, that they should not do like them. And they left all the commandments of the Lord their God, and made them molten images, even two calves, and made a grove, and worshipped all the host of heaven, and served Baal. And they caused their sons and their daughters to pass through the fire, and used divination and enchantments, and sold themselves to do evil in the sight of the Lord, to provoke him to anger. Therefore the Lord was very angry with Israel, and removed them out of his sight: there was

none left but the tribe of Judah only. Also Judah kept not the commandments of the Lord their God, but walked in the statutes of Israel which they made. And the Lord rejected all the seed of Israel, and afflicted them, and delivered them into the hand of spoilers, until he had cast them out of his sight.

If the Israelites to whom the Torah was given were unable to follow the commandments of God, what makes these Hebrew Roots people think they can follow all the laws of God perfectly? God does indeed demand perfect obedience in his word. The Bible says,

Galatians 3:10 - For as many as are of the works of the law are under the curse: for it is written, Cursed is every one that continueth not in all things which are written in the book of the law to do them.

This quotes from Deuteronomy 27:26, which says "Cursed be he that confirmeth not all the words of this law to do them." In the next chapter, God says,

Deuteronomy 28:15 - But it shall come to pass, if thou wilt not hearken unto the voice of the Lord thy God, to observe to do all his commandments and his statutes which I command thee this day; that all these curses shall come upon thee, and overtake thee.

Once again, God demands perfect obedience to all the words of his law and all of his commandments. Without following all of his commandments, God promises that curses will come on the Israelites, a promise which he did fulfill. Furthermore, the Bible says,

James 2:10-11 - For whosoever shall keep the whole law, and yet offend in one point, he is guilty of all. For he that said, Do not commit adultery, said also, Do not kill. Now if thou commit no adultery, yet if thou kill, thou art become a transgressor of the law.

Those Hebrew Roots people who think that they can justify themselves by keeping the law need to understand: unless they perfectly obey every single commandment of God, they are guilty of all. This principle is simple - God demands perfect obedience to his law, so even if a person offends in one point, they are still a sinner, and still a transgressor. God does not treat our sins like gods in the pagan religions, weighing our good and our bad deeds. He sees us as wicked and evil even if we do only *one* sin. One sin is enough to make us a transgressor of the law.

Consider this along with the fact that the Bible repeatedly tells us that every single man on earth is a sinner (1 Sam. 8:46, Psa. 14:1, Eccl. 7:20, Romans 3:10-23), and we see that in God's eyes, everybody is a transgressor of the law, and everybody is under a curse. The universality of sin applies even to believers, for John said, "If we say we have no sin, we deceive ourselves, and the truth is not in us (1 John 1:8)." Everybody has sin, regardless of how righteous they *think* they are.

Since everybody is a sinner, everybody also has the same fate, in hell and the lake of fire. This is something the Hebrew Roots agrees on, boldly declaring that if we Christians don't start following the law of God, that we'll end up in the lake of fire. What they foolishly refuse to realize is that they, trusting in their obedience to the law to save them, are the ones headed for the lake of fire. These people are not special, they're included in the 'all' of Romans 3:23, where it says "All have sinned, and come short of the glory of God." Because we have sinned, this is our natural fate:

> Ezekiel 18:4 - Behold, all souls are mine; as the soul of the father, so also the soul of the son is mine: the soul that sinneth, it shall die.

> Romans 6:23a - For the wages of sin is death;

> Revelation 20:11-15 - And I saw a great white throne, and him that sat on it, from whose face the earth and the heaven fled away; and there was found no place for them. And I saw the dead, small and great, stand before God; and the books were opened: and another book was opened, which is the book of life: and the dead were judged out of those things which were written in the books, according to their works. And the sea gave up the dead which were in it; and death and hell delivered up the dead which were in them: and they were judged every man according to their works. And death and hell were cast into the lake of fire. This is the second death. And whosoever was not found written in the book of life was cast into the lake of fire.

> Revelation 21:8 - But the fearful, and unbelieving, and the abominable, and murderers, and whoremongers, and sorcerers, and idolaters, and all liars, shall have their part in the lake which burneth with fire and

brimstone: <u>which is the second death.</u>

The punishment, or wages of sin, is always given as death in the scriptures. The word 'wages' means what we earn. At a job, our wages are the money we receive for the work we do. Likewise, for the evil works we do on the earth (sin), we receive death as our wage. We deserve nothing else. To God, who is holy (Lev. 19:2), our righteousnesses are nothing but filthy rages (Isa. 64:6). We're nothing but wicked sinners, and as a result, we will receive nothing but what we deserve: death.

This death in the Bible is defined in two ways: the physical death of the body, which results in the descent into hell (Rev. 20:13), and the second death, which is the judgment in the lake of fire. Revelation 21:8 makes it very clear that all sinners, even 'all liars' will have their part in the lake which burneth with fire and brimstone. Even lying, which is a sin everybody is guilty of ("The heart is deceitful above all things, and desperately wicked," Jer. 17:9), is enough to send somebody to the lake of fire.

Therefore, the Bible shows us beyond a shadow of a doubt that every person is a sinner in God's eyes, and every sin has the potential for sending somebody to hell. Nobody is good enough to escape death and the lake of fire. Nobody can be good enough to earn their salvation by their obedience to the law. In fact, it matters not whether somebody makes a change for the better or decides to start obeying the law at some point in their life. The Bible teaches that when we first sin, there is an inward death of the spirit:

> Romans 7:7-13 - What shall we say then? Is the law sin? God forbid. Nay, I had not known sin, but by the law: for I had not known lust, except the law had said, Thou shalt not covet. But sin, taking occasion by the commandment, wrought in me all manner of concupiscence. For without the law sin was dead. For I was alive without the law once: but when the commandment came, sin revived, and I died. And the commandment, which was ordained to life, I found to be unto death. For sin, taking occasion by the commandment, deceived me, and by it slew me. Wherefore the law is holy, and the commandment holy, and just, and good. Was then that which is good made death unto me? God forbid. But sin, that it might appear sin, working death in me by that which is good; that sin by the commandment might become exceeding sinful.

When Adam transgressed the law of God in the Garden of Eden, his eyes were opened, so that he knew both good and evil (Gen. 3:7). It was this transgression which brought sin, and therefore, death into the world. The Scriptures say:

> Romans 5:12-14 - Wherefore, as <u>by one man sin entered into the world, and death by sin; and so death passed upon all men, for that all have sinned:</u> (For until the law sin was in the world: but sin is not imputed when there is no law. Nevertheless death reigned from Adam to Moses, even over them that had not sinned after the similitude of Adam's transgression, who is the figure of him that was to come.

Adam's trangression brought death into the world, and by it, the Bible says "death passed upon all men, for that all have sinned." It is absurd to assume that one can be righteous enough in God's eyes when the scriptures show us that man is by their very nature inclined to sin. Going back to Romans 7, Paul writes that the very presence of the commandments of God (a knowledge of what's right and what's wrong) is what allows sin to take advantage of us and kill us. Therefore, Paul says "I died."

Paul was not physically dead, but spiritually, due to the presence of sin in his life. Even just one sin, the first sin which comes into your life, is enough to send you to the lake of fire. Therefore, the Bible teaches, "we were dead in trespasses and sins," and "were by nature the children of wrath, even as others (Eph. 2:1-3)." By nature, our sinful flesh is not in obedience to God, so we cannot hope to be declared righteous by our observance of the commandments of the LORD. Any attempt to do so is utterly futile, for all will fail, and even in just offending at one point, will be guilty of all (James 2:10). For this reason the Bible says,

> Romans 8:7-8 - Because the carnal mind is enmity against God: for it is not subject to the law of God, neither indeed can be. So then they that are in the flesh cannot please God.

The word 'carnal' means 'fleshly.' The natural mind which man has, which dies due to sin, according to the previous chapter, cannot be subject to the law of God. It is an inescapable fact that we cannot serve God due to the presence of the sinful flesh which we have. Therefore, it is not only a fact that all have sinned, and that any sin is enough to send one's soul to the lake of fire; it is also a fact that it is impossible to escape from the hold of sin, as it is human nature, as a result of the flesh which we have, to disobey God's law.

So, in summary thus far, here's what the Scriptures teach: that firstly, we are all sinners. This is a result of the transgression of Adam. Our nature has become disobedient to the law of God so that we cannot hope to obey his commandments due to our fleshly nature. Secondly, the punishment of sin, regardless of *how sinful* one is, is both physical death and the second death, which is the lake of fire. He who breaks one point of the law is guilty of all, still being a sinner in God's eyes, and therefore, will still end up in hell and the lake of fire.

Since this is the truth, the Bible tells us furthermore:

> Galatians 3:21-22 - Is the law then against the promises of God? God forbid: for if there had been a law given which could have given life, verily righteousness should have been by the law. But the scripture hath concluded all under sin, that the promise by faith of Jesus Christ might be given to them that believe.

We Christians hold to what the Bible says: there's nothing wrong with the law, but, there's a problem with mankind and his sinful condition. The Hebrew Roots do not seem to understand this. Here it is written that "IF there had been a law given which could have given life" (which implies there isn't), "verily righteousness SHOULD have been by the law." However, it goes on to say, "but the scripture hath conclude all under sin, that the promise by FAITH of Jesus Christ might be given to them that believe." There exists a very logical progression in this passage. First, it tells us that righteousness should be by obedience to the law, but only if such a law existed which could have given life.

However, since we are all under sin, the law cannot declare us right, or justify us. Instead, the Bible says here that it's by the 'faith of Jesus Christ.' The Hebrew Roots attack and mock the Christian message of the Gospel, which declares that justification and salvation is only by faith in Christ, and not by obedience to the law. This is the only way we can hope to achieve righteousness. If everybody is a sinner and guilty of breaking God's commandments, how does it make any sense to teach that we can be justified by our obedience to the law? That's an oxymoronic statement.

But rather, as will be shown, God prepared a way for salvation which has nothing to do with our own holiness and supposed righteousness (which is non-existent), but rather, entirely on the righteousness of Jesus Christ. We know that the curse of sin and death has passed upon all men (Rom. 5:12). However, "we have seen and do testify that the Father sent the Son to be the Saviour of the world (1 John 4:14)." What the Son was sent to save us from is stated clearly in the very first chapter of the New Testament:

> Matthew 1:21 - And she shall bring forth a son, and thou shalt call his name Jesus: for he shall save his people from their sins.

This is a verse which the Hebrew Roots should know well: for the name of Jesus, as shown earlier, is the Greek form of the Hebrew name Yeshua. This word, *yeshua*, means "salvation." Jesus Christ has this name because the purpose of his first coming to this earth was to "seek and save that which was lost (Luke 19:10)," which is defined here as saving "his people from their sins." We all have sinned, and thus all deserve death, but a Saviour came to deliver us from both.

This Saviour we know to be the Word made flesh (John 1:14) and the Son of God (Matt. 3:17, 17:5, Mark 1:11, 5:7, 9:7, 14:61-62, Luke 3:22, 9:35, John 10:36), and the prophesied Messiah, or Christ (John 1:41). His name was Jesus Christ, who was sent because God "loved us, and sent his Son to be the propitiation for our sins (1 John 4:10)." The word 'propitiation' means 'appeasing or satisifying.' We owe our lives to God, and deserve the punishment of death and hell for our sins, but Jesus Christ came to remove our guilt and therefore, this disastrous fate from us.

So, how was Jesus our 'propitiation?' How exactly did he save us from our sins?

> 1 Corinthians 15:1-4 - Moreover, brethren, <u>I declare unto you the gospel</u> which I preached unto you, which also ye have received, and wherein ye stand; By which <u>also ye are saved,</u> if ye keep in memory what I preached unto you, unless ye have believed in vain. For I delivered unto you first of all that which I also received, how that Christ died for our sins according to the scriptures; And that he was buried, and that he rose again the third day according to the scriptures:

The Scriptures declared that we are saved by the gospel, which it defines as the death, burial, and resurrection of Christ. The word gospel means 'good news,' or as the scriptures put it, 'glad tidings' or 'good tidings.' In Isaiah 61, which is a prophecy of the Lord Jesus Christ, and the chapter Jesus read in the synagogue in Luke 4, it says "The Spirit of the Lord GOD is upon me; because the LORD hath anointed me to preach good tidings unto the meek." This is the gospel which Jesus was sent to preach, which is the message of salvation through himself, the Son of God who was sent by the Father to deliver us from our sins.

Here in 1 Corinthians it says first that "Christ died for our sins according to the scriptures." This is the first part of the gospel, which consists in Christ's crucifixion. His death was more than just an event or a fulfillment of prophecy. This is how many in the Hebrew Roots movement treats it. Rather, the purpose of Christ's death was to take away our sins, by the shedding of his living blood. In the Old Testament there are pictures of Christ's sacrifice, which consisted in the animal sacrifices done at the tabernacle and the temple. The scriptures say:

> Leviticus 17:11 - For the life of the flesh is in the blood: and I have given it to you upon the altar to make an atonement for your souls: for it is the blood that maketh an atonement for the soul.

Without the shedding of blood, there is no remission of sins (Heb. 9:22). It was by the shedding of the blood of Christ that our sins are remitted and atoned for (meaning, covered). The Bible says:

> Romans 5:8-9 - But God commendeth his love toward us, in that, while we were yet sinners, Christ died for us. Much more then, being now justified by his blood, we shall be saved from wrath through him.

Even though we were sinners in God's eyes and deserving of the punishment of hell, God sent his Son to die for us, meaning, to die in place of us and to atone for our sin. This same simple truth is repeated in 1 Peter:

> 1 Peter 2:21-24 - For even hereunto were ye called: because Christ also suffered for us, leaving us an example, that ye should follow his steps: Who did no sin, neither was guile found in his mouth: Who, when he was reviled, reviled not again; when he suffered, he threatened not; but committed himself to him that judgeth righteously: Who his own self

bare our sins in his own body on the tree, that we, being dead to sins, should live unto righteousness: by whose stripes ye were healed.

Here the importance of Christ's death is outlined. Christ, being God in the flesh and not sharing of the sinful blood of Adam according to the flesh, lived a perfect life without sin (Heb. 4:15), yet despite his perfect obedience to God's law, was put to death for our own sins. While on the cross, he 'bare our sins in his own body.' Therefore, when Christ died, his sacrifice was a substitution. Even though we deserve to die for our sins, Christ gave his life to satisfy the debt owed to God instead. He did so that we "should live unto righteousness."

Here Peter quotes from the Old Testament, in which a prophecy of Christ's death on the cross is given, which explains this doctrine of substitutionary atonement very clearly. In this following passage, we see that the Saviour perished to remove our transgressions from us, through the imputation of our sin onto him, and the shedding of his blood which maketh atonement for the soul.

> Isaiah 53:1-12 - Who hath believed our report? and to whom is the arm of the Lord revealed? For he shall grow up before him as a tender plant, and as a root out of a dry ground: he hath no form nor comeliness; and when we shall see him, there is no beauty that we should desire him. He is despised and rejected of men; a man of sorrows, and acquainted with grief: and we hid as it were our faces from him; he was despised, and we esteemed him not. Surely he hath borne our griefs, and carried our sorrows: yet we did esteem him stricken, smitten of God, and afflicted. But he was <u>wounded for our transgressions, he was bruised for our iniquities</u>: the chastisement of our peace was upon him; and with his stripes we are healed. All we like sheep have gone astray; we have turned every one to his own way; and <u>the Lord hath laid on him the iniquity of us all</u>. He was oppressed, and he was afflicted, yet he opened not his mouth: he is brought as a lamb to the slaughter, and as a sheep before her shearers is dumb, so he openeth not his mouth. He was taken from prison and from judgment: and who shall declare his generation? for he was cut off out of the land of the living: <u>for the transgression of my people was he stricken</u>. And he made his grave with the wicked, and with the rich in his death; because he had done no violence, neither was any deceit in his mouth.

> Yet it pleased the Lord to bruise him; he hath put him to grief: <u>when thou shalt make his soul an offering for sin</u>, he shall see his seed, he shall prolong his days, and the pleasure of the Lord shall prosper in his hand. He shall see of the travail of his soul, and shall be satisfied: by his knowledge shall my righteous servant justify many; for <u>he shall bear their iniquities</u>. Therefore will I divide him a portion with the great, and he shall divide the spoil with the strong; because he hath poured out his soul unto death: and he was numbered with the transgressors; <u>and he bare the sin of many, and made intercession for the transgressors</u>.

This is an amazing chapter which describes in detail what would happen to our Messiah, and the reason why it happened. Just as in the New Testament, this chapter repeats over and over again that the purpose of Jesus' death was to take our sins away. In verse 5, it says "he was wounded for our transgressions." Our own sins are what led Jesus to die on the cross. That's why Romans 5:8 says, "while we were yet sinners, Christ died for us." Despite being sinners who don't deserve anything but hell, Christ came to die in our place.

In verse 6, the scriptures say that "the Lord hath laid on him the iniquity of us all." This shows exactly what 1 Peter 2 says, that he bore all of our sins in his own body on the tree. This does not apply to only certain people, but to 'all' as it says. All the sins of mankind were laid upon this one sinless man on the cross (see also Titus 2:11, Heb. 2:9, 1 John 2:2) . In verse 10, it says that his soul was made 'an offering for sin,' and in verse 11, that he will justify many by bearing their iniquities. This is the amazing Gospel, that when Christ was put to death, he became a sacrifice for our sins, and bore all the sins WE have committed, despite being innocent himself.

This is why the Bible says:

> 2 Corinthians 5:21 - For he hath made him to be sin for us, who knew no sin; that we might be made the righteousness of God in him.

Christ, who knew no sin, was made as a sinner to God, and died in our place, so that we can be justified (or declared righteous), through him and him alone. His shed blood has made atonement for our sins eternally. The scriptures say,

Hebrews 9:11-14 - But Christ being come an high priest of good things to come, by a greater and more perfect tabernacle, not made with hands, that is to say, not of this building; Neither by the blood of goats and calves, but by his own blood he entered in once into the holy place, having obtained eternal redemption for us. For if the blood of bulls and of goats, and the ashes of an heifer sprinkling the unclean, sanctifieth to the purifying of the flesh:How much more shall the blood of Christ, who through the eternal Spirit offered himself without spot to God, purge your conscience from dead works to serve the living God?

Here it says that Christ's blood has given us "eternal redemption." Both of these words are powerful to understanding the greatness of the Gospel. The word eternal means "forever" and the word redemption means "the act of paying off a debt and thus purchase freedom." The Bible describes our inability to follow God as bondage to sin. Jesus said, "whosoever commiteth sin is a servant to sin (John 8:34)." Knowing that we are all sinners and have all transgressed God's law (Eccl. 7:20, Rom. 3:10-18, 23, 1 John 1:8), we are all, when dead in our sins, a servant to sin. However, God has redeemed us from the bondage of sin by his own blood. This is why the Bible says:

Galatians 3:13 - Christ hath redeemed us from the curse of the law, being made a curse for us: for it is written, Cursed is every one that hangeth on a tree:

Ephesians 1:7 - In whom we have redemption through his blood, the forgiveness of sins, according to the riches of his grace

Colossians 1:14 - In whom we have redemption through his blood, even the forgiveness of sins:

With the precious blood of Christ we have been redeemed, according to the word of God (1 Peter 1:18-19). The emphasis on Christ's shed blood cannot be taken out. It is blood that makes atonement for the soul (Lev. 17:11), and it is by the sacrifice of the Son of God and the shedding of his blood that we have had our sins atoned for, to redeem us from the curse and give us forgiveness of sins (Eph. 1:7, Col. 1:14). This blood is referred to by Christ as the blood of the new testament (Matt. 26:28), which was prophesied by Jeremiah (Jer. 31:31-34), and which the Bible also calls the 'blood of the everlasting covenant' (meaning, it lasts forever) in Hebrews 13:20.

Christ completed the Gospel (1 Corinthians 15) not by his death only, but by his burial and resurrection. After being dead for three days, the Lord rose from the dead, as he had predicted (John 2:20-21). This resurrection is necessary also for our salvation, for it is because of his rise from the dead that he ascended into heaven to be our eternal intercessor. The Scriptures say:

> Romans 8:34 - Who is he that condemneth? It is Christ that died, yea rather, that is risen again, who is even at the right hand of God, who also maketh intercession for us.

After Christ rose from the dead, he ascended into heaven to sit at the right hand of the God, where he's our intercessor. The Bible says that he was "raised again for our justification" in Romans 4:25. The resurrection of Christ showed the Lord's victory over death and exalted him on high as our Messiah, who ever lives and gives us the gift of eternal life.

Recall in 1 Corinthians 15 that this message of Christ's death for our sins, his burial, and his resurrection for our justification, is the Gospel by which we are saved. This salvation is a salvation from sin (Matt. 1:21). All this was done so that Christ could save us from our sins; the very sins which we as mankind cannot naturally turn from, and which has caused death to pass upon all mankind. Our sins have already been paid for by Christ. It's abundantly clear in the Scriptures that Christ's shed blood both redeems us and forgives us of our sins. Why then, do we assume that our salvation is based on our own human effort?

> Romans 5:14-21 - Nevertheless death reigned from Adam to Moses, even over them that had not sinned after the similitude of Adam's transgression, who is the figure of him that was to come. But not as the offence, so also is the free gift. For if through the offence of one many be dead, <u>much more the grace of God, and the gift by grace, which is by one man, Jesus Christ, hath abounded unto many</u>. And not as it was by one that sinned, so is the gift: for the judgment was by one to condemnation, but the <u>free gift is of many offences unto justification</u>. For if by one man's offence death reigned by one; much more they which <u>receive abundance of grace and of the gift of righteousness shall reign in life by one, Jesus Christ</u>.) Therefore as by the offence of one

133

judgment came upon all men to condemnation; even so by the righteousness of one the free gift came upon all men unto justification of life. For as by one man's disobedience many were made sinners, so by the obedience of one shall many be made righteous. Moreover the law entered, that the offence might abound. But where sin abounded, grace did much more abound: That as sin hath reigned unto death, even so might grace reign through righteousness unto eternal life by Jesus Christ our Lord.

It is not our own righteousness which saves us. Our righteousnesses are as filthy rags (Isa. 64:6). We are all sinners, regardless of how righteous we think we are. It was Christ who was righteous, and by him are we saved. In the passage above, read how it speaks clearly of the amazing grace of Christ: that the righteousness of ONE (that is, Christ) provides for us what the Bible calls "the free gift." The language used here is very clear. A gift is not something which one earns, it is something provided freely. Likewise, grace is not earned. It is unmerited favour provided through love and graciousness.

Christ says in the closing chapter of Revelation, "Whosoever will, let him take the water of life freely (Revelation 22:17)." Our salvation and eternal life is a free gift, which is offered to us on the basis of the obedience of one (Rom. 5:19), which makes us righteous. This is justification. Christ died on the cross, and his shed blood made atonement for our sins and redeemed us unto God. He rose from the dead, and now offers to us a free gift, the gift of salvation, in which our sins are forgiven and we are declared righteous. Romans 6:23 defines the gift of God as "eternal life through Jesus Christ our Lord."

"NOT by works of righteousness which we have done, but according to his mercy he saved he saved us (Titus 3:5)," the word of God says. The Hebrew Roots movement mocks us Christians for proclaiming the simplicity of the Gospel, by claiming that we have to do something righteous ourselves to escape the punishment of hell. The truth is, our sinful nature and wicked flesh prohibits us from being subject to the law of God. But Christ, by his death, burial, and resurrection, and by his own obedience, justifies us by grace.

The only thing we have to do is accept the free gift which Christ offers by grace. We accept this gift by faith. Although the Hebrew Roots movement denies this, there's an abundant amount of clear Scriptures which tell us that we are justified the moment we believe on the Lord Jesus Christ. Jesus himself said:

Mark 16:16 - He that believeth and is baptized shall be saved; <u>but he that believeth not shall be damned.</u>

Luke 8:12 - Those by the way side are they that hear; then cometh the devil, and taketh away the word out of their hearts, lest they should <u>believe and be saved.</u>

Luke 18:42 - And Jesus said unto him, Receive thy sight: <u>thy faith hath saved thee.</u>

John 3:16 - For God so loved the world, that he gave his only begotten Son, that <u>whosoever believeth in him</u> should not perish, but have everlasting life.

John 3:18 - <u>He that believeth on him is not condemned</u>: but he that believeth not is condemned already, because he hath not believed in the name of the only begotten Son of God.

John 5:24 - Verily, verily, I say unto you, He that heareth my word, and <u>believeth on him that sent me, hath everlasting life,</u> and shall not come into condemnation; but is passed from death unto life.

John 6:35 - And Jesus said unto them, I am the bread of life: he that cometh to me shall never hunger; and <u>he that believeth on me shall never thirst.</u>

John 6:40 - And this is the will of him that sent me, that <u>every one which seeth the Son, and believeth on him, may have everlasting life</u>: and I will raise him up at the last day.

John 6:47 - Verily, verily, I say unto you, <u>He that believeth on me hath everlasting life.</u>

John 8:24 - I said therefore unto you, that ye shall die in your sins: for <u>if ye believe not that I am he, ye shall die in your sins.</u>

John 11:25-26 - Jesus said unto her, I am the resurrection, and the life: <u>he that believeth in me, though he were dead, yet shall he live: And whosoever liveth and believeth in me shall never die.</u> Believest thou this?

John 12:36 - While ye have light, <u>believe in the light, that ye may be the children of light</u>. These things spake Jesus, and departed, and did hide himself from them.

John 12:46 - I am come a light into the world, that <u>whosoever believeth on me should not abide in darkness</u>.

Christ said over and over again that the only requirement for eternal life was faith in him: that once somebody believed on him, they would have everlasting life. In John 3:16, Christ says simply, "whosoever believeth in him should not perish, but have everlasting life." The word 'whosoever' means anybody. He is guaranteeing that no matter what else the person may do, if they believe in him, they have the gift of everlasting life. In case this wasn't clear, he says to Martha, "whosoever liveth and believeth in me shall never die." The Hebrew Roots movement has the wrong opinion that one must live a good life of obedience to God's commandments in order to escape the second death. However, Jesus says that belief is the only thing required for one to avoid the judgment of death.

Therefore, when one has faith, they are saved (Luke 18:42), they have everlasting life (John 3:16-18, 5:24, 6:40, 47, 11:25-26), they shall never hunger or thirst (John 6:35), they become the children of light (John 12:36) and they do not abide in darkness (John 12:46). When one does not have faith, they will be damned (Mark 16:16), condemned (John 3:18), and they die in their sins (John 8:24)." It's not difficult to understand the message which Jesus taught. The entire purpose of the Book of John being written was "that ye might believe that Jesus is the Christ, the Son of God; and that believing ye might have life through his name (John 20:31)." It's no wonder, then, that the word 'believe' appears over 80 times in the book of John!

In case the words of our Messiah himself are not enough, let's examine other scriptures and see what they have to say about salvation and eternal life. It's abundantly clear through the entirety of the Holy Bible that we are justified through nothing but our faith in the Lord Jesus Christ. The question is asked only once in the Bible, "What must I do to be saved?" The answer is given:

Acts 16:30-31 - And brought them out, and said, Sirs, what must I do to be saved? And they said, <u>Believe on the Lord Jesus Christ, and thou shalt be saved</u>, and thy house.

If there is some other requirement for salvation, whether it's baptism, good works, obedience to the commandments, are otherwise, then why is it left out of this answer? The answer is simply, 'Believe on the Lord Jesus Christ.' This is all the scriptures ever teach us about how we are saved from our sins. A similarly worded passage appears in the book of Romans, saying:

> Romans 10:9-10 - That if thou shalt confess with thy mouth the Lord Jesus, and shalt believe in thine heart that God hath raised him from the dead, <u>thou shalt be saved</u>. For with the heart man believeth unto righteousness; and with the mouth confession is made unto salvation.

Both of these passages share this as an absolute promise. If we believe on him, we shall be saved. There's no doubt about our salvation. There's no additional, "if thou obey the commandments" or "if thou serve God faithfully." Rather, if our heart puts our trust on the Lord Jesus Christ, we are saved, which is, salvation from sin.

It's not difficult to understand why this is necessary. As already shown, the scriptures hath concluded all under sin (Gal. 3:22). We cannot be justified by anything other than faith because we are unrighteous in God's eyes, because we've all sinned, and because we all die in Adam (Rom. 5:12). We therefore can only expect to be saved through our Saviour and through what he did, not what we do. In Romans, after a multitude of quotes from the Old Testament showing that all men are wicked (Rom. 3:10-18), the passage continues on with a crystal clear description of grace:

> Romans 3:19-28 - Now we know that what things soever the law saith, it saith to them who are under the law: <u>that every mouth may be stopped, and all the world may become guilty before God</u>. Therefore <u>by the deeds of the law there shall no flesh be justified in his sight</u>: for by the law is the knowledge of sin. But now the righteousness of God without the law is manifested, being witnessed by the law and the prophets; <u>Even the righteousness of God which is by faith of Jesus Christ unto all and upon all them that believe</u>: for there is no difference: For all have sinned, and come short of the glory of God; Being justified freely by his grace through the redemption that is in Christ Jesus: Whom God hath set forth to be <u>a propitiation through faith in his blood</u>, to declare his righteousness for the remission of sins that are past, through the forbearance of God; To declare, I say, at this

time his righteousness: that he might be just, and the <u>justifier of him which believeth in Jesus</u>. Where is boasting then? It is excluded. By what law? of works? Nay: but by the law of faith. Therefore we conclude that <u>a man is justified by faith without the deeds of the law</u>.

This passage is packed with important information, so let's break it down. After declaring the sinfulness of all people in the preceding verses (v. 10-18, "there is none righteous, no, not one"), it is written in verse 19 that the law says what it says to them which are under the law. Of those who are saved, we are "not under the law, but under grace (Rom. 6:14)." Jesus "redeemed them that were under the law (Gal. 4:5)." Thus, those referred to here in verse 19 are not those in the new testament, but who remain under the old testament, who have not yet come to Christ. The law is written to them for a purpose, and this purpose is "that every mouth may be stopped, and all the world may become guilty before God."

This means that the law was given so that we could understand our sinful condition. This applies to all people; notice the absolutes "every mouth" and "all the world." The law is not written for the purpose of making people righteous before God, but the very opposite: to make the world guilty before God. This is exactly what we see in multitudes of other scriptures. In Romans 5:20, it says "the law entered, that the offence might abound." God knew that mankind would not be able to obey his law, knowing that "the carnal mind is enmity against God (Rom. 8:7)." The law was not established because we could obey it, but in order that our transgressions would increase, and we would understand our sinful condition. It is written elsewhere, "the law was our schoolmaster to bring us unto Christ, that we might be justified by faith (Gal. 3:24)," showing us that the law was established to bring us to faith in Jesus Christ, not to justify us.

Therefore, the law says what it says to create a humble heart and to lead us to the acknowledgement of our sinful condition. After all, without understanding why we need a saviour, we cannot be saved - "If we say that we have not sinned, we make him a liar, and his word is not in us (1 John 1:10)." Romans 3 goes on to say in the following verse, "Therefore by the deeds of the law there shall no flesh be justified in his sight: for by the law is the knowledge of sin." Once again, this makes sense and is in agreement with the rest of Scripture.

The verse starts off with the adverb 'therefore' which means "for this reason." For the reason just written: that everybody is a sinner, and thus, the law only helps man to understand his sinful condition, man cannot be saved by deeds of the law. Once again, absolutes are used in this scripture, saying "there shall no flesh be justified in his sight." There's no exception. Nobody on earth can be declared righteous by God through their observance of the law: that includes the Hebrew Roots movement.

The next verse establishes the alternative, then: that though we are not justified by the deeds of the law, there is a way in which we can be declared righteous. Verse 22 says, that this righteousness "is by faith of Jesus Christ unto ALL and upon ALL them that believe." Isn't this what Jesus spoke clearly in John 3:16, 6:47, and 11:26, that whosoever (meaning all) believes on him would have everlasting life? This means that I, since I put my trust in Christ, have been justified. This means that any person out there, regardless of their obedience or disobedience to the commandments of the Torah, is justified by their faith in Christ.

In verse 23, the reason for this is again stated: "For all have sinned and come short of the glory of God." Verse 24 goes on to say that these are justified "freely" through the redemption which is in Christ Jesus. Once again, salvation is referred to as a free gift of God and not something which we have to earn. We do not have to pay for anything ourselves, because Christ has already paid off this debt (redeemed us). Not only that, but this Christ Jesus is "set forth to be a propitiation, through faith in his blood." Remember, the word "propitiation" means "appeasing or satisfying." God is satisfied by our faith in the blood which Christ shed on the cross, the same blood discussed earlier which is said to give us redemption and forgiveness of sins (Eph. 1:7, Col. 1:14).

We are "justified by his blood (Romans 5:9)." Since Christ already died on the cross for our sins and then rose again, we do not need to do anything ourselves for salvation. Once we rest upon his finished work, God imputes to us his righteousness and is propitiated. His wrath is no longer upon us (the forbearance of God in v. 25, which is, the removal of enforcing a debt), because we have faith in his Son, Jesus Christ.

In verse 26, we see that God is the "justifier of him which believeth in Jesus." We are declared as just in the eyes of God if we believe on Jesus Christ. It's not difficult to understand what's being laid out here. Verse 28 concludes the whole matter, saying "Therefore we conclude that a man is justified by faith WITHOUT the deeds of the law."

God does not accept us based on how much good we have done, or whether we obey his commandments. He accepts us based on our trust in Jesus Christ, and that's it. If we are justified by faith but not justified by the deeds of the law, then we are justified by nothing but faith: or in other words, the simple Christian declaration of *faith alone*. This is what Jesus preached, this is what Paul preached, this is what John preached, and what Peter (Acts 10:43, 1 Peter 1:5, 9) preached.

Moreover, as stated here in Romans 3, this simple truth is "witnessed by the law and the prophets (v. 21)." Peter said also, "To him give all the prophets witness, that through his name whosoever believeth in shall receive remission of sins (Acts 10:43)." Since the Hebrew Roots movement often places more emphasis on the Old Testament than the words of our Saviour himself, we shall also examine the Tanakh, and see that the doctrine of the New Testament concerning justification by faith alone is not a new doctrine, but one which was preached clearly even in the days of the Sinai covenant.

Firstly, it is outlined in the New Testament that salvation has always been by grace through faith, by showing several examples of how people were justified in the Tanakh. Concerning both Abraham and David, it is written:

> Romans 4:1-8 - What shall we say then that Abraham our father, as pertaining to the flesh, hath found? For if Abraham were justified by works, he hath whereof to glory; but not before God. For what saith the scripture? <u>Abraham believed God, and it was counted unto him for righteousness</u>. Now to him that worketh is the reward not reckoned of grace, but of debt. But to him that worketh not, but believeth on him that justifieth the ungodly, his faith is counted for righteousness. Even as David also describeth the blessedness of the man, unto whom God imputeth righteousness without works, Saying, <u>Blessed are they whose iniquities are forgiven, and whose sins are covered.</u> <u>Blessed is the man to whom the Lord will not impute sin.</u>

Verses 3, 7, and 8 all quote from the Old Testament to establish the point that justification does not come by works, but by the righteousness of faith.

140

Genesis 15:6 - And he believed in the Lord; and he counted it to him for righteousness.

Psalm 32:1-2 - Blessed is he whose transgression is forgiven, whose sin is covered. Blessed is the man unto whom the LORD imputeth not iniquity, and in whose spirit there is no guile.

Here we see examples in the Old Testament of the forgiveness of sins, which is by faith. As pointed out in the remainder of Romans 4, this above passage (Gen. 15:6) is prior to Abraham's circumcision or his good works for God. All he did was believe the promise of God, and this faith was reckoned to him for righteousness. Isn't that exactly what we've seen so far in the New Testament? The Bible is in agreement. These passages are not alone, however. The Scriptures say also:

Psalm 25:18-20 - Look upon mine affliction and my pain; and forgive all my sins. Consider mine enemies; for they are many; and they hate me with cruel hatred. O keep my soul, and deliver me: let me not be ashamed; for I put my trust in thee.

Psalm 32:10 - Many sorrows shall be to the wicked: but he that trusteth in the LORD, mercy shall compass him about.

Psalm 34:22 - The LORD redeemeth the soul of his servants: and none of them that trust in him shall be desolate.

Psalm 37:39-40 - But the salvation of the righteous is of the LORD: he is their strength in the time of trouble. And the LORD shall help them, and deliver them: he shall deliver them from the wicked, and save them, because they trust in him.

Psalm 55:16 - As for me, I will call upon God; and the LORD shall save me.

Psalm 78:21-22 - Therefore the LORD heard this, and was wroth: so a fire was kindled against Jacob, and anger also came up against Israel; Because they believed not in God, and trusted not in his salvation:

Psalm 86:2-5 - Preserve my soul; for I am holy: O thou my God, save thy servant that trusteth in thee. Be merciful unto me, O Lord: for I cry unto thee daily. Rejoice the soul of thy servant: for unto thee, O

Lord, do I lift up my soul. For thou, Lord, art good, and ready to forgive; and plenteous in mercy unto all them that call upon thee.

Psalm 107:1-6 - O give thanks unto the Lord, for he is good: for his mercy endureth for ever. Let the redeemed of the Lord say so, whom he hath redeemed from the hand of the enemy; And gathered them out of the lands, from the east, and from the west, from the north, and from the south. They wandered in the wilderness in a solitary way; they found no city to dwell in. Hungry and thirsty, their soul fainted in them. Then they cried unto the Lord in their trouble, and he delivered them out of their distresses.

Psalm 107:17-21 - Fools because of their transgression, and because of their iniquities, are afflicted. Their soul abhorreth all manner of meat; and they draw near unto the gates of death. Then they cry unto the Lord in their trouble, and he saveth them out of their distresses. He sent his word, and healed them, and delivered them from their destructions. Oh that men would praise the Lord for his goodness, and for his wonderful works to the children of men!

It is proclaimed repeatedly that the LORD saves his people and forgives the sins of those who trust in him. This is what we ought to believe, for it is the clear proclamation in all of the Word of God: that whoever trusts in the Lord for their salvation will be forgiven of their sins and receive everlasting life. In conclusion,

1 John 5:10-13 - He that believeth on the Son of God hath the witness in himself: he that believeth not God hath made him a liar; because he believeth not the record that God gave of his Son. And this is the record, that God hath given to us eternal life, and this life is in his Son. He that hath the Son hath life; and he that hath not the Son of God hath not life. These things have I written unto you that believe on the name of the Son of God; that ye may know that ye have eternal life, and that ye may believe on the name of the Son of God.

Those who make God a liar are those who reject the clear record which God gave of his Son, the very record which, by the context, is borne by the Father, the Word, and the Holy Ghost (v.7), and the Spirit, the water, and the blood (v. 8). All of these testify of this evident truth: that God hath given to us eternal life, and this life is in his Son. Do you believe this? Do you believe that eternal life is a gift (meaning, it is given by God freely and not earned)? Do you believe that this life is eternal (meaning, it doesn't end)? Do you believe that this life is in his Son (meaning, we have eternal life through Jesus Christ and nothing else)?

The Hebrew Roots exalt themselves as the true followers of Yeshua, falsely proclaiming a false Gospel of salvation by obedience to the Torah. They often believe that the Messiah did not come to be the Saviour of the world and to die for our sins, but to turn Israel back to following the law of God. Those in the Hebrew Roots movement thus teach that if you willingly break God's commands, you will end up in the lake of fire. This, as we have seen, is contary to a multitude of Scriptures, which show that we are "justified by faith without the deeds of the law (Rom. 3:28)." However, just to destroy any additional doubts about the unmistakable truth of the Gospel, we'll take a look at more scriptures which specifically tell us that we are NOT saved by obedience to the law, works, or anything other than faith, and then will proceed to address the 'proof texts' which are often advance by their movement.

Not of Works

Besides some of the passages in the scriptures we've already looked at, like Romans 3:19-28 and Galatians 3:21-22, which show that we are justified without the deeds of the law, there are plenty of additional scriptures which show the absence of good works and obedience to the salvation plan. For example, in Romans 4, quoted previously, it states, "But to him that worketh not, but believeth on him that justifieth the ungodly, his faith is counted for righteousness (Rom. 4:5)." This means that even to those who don't do any works (worketh not), if they believe, they are still justified by their faith. It doesn't matter how many good things I've done, if I have the faith, I am still righteous to God. Furthermore, the Bible says:

> Galatians 2:16 - Knowing that a man is not justified by the works of the law, but by the faith of Jesus Christ, even we have believed in Jesus Christ, that we might be justified by the faith of Christ, and not by the works of the law: for by the works of the law shall no flesh be justified.

This verse couldn't make it any clearer. We are not justified by the works of the law, but by faith in Christ. Again, even if we repent and try to follow the law of God, we are still sinners, our righteousnesses are still as filthy rags (Isa. 64:6). We can only be righteous through our faith, in which Christ's righteousness is imputed onto us (2 Cor. 5:21). Several verses later in Galatians 2, it says "If righteousness come by the law, then Christ is dead in vain."

What an amazing truth! Indeed, since Christ was sent to save us from our sins (Matt. 1:21), it makes no sense to teach that we are saved by the very thing which causes us to sin. The scriptures say, "When the commandment came, sin revived, and I died... For sin, taking occasion by the commandment, deceived me, and by it slew me (Rom. 7:9-11)." Our fleshly nature cannot be subject to the law of God, and this is why we are all under sin. With the law, all which happens is that we gain a knowledge of our sin (Rom. 3:19-20). Christ came to save us from the sin which has brought death upon us, and to "redeem them that were under the law (Gal. 4:5)."

Some in the Hebrew Roots movement will raise the erroneous objection that the "deeds of the law" and "works of the law" only refers to Jewish customs or rituals and not to observance of the actual law of Moses (the Torah). However, this idea is nowhere taught in the Bible, but is completely made-up. The term "works of the law" is defined in the book of Galatians:

> Galatians 3:10 - For as many as are of the works of the law are under the curse: for it is written, Cursed is every one that continueth not in all things which are written in the book of the law to do them.

Here 'works of the law' is defined as "all things which are written in the book of the law." Therefore, whenever this phrase appears, such as in Gal. 2:16, where it says that we are not justified by the works of the law, the Bible is telling us that nothing written in the book of the law can justify us. This is made evident also by the fact that several scriptures simply just say 'law' and not 'works of the law' (Gal. 2:21, 5:4, Phil. 3:9).

Let's move on to another scripture:

> Ephesians 2:8-9 - For by grace are ye saved through faith; and that not of yourselves: it is the gift of God: Not of works, lest any man should boast.

Here is quite an efficient summary of how we are saved: in accordance to what has been delivered so far in this essay: that we are saved by grace through faith, and that it is not of works. Works are absent from our salvation.

Let's stop for a moment to consider the contradictory nature of grace and works. The Hebrew Roots movement does not entirely remove grace out of the equation or reject it (since they claim to believe the Bible), but are guilty of adding works onto salvation. What's the problem with this? The statement "We are saved by grace and works" is an oxymoron. By definition, grace and works are opposites. Grace is unmerited favour. If we are saved by grace, then we do not earn it. On the contrary, if salvation is something gained by our obedience and good works, then it is merited and earned.

Furthermore, as stated in this verse as well as other scriptures (Rom. 5:15-18, 6:23), salvation is a gift of God. Once again, the very definition of a gift is contradictory to works. If we are saved by works, then salvation is not a gift, it is a compensation. This is exactly what Paul writes about in Romans 4:4 - he acknowledges that there is a place for works, and there are rewards given out of debt. Just like when we work on earth, we receive a debt of compensation for the labour which we've done. However, the money which we earn at our jobs is not a 'gift.' It is not given out of the grace of our superiors, but given because they earned it.

We cannot earn our salvation. The only one who was able to earn it and pay the debt was Jesus Christ, who through his own righteousness (Rom. 5:18) redeemed us. This contradiction between grace and works is clearly shown in several scriptures, such as the following:

> Romans 11:5-6 - Even so then at this present time also there is a remnant according to the election of grace. <u>And if by grace, then is it no more of works: otherwise grace is no more grace. But if it be of works, then it is no more grace: otherwise work is no more work</u>.

> Titus 3:5-7 - <u>Not by works of righteousness which we have done, but according to his mercy he saved us</u>, by the washing of regeneration, and renewing of the Holy Ghost; Which he shed on us abundantly through Jesus Christ our Saviour; That being justified by his grace, we should be made heirs according to the hope of eternal life.

We already examined Romans 11:5-6 in the earlier section about the nation of Israel. The passage makes it clear that there is no intermixing between grace and works. Just as I pointed out, if our election is of grace, then it is "no more of works." If it were of works, "grace is no more grace." It is an undeniable fact of the Bible that our salvation is by grace; even the Hebrew Roots acknowledge this. Denying this would be to deny what the Bible says clearly in dozens of verses. Therefore, since we are most certainly justified by grace (as it says in Titus 3:7), we are not justified by works. It's simple.

Instead of having confidence in the teachers of the world, why not rely on what the Bible says? There's no need for special teachings by "Torah teachers" or any twisting of the scriptures. What the Bible says overwhelmingly is that we are NOT saved by the law, that we are NOT saved by works, that we are NOT saved by obedience, but entirely by the grace of God which is bestowed upon us once we trust in Jesus Christ and his work in his death, burial, and resurrection. This is the only way to receive eternal life and escape from the damnation of hell and the lake of fire.

Why then, are there apparent scriptures which teach otherwise? I was confident in my beliefs during my time in the Hebrew Roots movement, being ignorant of these verses but knowledgable in passages which are twisted by the Messianics to teach that without the Torah, one will end up in the lake of fire. There are quite a few of these, and without comparison to other scriptures (spiritual to spiritual, 1 Cor. 2:13) or even to the context, they can be easily misunderstood.

I'll give a few examples of this. Many of these were my favorite to use against Christians who I believed were in error. Considering that the message of salvation in the Bible is clear, and that the Bible is perfect, without contradictions, we ought to examine these scriptures, and in doing so, we'll find that they do not contradict the message of grace through faith. Perhaps the most recognizable of these passages is James 2:14-24, which says:

> James 2:14-24 - What doth it profit, my brethren, though a man say he hath faith, and have not works? can faith save him? If a brother or sister be naked, and destitute of daily food, And one of you say unto them, Depart in peace, be ye warmed and filled; notwithstanding ye give them not those things which are needful to the body; what doth it profit? Even so faith, if it hath not works, is dead, being alone. Yea, a

man may say, Thou hast faith, and I have works: shew me thy faith without thy works, and I will shew thee my faith by my works. Thou believest that there is one God; thou doest well: the devils also believe, and tremble. But wilt thou know, O vain man, that faith without works is dead? Was not Abraham our father justified by works, when he had offered Isaac his son upon the altar? Seest thou how faith wrought with his works, and by works was faith made perfect? And the scripture was fulfilled which saith, Abraham believed God, and it was imputed unto him for righteousness: and he was called the Friend of God. Ye see then how that by works a man is justified, and not by faith only.

The Hebrew Roots are not alone in using this passage and twisting it in an attempt to prove that we need works as well in order to be saved. The interpretation usually comes in two forms: either it means "we need works in order to be saved" or "if we have faith but do not do the good works to prove it, then we don't have real faith." Both of these interpretations are extreme misunderstandings of the text. Let's examine it deeply, and then compare spiritual with spiritual.

First, in verse 14, the passage starts with the question, "can faith save him?" We need to understand that the salvation of the soul from sin is not the only context in which the word 'save' appears. There are numerous examples in the scriptures in which the word 'save' does not have a spiritual application, even in the New Testament. For example, in 1 Peter 3:20, it is stated, "eight souls were saved by water." This, referring to Noah and his family, of course is not saying that everybody on board the ark was spiritually saved, but rather refers to the salvation or deliverance of the flesh. In Luke 9:24, Jesus says "Whosoever will save his life shall lose it," referring to the salvation of his fleshly life; our life here on earth.

Likewise, in James 2:14, the word 'save' is not about spiritual salvation, but about the body. We see this is evident as we continue to read. The following verses all talk about provisions for the body, such as food and warmth, to fellow brethren. James is making a point here: that faith is not profitable for the body (which is the temple of Holy Ghost). This is why James asks the question, "What doth it profit?" Indeed, what does it profit anybody if we believe but don't do the works? As in the illustration used here by James, we may have the right attitude and have faith that one could be "warm and filled," but unless we actually provide such food and warmth which is necessary for doing so, our faith is unprofitable.

This entire passage makes sense once we consider that this is from the perspective of man. In verse 18, James starts out by writing "A man may say." The subject here is not God. There's no indication that God wants us to prove our faith by our works. This hypothetical man says, "Thou hast faith, and I have works: shew me thy faith without thy works, and I will shew thee my faith by my works." This hypothetical man, because he is not God, cannot see the faith of a man. It is impossible for the world to know for a truth that we have faith in Christ; the only way which we can prove our faith to *man* is by showing it with works: "I will shew thee my faith by my works."

For example, I may say that I have faith, but this undoubtedly is not enough for you nor anybody else to see my faith. I show my faith by works. I could go out, and use my energy, time, and resources to share the Gospel with the world as Jesus commanded in Mark 16:15. In doing so, I prove that I really believe what I say that I believe, for logically, I would not be wasting my time soul-winning and preaching (especially since it's not lucrative, and the world opposes such) if I did not truly believe it.

James himself gives an example of what he's speaking of here in the person of Abraham. Before discussing Abraham's faith and works, let's quickly address a common argument which arises from verse 19: it is commonly misquoted as simply "Thou believest." That's not what it says. It says "Thou believest there is one God." Believing there is One God is not what saves us. James points out that even the devils believe, but this belief is in one God. So far in this book, I have never stated that the requirement for salvation is monotheism. Muslims believe in one God: this does not mean they are saved. You must put your trust in the Lord Jesus Christ, and that he has paid for your sins and risen from the dead, in order to be saved. This is the faith we preach, according to what's written in the scriptures.

Now, the example of Abraham: He was justified by works when he offered Isaac upon the altar. Does this mean that Abraham was saved only because he did this? No, it does not. This took place many decades after it is stated in Genesis 15:6, "And he believed in the Lord, and it was counted to him for righteousness." The definition of justification itself is "to become just." Abraham's faith in the LORD is what made him just, or righteous, to God. So why then does James say that Abraham was justified by works, even though he himself quotes this above verse in v. 23?

As already pointed out, this justification is justification in the eyes of man. Verse 18 says "A man may say," not, "God may say." This whole passage is about proving faith and being profitable to man with works. In the book of Romans, we see:

> Romans 4:1-2 - What shall we say then that Abraham our father, as pertaining to the flesh, hath found? <u>For if Abraham were justified by works, he hath whereof to glory; but not before God.</u>

Verse 2 is the key here: "if Abraham were justified by works." James tells us that Abraham was indeed justified by works, when he offered his son Isaac upon the altar (v. 21). Therefore, Abraham hath whereof to glory (meaning, something to glory in or to boast about), but NOT BEFORE GOD. Abraham was indeed justified by works, but he was not justified before God, for the scripture says evidently, that salvation is "not of works, lest any man should boast."

Therefore, the subject of James is man's outward judgment of the flesh, and not God's searching of the heart. The LORD does not need to see our works, because the Scriptures tell us "God knoweth the secrets of the heart (Psa. 44:21) and "the LORD seeth not as man seeth; for man looketh on the outward appearance, but the LORD looketh on the heart." We as men, unable to see the heart, do not know faith unless there are works to prove the faith. This is why, in Hebrews 11, it is written "faith is the substance of things hoped for, the evidence of things not seen." This chapter lists the good works of the holy men of the Old Testament, explaining that these are examples for us, and by these works, we know of the faith which they have in God.

> Hebrews 11:17-19 - By faith Abraham, when he was tried, offered up Isaac: and he that had received the promises offered up his only begotten son, Of whom it was said, That in Isaac shall thy seed be called: Accounting that God was able to raise him up, even from the dead; from whence also he received him in a figure.

Here we see that Abraham offered Isaac by faith. He had faith in God, that even if he killed his son Isaac, he would be able to be raised from the dead. We know of Abraham's faith because of this example. This work demonstrates Abraham's faith to us, but did not justify him in the eyes of

God. To God, he was justified decades before when he believed God in Genesis 15.

Therefore, James 2 does not teach that we are saved by works. The phrase "faith without works is dead," simply means that faith is unprofitable without works. Verse 26 says "For as the body without the spirit is dead, so faith without works is dead also." When our body dies, the spirit departs (Eccl. 12:7, Acts 7:59). This does not mean that the body was never alive or that the body doesn't exist. Likewise, if we have faith but don't have works, this doesn't mean "it's not real faith" as many like to say, or that it doesn't exist at all.

Another passage which is used in an attempt to prove that we must have obedience to the commandments of God in order to be saved or stay saved is this:

> Matthew 7:21-23 - Not every one that saith unto me, Lord, Lord, shall enter into the kingdom of heaven; but he that doeth the will of my Father which is in heaven. Many will say to me in that day, Lord, Lord, have we not prophesied in thy name? and in thy name have cast out devils? and in thy name done many wonderful works? And then will I profess unto them, I never knew you: depart from me, ye that work iniquity.

In reality, this passage instead refutes the Hebrew Roots position. The twisting of this passage comes from verses 21 and 23; the claim is that the "will of my Father" refers to obedience to God's commands, while "ye that work iniquity" refers to those who have refused to follow God's law. However, those in the Hebrew Roots movement typically ignore the middle verse, which includes the boasting of men who have done "many wonderful works."

Thus, what this is picturing are those who call Jesus Lord, and who have done many works in his name, but who Jesus does not let enter into the kingdom of heaven. The implied reason for this is because they did not do the will of the Father. Those in the Hebrew Roots movement immediately assume that this will of the Father must be God's commandments: since God commanded them, it is his will. However, Jesus specifically defines what he's talking about elsewhere, saying,

> John 6:39-40 - And this is the Father's will which hath sent me, that of

150

all which he hath given me I should lose nothing, but should raise it up again at the last day. <u>And this is the will of him that sent me</u>, that every one which seeth the Son, and believeth on him, may have everlasting life: and I will raise him up at the last day.

The will of God the Father is our faith, and that through our faith, we would have everlasting life. It's not about observing the commandments or living a good life. Rather, those who try to enter in through their good works are cast out before Jesus. Why is that? Because as the Scripture says in Hebrews 6:1, the foundation of the doctrine of Christ is "repentance from dead works, and faith toward God." In turning to Christ in faith, we turn away from our dead works (works which do not profit anything). Those in the Matthew 7 passage are those who are trusting in their works and not in Christ for their salvation, just as Ephesians 2:9 says - "Not of works, lest any man should boast."

Therefore, the will of God, as expressed in numerous other passages, is our repentance and faith, not our attempt to follow the Torah. These workers of iniquity, being unjustified, are "guilty of all (James 2:10)," because they have not had their sins forgiven by the blood of Christ. The commandment we are given is not to obey his whole law in every precept, but "that we should believe on the name of his Son Jesus Christ (1 John 3:23)." Therefore, this passage does not teach that we are saved by our works or obedience to the law. Another passage used, also in the book of Matthew, is this:

> Matthew 13:41-42 - The Son of man shall send forth his angels, and they shall gather out of his kingdom all things that offend, <u>and them which do iniquity</u>; And shall cast them into a furnace of fire: there shall be wailing and gnashing of teeth.

Often this passage is taken out of the context of a parable which Jesus tells. This is part of the explanation of the parable. Looking earlier in the chapter, Christ said,

> Matthew 13:24-30 - The kingdom of heaven is likened unto a man which sowed good seed in his field: But while men slept, <u>his enemy came and sowed tares among the wheat</u>, and went his way. But when the blade was sprung up, and brought forth fruit, then appeared the tares also. So the servants of the householder came and said unto him, Sir, didst not thou sow good seed in thy field? from whence then hath it

tares? He said unto them, An enemy hath done this. The servants said unto him, Wilt thou then that we go and gather them up? But he said, Nay; lest while ye gather up the tares, ye root up also the wheat with them. Let both grow together until the harvest: and in the time of harvest I will say to the reapers, <u>Gather ye together first the tares, and bind them in bundles to burn them</u>: but gather the wheat into my barn.

Matthew 13:37-40 - He answered and said unto them, He that soweth the good seed is the Son of man; The field is the world; the good seed are the children of the kingdom; <u>but the tares are the children of the wicked one; The enemy that sowed them is the devil</u>; the harvest is the end of the world; and the reapers are the angels. As therefore <u>the tares are gathered and burned in the fire</u>; so shall it be in the end of this world.

Jesus makes it clear from this parable that at the end of the world, when the harvest takes place, there will be some false Christians who are among the true children of the kingdom, who will be gathered and thrown into the fire. The key details to make note of here is that the enemy, defined as the devil, sowed these tares among the wheat, and that these tares are the children of the wicked one. This passage does not indicate whatsoever that this has anything to do with obedience to the commandments.

We see elsewhere in Scripture that anybody who believes on Christ becomes a son of God. It is written, "As many as received him, to them gave he power to become the sons of God, even to them that believe on his name (John 1:12)," and "For ye are all children of God by faith in Christ Jesus (Gal. 3:26)." We are God's children when we have faith in his Son Jesus Christ. Therefore, just as in the Matthew 7 passage, "them which do iniquity," are not those who have faith but do not obey the Torah, but rather, those who have not put their full trust on Christ for their salvation, and thus, their sin is still imputed.

John 1:13 says that these who received Christ and became his sons are those "who were born not of blood, nor of the will of the flesh, nor of the will of man, but of God." We see later in 1 John 3:9 that it says "Whosoever is born of God doth not commit sin." This shows us that everybody who has faith in the name of Christ, becomes born of God (or born again, John 3:3-7), and in doing so, they do not commit sin. This of course is referring to the inward man and not the flesh, for Paul writes in Romans 7, "Now it is no more I that do it, but sin that dwelleth in me. For I know that in me (that is, in my flesh) dwelleth no good thing)."

There is an inward change in the heart when one is born again. Christ even said "That which is born of the Spirit is Spirit." When we receive the gift of the Spirit within ourselves, a promise made to every believer (John 7:38-39), we are born again. This is an inward transformation which establishes that one does not hold sin in their heart. Although the believer may still sin outwardly (since there is no change in the flesh), it is the spirit which is born again, and it is the spirit which does not sin.

Therefore, in Matthew 13, the subject cannot possibly be believers in Christ. All believers, according to the word of God, are not those who do iniquity. Rather, the children of the devil, who are not the children of God, have not had their sins forgiven. Believers have had their sins forgiven and will not have them imputed unto them (Rom. 4:7-8). Therefore, they are still evildoers in the eyes of the LORD, and will therefore be cast into the Lake of Fire. These are false Christians, those who claim the name of the LORD but have not been born again by their faith alone in Christ.

Another passage which is twisted often is the following:

> Matthew 19:16-22 - And, behold, one came and said unto him, Good Master, what good thing shall I do, that I may have eternal life? And he said unto him, Why callest thou me good? there is none good but one, that is, God: but if thou wilt enter into life, keep the commandments. He saith unto him, Which? Jesus said, Thou shalt do no murder, Thou shalt not commit adultery, Thou shalt not steal, Thou shalt not bear false witness, Honour thy father and thy mother: and, Thou shalt love thy neighbour as thyself. The young man saith unto him, All these things have I kept from my youth up: what lack I yet? Jesus said unto him, If thou wilt be perfect, go and sell that thou hast, and give to the poor, and thou shalt have treasure in heaven: and come and follow me. But when the young man heard that saying, he went away sorrowful: for he had great possessions.

It can be understandable how this Scripture can be misinterpreted, if one does not pay attention to the words used in this text. Jesus is simply answering the question of this young ruler who comes to him. The question is

"What good thing shall I do, that I may have eternal life (v. 16)?" Thus, the assumption of this young man is already that one must do a good thing. The Bible says,

> Galatians 3:21 - Is the law then against the promises of God? God forbid: for if there had been a law given which could have given life, verily righteousness should have been by the law.

Hypothetically, if the law could have given us life, God would have rather established righteousness by the law. This "if" shows that this is a conditional statement. If the law could give life, then righteousness should have been by the law. However, the very next verse says:

> Galatians 3:22 - But the scripture hath concluded all under sin, that the promise by faith of Jesus Christ might be given to them that believe.

Therefore, the problem is not the law itself, but that every man is a sinner by nature. We have all sinned, as shown earlier (Eccl. 7:20, Rom. 3:10-18, 23, 1 John 1:8). Therefore, since we are all sinners, and our disobedience to the law leads to death (Rom. 6:23), the only way we can be declared righteous is through the faith of Jesus Christ. The words which Jesus spake to the rich young ruler are not false. The only way to enter into life by doing a 'good thing' is by keeping the commandments. However, the evident problem is that one cannot keep the commandments. Remember, the carnal mind cannot be subject to the law of God (Rom. 8:7).

Therefore, after the young man boasts of keeping the whole law from his youth (which is most likely false, if we are to believe the testimony of scripture), Jesus says, "If thou wilt be perfect..." After this, the young man shows that he is not perfect by his refusal to obey this last commandment of Jesus. This demonstrates again, that nobody is perfect, even those who boast in keeping the law. As mentioned earlier, this is exactly what the purpose of the law was: to show the sinfulness of man. Romans 3:19 says "What things soever the law saith, it saith to them who are under the law, that every mouth may be stopped, and all the world may become guilty before God." When Christ spoke the commandment of "give to the poor," this rich man's mouth was stopped, and he thus became guilty before God. At this moment, he knew that he was not perfect, and could not be perfect.

Another verse which is twisted by the Hebrew Roots movement to teach a works-based salvation, or to attack the free grace Gospel, is the following:

> Matthew 24:13 - But he that shall endure unto the end, the same shall be saved.

This, of course, is taken out of the context of the Olivet Discourse, in which Jesus describes the end times and the events leading up to his Second Coming. As mentioned earlier, we should let the context determine what the word 'saved' means. If it's not talking about everlasting life or salvation from sin, then this verse is irrelevant to the conversation about how we are justified. Later in the sermon, Jesus says,

> Matthew 24:21-22 - For then shall be great tribulation, such as was not since the beginning of the world to this time, no, nor ever shall be. And except those days should be shortened, there should no flesh be saved: but for the elect's sake those days shall be shortened.

This is not talking about spiritual salvation, but the salvation of the flesh. This is talking about the great tribulation, during which, according to the Book of Revelation, the Beast shall "make war with the saints (Rev. 13:7)." If the days of this tribulation were not shortened by the coming of Christ, all Christians would be put to death during this tyrannical reign of the Beast, who puts to death all those who refuse to worship him. Therefore, in context, verse 13 is talking about enduring to the end of the tribulation; in other words, surviving until the coming of Christ.

It is an undeniable truth that the testimony of the Bible is that the obedience to the law, or our attempts to obey God in everything which he has commanded is simply impossible, and that the only way to be saved is to "Believe on the Lord Jesus Christ (Acts 16:31)." It's dangerous to trust in anything other than Christ, who gave his life for us that we might be saved. The Bible states,

> Galatians 5:4 - Christ is become of no effect unto you, whosoever of you are justified by the law; ye are fallen from grace.

Those who believe that they are righteous in the eyes of God because of their observance of the law, they are fallen from grace, according to the scriptures. This means that the Hebrew Roots movement, because they're trusting in the law to save them from death and hell, do not have the grace of God bestowed upon them. They will end up just like the Pharisees, who according to Jesus Christ, will be accused by Moses, "in whom ye trust." We are saved by grace, through faith (Eph. 2:8), and if it is of grace, it is no more of works (Rom. 11:6). This is the simple truth of how we are justified. Unless one is justified according to faith in the promises of God, they are not justified at all.

Eternal Life

Eternal life is a free gift which is given to us all. Jesus Christ calls to all at the end of the Book of Revelation, "Whosoever will, let him take the water of life freely!" The Bible says also,

> Romans 6:23 - For the wages of sin is death; but the gift of God is eternal life through Jesus Christ our Lord.

The gift which is given by God is eternal life, or as the Bible describes it in some places, everlasting life. Once we are justified and 'saved', we have everlasting life. This is not a promise that we will one day have everlasting life, but rather, a promise that we have this gift of God the moment we decide to receive it by faith.

> John 3:36 - He that believeth on the Son hath everlasting life: and he that believeth not the Son shall not see life; but the wrath of God abideth on him.

> John 5:24 - Verily, verily, I say unto you, He that heareth my word, and believeth on him that sent me, hath everlasting life, and shall not come into condemnation; but is passed from death unto life.

> John 6:47 - Verily, verily, I say unto you, He that believeth on me hath everlasting life.

The promise is that we have everlasting life the moment we believe. Therefore, the moment I decided to put my trust in the Son of God, Jesus Christ, I had everlasting life. Likewise, the Bible also talks about those which "are saved" (1 Cor. 1:18, 15:2, 2 Cor. 2:15, 2 Tim. 1:9, Rev. 21:24). Hebrew Roots teachers, especially Michael Rood, claim that salvation does not happen until the resurrection. This contradicts the plenty of clear scriptures which shows that we are justified, have eternal life, and are saved the moment that we believe.

The fact that we have everlasting life the moment we believe guarantees also that we are eternally secure. This is another problem which many Messianics have with Christianity and the free grace Gospel. Some may even claim that salvation is by faith alone, but take the Arminian position that one will still have to live a good life after justification in order to keep their salvation. This is demonstrable nonsense for two reasons: Firstly, if we could not be justified in the first place by our obedience to the law, and if we are all by nature sinners, then why would we be expected to obey the law in order to keep our salvation?

Secondly, how can our eternal life be eternal if it ended? The word 'eternal' means "without end." The synonym 'everlasting' means "lasts forever." If we had everlasting life the moment we believed, but somehow could do something to lose that life, then was the life which we received truly everlasting? Is not "the record which God gave of his Son" that "God hath given to us eternal life", according to 1 John 5:10-11? Therefore, what we are to believe is that Christ's sacrifice and resurrection was sufficient to not just give us life, but life which lasts forever. This is why he himself says:

> John 11:25-26 - Jesus said unto her, I am the resurrection, and the life: he that believeth in me, though he were dead, yet shall he live: <u>And whosoever liveth and believeth in me shall never die.</u> Believest thou this?

Just like the promise in John 3:16 by Jesus that "whosoever believeth in him should not perish, but have everlasting life," here, Christ promises that whosoever, or anybody, who believes in him shall never die. In case the word 'everlasting' wasn't clear enough, Christ put the meaning into different terms: that if we believe on him, we will never die! This is an absolute guarantee, a promise by Christ. If we believe Christ's words, we ought to believe that the gift we are given is truly eternal.

Therefore, I believe, based on the promise of the scriptures, that when I put my faith in Christ, I received everlasting life, and that there is nothing I can do to lose it. If I believed that there was something which I could do to lose it, then I would be calling Christ a liar, because he declared that those who believe would never die. He didn't say "They might die, depending on how obedient they are." Those in the Hebrew Roots movement who reject eternal security and believe that they must do something good to gain or keep eternal

157

life are thus not saved, and have not been delivered from the punishment of the lake of fire.

In John 5:24 (quoted a couple pages ago), Christ said also that we are "passed from death unto life." Rather than fearing the wages of sin, we trust that we have been forgiven of our sins and that they have been remitted by the blood of Christ. Death is not to be feared, for we have been delivered from death (2 Cor. 1:10).

There are plenty of other passages in the scriptures which provide the testimony that once we are saved, we are always saved. This is the promise which God, who cannot lie, hath promised us, that we would have eternal life (Titus 1:2, 1 John 2:25). Therefore, we should expect there to be sufficient evidence in the Bible that it is impossible to lose our salvation. This is indeed what we find in the scriptures, for it says,

> Romans 8:38-39 - For I am persuaded, that neither death, nor life, nor angels, nor principalities, nor powers, nor things present, nor things to come, Nor height, nor depth, nor any other creature, shall be able to separate us from the love of God, which is in Christ Jesus our Lord.

According to these clear verses, there is absolutely nothing which can separate us from the love of God which is in Christ Jesus. There is nothing present nor anything which will come that can separate us from God. This means that despite anything that may happen, we can still be confident that God will still love us as his children. Similarly, God says, "I will never leave thee, nor forsake thee (Hebrews 13:5)." If God says never, that means never.

Some make the erroneous claim that even though God will never leave us or let go of us, we can let go of him by turning from our faith. This is contradictory to the promises of Jesus in which he promises everlasting life, in which he says "Whosoever liveth and believeth in me shall never die." Once we believe, we have everlasting life, and it is promised that we have this life for eternity. No condition is ever given by Jesus; he never says "He that believeth in me hath temporary life." Furthermore, we can conclude by studying the Bible that no genuinely saved person will stop believing, for Jesus said also,

> John 3:18 - He that believeth on him is not condemned: but he that believeth not is condemned already, because he hath not believed in the

name of the only begotten Son of God.

Christ tells us that there are two types of people: he that believeth and he that believeth not. The former is not condemned (again, with no condition), just as John 5:24 says that those who believe "shall not come into condemnation." It doesn't say 'might not.' Then, there are those who don't believe. Jesus says of them, that they "hath not believed..." If it were true that one could believe in the name of the only begotten Son of God, but could turn back and lose their salvation, then it wouldn't be true to say that they 'hath not believed.' The Hebrew Roots and other false religions who teach conditional security add a third person who believes not, but who used to believe. Jesus tells us that those who don't believe have never believed: thus, if one falls away and no longer believes in Christ, it is not because they lost their salvation, but because they never had faith in the first place.

The same point is proved from Matthew 7:23, which was quoted earlier. Jesus says to those who try to enter the kingdom of heaven, "I never knew you." Christ is not a liar, for his Father is God, who cannot lie (Titus 1:2), and not the devil, the father of lies (John 8:44). Thus, if Christ says to those who are barred from entering the kingdom, "I never knew you," it truly means that he never knew them. There was never a point in which he knew these people. They proclaimed the name of Christ and they did works in his name, but because they tried to justify themselves by their works and not by faith, they were not God's people.

Another verse which demonstrates that one who truly believes in Christ will always be in Christ is this:

> John 6:38-39 - For I came down from heaven, not to do mine own will, but the will of him that sent me. And this is the Father's will which hath sent me, that of all which he hath given me I should lose nothing, but should raise it up again at the last day.

The Father's will was that nothing of what had been given to Jesus should be lost. If we truly belong to Christ, Christ will not lose us, but will raise us again in the last day. This is a guarantee by Jesus. In the very next verse, he tells us that this includes "every one which seeth the Son, and believeth on him (v. 40)." There are no exceptions.

> John 10:28-29 - My sheep hear my voice, and I know them, and they

follow me: And I give unto them eternal life; and they shall never perish, neither shall any man pluck them out of my hand. My Father, which gave them me, is greater than all; and no man is able to pluck them out of my Father's hand.

Just as Jesus said we will "never die," he says also that we will "never perish." If we are of the fold of Christ, we are secured by both him and his Father. The Father is greater than all. We are not greater than him. Even if we wanted to leave, we are secure in his hand, and we cannot pluck ourselves out, neither can anybody else pluck us out. As Paul said in Romans 8, there is *nothing* which can separate us from the love of Christ.

Once somebody understands this truth and believes it, they believe the record that God gave of his Son. Without having faith that the gift of God is eternal life, one cannot be saved. The Hebrew Roots movement, and all in it, need to lay aside their pride, thinking they can be righteous enough to escape the judgment of the lake of fire. Nobody was righteous enough to ever earn eternal life; it was paid for by Jesus Christ, who through his own righteousness forgives our sins and quickens us, so that we can forever be the children of God.

It is no mystery of why eternal life is a necessity. One of the promises of the new covenant is that we would be given a new spirit. This was a promise made in the old testament (Eze. 36:26-27), but also promised by Christ himself, when he shouted in the temple, "He that believeth on me, as the scripture hath said, out of his belly shall flow rivers of living water. But this spake he of the Spirit, which they that believe on him should receive (John 7:38-39)." Once we believe on him, we are given the spirit of God. In Christ's last sermon to his disciples before his betrayal, he said,

> John 14:16-17 - And I will pray the Father, and he shall give you another Comforter, that <u>he may abide with you for ever</u>; Even the Spirit of truth; whom the world cannot receive, because it seeth him not, neither knoweth him: but ye know him; for he dwelleth with you, and shall be in you.

The key phrase here is that when the Spirit came, also identified to be the Holy Ghost in verse 26, he abides with us forever. Thus, we see from comparing scripture with scripture that of all those who believe, the Spirit comes and abides with them forever. Again, no condition is given here for why the Spirit might depart from them. The gift of the Holy Ghost is our inward sign of our salvation; it is what renews us, and the fulfillment of the promise of God to put a new spirit within us. 2 Corinthians 1:22 calls this gift "the earnest of the Spirit." The word 'earnest' means "a sign of a promise." The Bible also says,

> Ephesians 1:12-14 - That we should be to the praise of his glory, who first trusted in Christ. In whom ye also trusted, after that ye heard the word of truth, the gospel of your salvation: in whom also after that ye believed, ye were sealed with that holy Spirit of promise, Which is the earnest of our inheritance until the redemption of the purchased possession, unto the praise of his glory.

When we trust in Christ and are saved, at that point we are sealed with the Holy Spirit. This spirit serves as the sign that we are saved, and that we have indeed inherited what God promised; that is, eternal life. Verse 14 also tells us that this earnest remains with us until the redemption of the purchased possession. This refers to the redemption of our bodies, which the Bible says we are still waiting for (Rom. 8:23), and which Jesus said takes places at the coming of Christ (Luke 21:28). Since this is so, then we can be assured that the Spirit will remain in us forever, as Christ promised. From the day one believes and receives the Spirit, they are sealed, and that Holy Ghost abides in them. This truth is repeated later in the book of Ephesians:

> Ephesians 4:30 - And grieve not the holy Spirit of God, whereby ye are sealed unto the day of redemption.

Again, the scriptures tell us that the holy Spirit of God seals us to the day of redemption. Why then, should we be fearful that the spirit will depart from us? It is the spirit which bears witness that we are the children of God (Rom. 8:16-17), and the spirit by which we are born again. Christ said,

> John 3:3-7 - Jesus answered and said unto him, Verily, verily, I say unto thee, Except a man be born again, he cannot see the kingdom of God. Nicodemus saith unto him, How can a man be born when he is old? can he enter the second time into his mother's womb, and be born? Jesus answered, Verily, verily, I say unto thee, Except a man be born of water and of the Spirit, he cannot enter into the kingdom of

God. <u>That which is born of the flesh is flesh; and that which is born of the Spirit is spirit.</u> Marvel not that I said unto thee, Ye must be born again.

We have already been born of the flesh, being conceived in the likeness of human flesh. Now, as we receive the spirit, we are born again, this time in the spirit. Our spirit was dead in trespasses and sins (Eph. 2:1), but we are now quickened. We are now the sons of God, born in the spirit. It is written,

> John 1:12-13 - But as many as received him, to them gave he power <u>to become the sons of God</u>, even to them that believe on his name: <u>Which were born</u>, not of blood, nor of the will of the flesh, nor of the will of man, <u>but of God.</u>

Those who believe on the name of Jesus Christ are not only born of God, but they become the sons of God. "Ye are all children of God by faith in Christ Jesus (Gal. 3:26)." Therefore, we can understand how God can make the promise that he will never leave us nor forsake us. If a child sins against his parent, this doesn't make the child 'unborn', neither does it exile him from the family. A child may do all they can to separate themselves from a family, but it does not change the fact that they are the son of their father.

Likewise, there's nothing we can do to become 'unborn' or to lose our membership in the family. The Bible promises that since we are sons of God, we have now become joint-heirs with Christ (Gal. 4:7). We are brethren in Christ, and there's nothing we can do to change this. It is simply a Biblical fact that when we believe, we are justified, washed from our sins, we receive the Holy Ghost and are sealed by the Holy Ghost, we are born again, we become the children of God, and we have everlasting life.

Still, however, those who don't want to believe the Bible for what it says continue to attack this doctrine. There is no hope and no faith in the Hebrew Roots movement in the promises of God. To them, everything is about the Torah and about Israel. Any departure from following this Hebrew-centric nonsense is labelled as 'paganism,' despite this Gospel being based on the truth spoken by the Messiah Jesus Christ. There are several passages which they will twist in an attempt to refute eternal security, just like they twist to attack the doctrine of justification by faith alone.

Two great examples of this are in 2 Peter 2:20-22 and Hebrews 6:4-6, both which I used when I was in the Hebrew Roots movement to defend my belief that one needed to keep the commandments to maintain their salvation. The former says this:

> 2 Peter 2:20 -22 -For if after they have escaped the pollutions of the world through the knowledge of the Lord and Saviour Jesus Christ, they are again entangled therein, and overcome, the latter end is worse with them than the beginning. For it had been better for them not to have known the way of righteousness, than, after they have known it, to turn from the holy commandment delivered unto them. But it is happened unto them according to the true proverb, The dog is turned to his own vomit again; and the sow that was washed to her wallowing in the mire.

The problem with the misunderstanding of this passage is the practice of reading things into the text. The text does not mention terms like 'everlasting life' and 'saved' which are common in the Bible to describe those who are the children of God. The assumption then, is that these people are saved. First, let's look at what the text says itself, and then look at even the context to show this is not the case. In v. 20, we learn about those who escape the pollutions of the world through "knowledge of the Lord and Saviour Jesus Christ."

The doctrine of justification by faith is not justification by knowledge. We are not Gnostics. We do not believe that people are saved by having knowledge. Knowing and trusting are two entirely different things. We may know what the Bible says about salvation and understand the Gospel but not place our full trust on Jesus Christ for our salvation. Judas Iscariot, for example, was with Christ during his full ministry. He had no excuse not to know that Christ was Lord, and what he taught about the gift of everlasting life. Regardless of his knowledge, Judas did not believe (John 6:64).

In verse 21 it says that these subjects had "known the way or righteousness." Once again, there is no mention of these people having faith or receiving everlasting life. This type of person written about is one that knows about Christ, but does not believe. Those who know the way of righteousness, but who turn away from it, the Bible says, have a latter end worse than if they had not heard the commandment at all. In verse 21 it says also that they have turned "from the holy commandment delivered unto them." The commandment that was delivered was the commandment to repent and believe (Acts 17:30, 1 John 3:23), but they turned from the commandment and did not receive it.

This passage is not about those who have fallen away from or lost their salvation, but those who have never received it. These are referred to elsewhere in the Bible as 'reprobates.' In Romans 1, we learn about men who "hold the truth in unrighteousness; Because that which may be known of God is manifest in them (Rom. 1:18-19)." Like in 2 Peter 2, these are people who had a knowledge of the truth and of the things of God. However, it is written further that "when they knew God, they glorified him not as God, neither were thankful; but become vain in their imaginations, and their foolish heart was darkened (Rom. 1:21)."

These people, because they "changed the truth of God into a lie" were given up unto uncleanness through the lusts of their own hearts (Rom. 1:24)," "unto vile affections (Rom. 1:26)," and "over to a reprobate mind (Rom. 1:28)." Of this same category, those who are reprobates, the Bible says that they are "ever learning, but never able to come to the knowledge of the truth (2 Tim. 3:7)." This is the subject of 2 Peter. We see this in the context even,

> 2 Peter 2:18-19 - For when they speak great swelling words of vanity, they allure through the lusts of the flesh, through much wantonness, those that were clean escaped from them who live in error. While they promise them liberty, they themselves are the servants of corruption: for of whom a man is overcome, of the same is he brought in bondage.

In the immediate verses beforehand, it writes about those who are given constantly to the lusts of the flesh, because they are "servants of corruption." These people are not servants of God and of righteousness, as the Bible calls those who are saved (Rom. 6:18, 22). These are those who were never saved in the first place, who, with the knowledge of God and his gift of eternal life, refuse to believe and turn from the commandment. In doing so, they become reprobates, filled will "all unrighteousness (Rom. 1:29)." Similarly, Hebrews 6 covers the same topic, despite being twisted by those in the Hebrew Roots movement and others to teach that we can lose our salvation. The passage says,

> Hebrews 6:4-6 - For it is impossible for those who were once enlightened, and have tasted of the heavenly gift, and were made

partakers of the Holy Ghost, And have tasted the good word of God, and the powers of the world to come, If they shall fall away, to renew them again unto repentance; seeing they crucify to themselves the Son of God afresh, and put him to an open shame.

Just as with 2 Peter, first we'll take a look at the wording of these three misunderstood verses, but also show that the context proves that this does not teach conditional security. The language used here once again shows no clear indication of talking about those with everlasting life or salvation. These words are never used. Rather, the language shows instead that these people are not saved. These are those who are "enlightened" (meaning, the truth has been revealed to them). These are those who have "tasted of the heavenly gift," not received the heavenly gift, and have "tasted the good word of God," but not believed on the good word of God. These were made "partakers of the Holy Ghost," but did not fully receive the Holy Ghost.

These descriptions show that this is, just like Romans 1 and 2 Peter 2, talking about those who have the knowledge of the truth and thus are face-to-face with the call to believe. They understand the Gospel, now all they need to do is put their trust in Christ and receive the gift of God. A taste of the water of life is not the same thing as drinking the water of life, and a taste of the bread of God is not the same thing as eating the bread of God (John 4 and 6).

In regards to the Holy Ghost mentioned here; it should be noted that the unsaved need the Holy Ghost to reprove their hearts in order to be saved. Jesus promised that the Comforter would come to "reprove the world of sin" and explains that it is "because they believe not on me (John 16:7-9)." The scriptures even write about the unsaved who "resist the Holy Ghost (Acts 7:51)." The Holy Ghost works in the unbeliever and leads one to Christ through the preaching of the Gospel. Thus, in Hebrews 6, the mention of them being 'partakers of the Holy Ghost' does not mean that the Holy Ghost dwells in them due to their belief.

Thus, we can see from close examination of the language that this refers to men who have been enlightened, or as 2 Peter 2 puts it, have knowledge of the Lord Jesus Christ. However, in verse 6, it says that it is impossible for these people, who have fallen away to be renewed again to repentance. The obvious problem here is that this does not fit with the doctrine of conditional security. Many in the Hebrew Roots movement will use this verse to teach that some can fall away, while simultaneously telling them to repent and turn to the truth. However, these are people who cannot repent, who cannot turn to the truth. Again, the subject are reprobates, who are "never able to come to the knowledge of the truth (2 Tim. 3:7)."

The unsaved who have been given the knowledge of Christ, who have had God reveal the truth of that which may be known of him (Rom. 1:18-19), but who have rejected him and hardened their heart, cannot be saved once they are given up by God. This is what the Bible speaks of here, not of the born-again children of God becoming unborn. The context shows this as well. In the following verses, it is written

> Hebrews 6:7-8 - For the earth which drinketh in the rain that cometh oft upon it, and bringeth forth herbs meet for them by whom it is dressed, receiveth blessing from God: But that which beareth thorns and briers is rejected, and is nigh unto cursing; whose end is to be burned.

The key is verse 8 and the word 'rejected.' Rejected is a synonym for the word reprobate: see the first use of the term in the Bible, Jeremiah 6:30: "Reprobate silver shall men call them, because the LORD hath rejected them." In addition, these rejects of God, those who have been given up to a reprobate mind by God (Rom. 1:28), bear "thorns and briers." Jesus had words to say about those who bear these. He said,

> Matthew 7:15-19 - Beware of false prophets, which come to you in sheep's clothing, but inwardly they are ravening wolves. Ye shall know them by their fruits. <u>Do men gather grapes of thorns, or figs of thistles</u>? Even so every good tree bringeth forth good fruit; but a corrupt tree bringeth forth evil fruit. <u>A good tree cannot bring forth evil fruit, neither can a corrupt tree bring forth good fruit</u>. Every tree that bringeth not forth good fruit is hewn down, and cast into the fire.

Verse 19 is especially similar to Hebrews 6:8. Those trees which don't bring forth good fruit are cast into the fire, just as the author of Hebrews writes that those who bear thorns and briers are burned. Jesus says that it is impossible for a good tree to bring forth evil fruit. Therefore, if a good tree cannot bring forth evil fruit, we know that Hebrews 6 is not talking about those who are good trees, with roots in Christ (Col. 2:6-7), but are corrupt trees, or false prophets. These people were never saved; they bring forth these thorns because they have always been corrupted, not because they lost their salvation.

This is not the only example of a scripture used in the Book of Hebrews which is twisted to teach conditional security. There are two others in particular which should be addressed here; the first is Hebrews 3:14.

> Hebrews 3:12-14 - Take heed, brethren, lest there be in any of you an evil heart of unbelief, in departing from the living God. But exhort one another daily, while it is called To day; lest any of you be hardened through the deceitfulness of sin. For we are made partakers of Christ, if we hold the beginning of our confidence stedfast unto the end;

Once again, this scripture is taken out of context. Once we place it in the proper context, the message becomes abundantly clear.

> Hebrews 3:15-19 - While it is said, To day if ye will hear his voice, harden not your hearts, as in the provocation. For some, when they had heard, did provoke: howbeit not all that came out of Egypt by Moses. But with whom was he grieved forty years? was it not with them that had sinned, whose carcases fell in the wilderness? And to whom sware he that they should not enter into his rest, but to them that believed not? So we see that they could not enter in because of unbelief.

The passage is once again about those who have not believed, who the author commands to believe. The subject is not those who have believed, but those who provoke out of hearing the truth because of their unbelief (v. 15). Paul is not writing to individuals, but to the congregation as a whole, and warning them as a whole to beware that there might be unbelievers among them. Read the words used carefully. Paul says "take heed," a warning, "lest there be in any of you an evil heart of unbelief."

Therefore, he is not telling them to beware that they do not lose their salvation, but to beware that there might be some in the congregation who don't believe. This is why he tells them next to "exhort one another daily, while it is called To day." This is essentially the same as "Behold, now is the accepted time; behold, now is the day of salvation (2 Cor. 6:2)." In verse 15, he tells these people to not harden their hearts if they hear his voice. Hearing the word is not the same as being saved, but is necessary for faith (Rom.

10:17). Now that they have heard the word, they should not harden their hearts in unbelief.

There's nothing in this chapter which suggests one can lose their eternal life. Rather, Paul is warning those in the church, if there are some unbelievers among them, to believe and not to hear his word and pass it off. This is the same case in every congregation: there are people who may think they're saved, or who may be part of the congregation without ever being born-again. This has happened in my own church and in many others, where people attend services, they participate in what the church does, but they have not been saved by their faith. This is why we are to "exhort one another daily," to make sure that those among us who are called brethren have truly responded to the Gospel.

Another passage twisted by the Hebrew Roots and others is in John 15. The problem with this scripture, as with many others, is that it has nothing to do with salvation, but with discipleship. The unsaved often fail to make a distinction between these two. However, they are not the same. Let's see what the passage teaches:

> John 15:1-8 - I am the true vine, and my Father is the husbandman. Every branch in me that beareth not fruit he taketh away: and every branch that beareth fruit, he purgeth it, that it may bring forth more fruit. Now ye are clean through the word which I have spoken unto you. Abide in me, and I in you. As the branch cannot bear fruit of itself, except it abide in the vine; no more can ye, except ye abide in me. I am the vine, ye are the branches: He that abideth in me, and I in him, the same bringeth forth much fruit: for without me ye can do nothing. If a man abide not in me, he is cast forth as a branch, and is withered; and men gather them, and cast them into the fire, and they are burned. If ye abide in me, and my words abide in you, ye shall ask what ye will, and it shall be done unto you. Herein is my Father glorified, that ye bear much fruit; so shall ye be my disciples.

As usual, those who misunderstand this passage do not read what the text actually says. There are three types of people here, the first two in Christ, and the third is not. In verse 2, we see that there is such thing as a branch in Christ that does not bear fruit. These are those who God takes away (more on this later). Next, there are branches in Christ which do bear fruit, which are purged by God in order to help them bear more fruit. In other words, those who are doing the works that God has commanded will be helped by the LORD to remove the uncleanness out of their life, that they can be more effective.

These are those who have committed their life to Christ; a disciple, meaning 'taught one' or 'follower. According to verse 8, those who bear much fruit are the only ones considered to be the disciples of Christ, and when they do such, they glorify the Father. The meaning of 'bearing fruit' is simply that they will preach the Gospel and lead people to the LORD. In the book of Genesis, we learn that every fruit bears after its own kind (Gen. 1:11-12). Likewise, a believer will produce other believers. These would be their 'fruit.'

However, there's a third type of branch, mentioned in verse 6. Jesus makes it clear that these are those who do not abide in him. Many will twist this verse by comparing it with those mentioned in verse 2; however, there is a distinct difference. In verse 2, the branch is in Christ, but when it does not bear fruit, is taken away by God. In verse 6, these are branches which are not in Christ, and likewise, do not bear fruit for God. It's not because they lose their salvation, but once again, because these are unbelievers.

Jesus said that those who are true believers, or those who come to him, he "will in no wise cast out (John 6:37)." This is again an absolute. There is no condition given of, 'except if he bear fruit.' No, Jesus promised that if somebody comes to him by faith, they will never be cast out. Yet in John 15:6, the subjects are "cast forth as a branch", and end up being burned by the fire.

If this meant one could lose their salvation, Jesus would be contradicting a multitude of words which he spoke in this very same Gospel. As I've already pointed out, he promised that he will not cast out believers (John 6:37), that he should lose nothing of those who believe (John 6:39), and that those who believe will never perish (John 3:16, 10:28, 11:26)."

So, regarding the first branch mentioned, or those who are in Christ but do not bear fruit; these are taken away by God. This refers to discipline for those who don't obey the commands of God. The scriptures promise that believers who do not do what God says will be disciplined. This is something the Hebrew Roots do not understand either. They claim that in teaching that we are saved by grace through faith, somehow we teach that there is a license to sin. Their erroneous logic is the assumption that since we don't think the Torah saves us, we must believe that the Torah has no value at all, and that we believe in antinomianism, or that the law is abolished.

This is completely false, as I shall explain here momentarily. Before this, let's take a look at one more passage which is used in a futile attempt to refute eternal security, which ties in with this doctrine of discipline by God. The verses are very clear when put into the larger context of Scripture. It says,

> Hebrews 10:25-31 - For if we sin wilfully after that we have received the knowledge of the truth, there remaineth no more sacrifice for sins, But a certain fearful looking for of judgment and fiery indignation, which shall devour the adversaries. He that despised Moses' law died without mercy under two or three witnesses: Of how much sorer punishment, suppose ye, shall he be thought worthy, who hath trodden under foot the Son of God, and hath counted the blood of the covenant, wherewith he was sanctified, an unholy thing, and hath done despite unto the Spirit of grace? For we know him that hath said, Vengeance belongeth unto me, I will recompense, saith the Lord. And again, The Lord shall judge his people. It is a fearful thing to fall into the hands of the living God.

The claim that this teaches conditional security usually arises out of the misunderstanding of the phrase "there remaineth no more sacrifice for sins." They believe that this refers to Jesus' sacrifice on the cross, and assume that this means that those who willingly sin after being justified will fall from the grace given to us. This couldn't be further from the truth. The context makes it abundantly clear that the phrase "there remaineth no more sacrifice for sins" refers to the sacrifices of the Old Testament done to cover one's sins. Several verses earlier, it is written,

> Hebrews 10:5-18 - Wherefore when he cometh into the world, he saith, Sacrifice and offering thou wouldest not, but a body hast thou prepared me: In burnt offerings and sacrifices for sin thou hast had no pleasure. Then said I, Lo, I come (in the volume of the book it is written of me,) to do thy will, O God. Above when he said, Sacrifice and offering and burnt offerings and offering for sin thou wouldest not, neither hadst pleasure therein; which are offered by the law; Then said

he, Lo, I come to do thy will, O God. <u>He taketh away the first</u>, that he may establish the second. By the which will <u>we are sanctified through the offering of the body of Jesus Christ once for all.</u> And every priest standeth daily ministering and offering oftentimes the same sacrifices, which can never take away sins: <u>But this man, after he had offered one sacrifice for sins for ever,</u> sat down on the right hand of God; From henceforth expecting till his enemies be made his footstool. <u>For by one offering he hath perfected for ever them that are sanctified</u>. Whereof the Holy Ghost also is a witness to us: for after that he had said before, This is the covenant that I will make with them after those days, saith the Lord, I will put my laws into their hearts, and in their minds will I write them; And their sins and iniquities will I remember no more. Now where <u>remission of these is, there is no more offering for sin</u>.

When we read this passage in its context, it's evident what Paul is writing about here. In the New Testament, the sacrifices which are commanded as part of the old testament law are done away with: God has no pleasure in them, but rather, in the sacrifice and offering of Jesus Christ, which he did "once for all" and whose sacrifice for sins is "for ever." Since Jesus Christ has paid for our sins already in his own sacrifice, the Bible says he has, by his single offering, "perfected for ever them that are sanctified." Compare this to verse 29, which says that those who willingly sin were sanctified by the blood of the covenant. How can this be talking about losing salvation, if in the preceding verses it tells us that those who are sanctified are "perfected for ever?"

Verse 18 says "there is no more offering for sin." For those who are saved, who have had their sins remitted under the new testament, we no longer have the ordinance of the animal sacrifices, because we know that our sins have been eternally paid for at Calvary. This is thus what is being spoken of in verse 25 when it says "there remaineth no more sacrifice for sins." What the verse is saying is that we cannot go to an altar and offer up a sacrifice any more, because the commandments of sacrifices have been abolished. In the old testament, if one sinned, they gave an offering to appease God and cover their sins temporarily. In the new testament, there is no offering for sin, because our sins have been eternally remitted by the blood of Christ, and "he needeth not daily, as those high priests, to offer up sacrifice (Heb. 7:27)."

Therefore, the passage does not teach that Christ's atonement is no longer effective if we go against God's commandments. Instead, it teaches that God will have judgment on "his people (v. 30)." We are still his people, even when God judges us. The passage never says that we'll lose our eternal life, our salvation, or any other thing of the sort. Simply, it teaches that those who are saved who willfully sin will be punished by God on this earth. This same truth is said later in the book of Hebrews,

> Hebrews 12:5-11 - And ye have forgotten the exhortation which speaketh unto you as unto children, My son, despise not thou the chastening of the Lord, nor faint when thou art rebuked of him: <u>For whom the Lord loveth he chasteneth, and scourgeth every son whom he receiveth.</u> If ye endure chastening, <u>God dealeth with you as with sons; for what son is he whom the father chasteneth not?</u> But if ye be without chastisement, whereof all are partakers, then are ye bastards, and not sons. Furthermore we have had fathers of our flesh which corrected us, and we gave them reverence: shall we not much rather be in subjection unto the Father of spirits, and live? For they verily for a few days chastened us after their own pleasure; <u>but he for our profit, that we might be partakers of his holiness.</u> Now no chastening for the present seemeth to be joyous, but grievous: nevertheless afterward it yieldeth the peaceable fruit of righteousness unto them which are exercised thereby.

Just as a fleshly father should discipline his son through chastisement, God will chastise us if we go away from his will. After all, he is our Father, and we are the children of God (John 1:12). However, when a father disciplines his children, this does not make the child no longer his children. If God punishes us on this earth, that doesn't mean we are not longer his children or his people. This passage quotes from the statement in Proverbs 3:12, "For whom the LORD loveth he chasteneth." God still loves us, even when we sin against him, and he executes punishment on us for the purpose of putting us back on the right path.

Therefore, it is written that he does this "for our profit, that we might be partakers of his holiness." God's intention is to bring up back to holiness. If we have fallen from him by our disobedience and sin, he wants to bring us back to holiness, and does so through chastening. However, that doesn't mean he will cast us away and abandon us. He says in the very next chapter, "I will never leave thee, nor forsake thee (Heb. 13:5)." Rather, only those who receive NO punishment from God are those who should be afraid, because they are "bastards, and not sons (v. 8)." People who receive no discipline from God don't receive discipline because they're not his sons, and because he doesn't chasten them as he would to a son.

Therefore, grace is not a license to sin. Not only do we have the spirit living inside of us, which means that we will naturally resist sin (see Romans 7), but God will discipline us if we disobey him. The Bible says "Shall we sin because we are not under the law, but under grace? God forbid (Rom. 6:15)." There's still no doubt that we are no longer under the law. We are under grace, and are saved by grace through faith (Eph. 2:8). This does not mean that we should disobey God. Examining this very chapter, the change in the New Testament is made evident:

> Romans 6:14-22 - For sin shall not have dominion over you: for ye are not under the law, but under grace. What then? shall we sin, because we are not under the law, but under grace? God forbid. Know ye not, that to whom ye yield yourselves servants to obey, his servants ye are to whom ye obey; whether of sin unto death, or of obedience unto righteousness? But God be thanked, that ye were the servants of sin, but ye have obeyed from the heart that form of doctrine which was delivered you. Being then made free from sin, ye became the servants of righteousness. I speak after the manner of men because of the infirmity of your flesh: for as ye have yielded your members servants to uncleanness and to iniquity unto iniquity; even so now yield your members servants to righteousness unto holiness. For when ye were the servants of sin, ye were free from righteousness. What fruit had ye then in those things whereof ye are now ashamed? for the end of those things is death. But now being made free from sin, and become servants to God, ye have your fruit unto holiness, and the end everlasting life.

Since we are born again, there is an inward change within us which allows us to serve God. Being under the law meant that sin did indeed have dominion over us, for "by the law is the knowledge of sin (Romans 3:20)." However, since we are freed from such bondage, we now have the liberty to serve God in the spirit. With this new liberty, which only exists where the Spirit of the Lord is (2 Corinthians 3:17), we are commanded to yield our members, or give our members to obey the spirit and not the flesh, for we are become "the servants of righteousness" and the "servants of God."

The Lord expects us to love him now that he's saved us. Jesus died to save us from our sins, but also to "purify unto himself a peculiar people, zealous of good works (Titus 2:14)." Works are not necessary to be saved nor to stay saved, but something we should do as a result of being saved. Nevertheless, if one does not have good works, this does not mean they have not believed, neither does it mean they will lose their salvation (Rom. 4:5). The result of good works is not to earn grace: "for to him that worketh, is the reward not reckoned of grace, but of debt (Rom. 4:4)."

If we faithfully obey the commandments of God, we are given rewards for our work at the judgment seat of Christ. Jesus said that when he comes, he will "reward every man according to his works (Matt. 16:27)." It is written that if our work abides in the day of the Lord, we "shall receive a reward (1 Cor. 3:14)." Therefore, serving God is not useless. God is not unjust or unfair; if we serve him, he gives to us based on that we have done when the kingdom of heaven comes. Jesus explained this in many of his parables.

> Luke 19:14-27 - He said therefore, A certain nobleman went into a far country to receive for himself a kingdom, and to return. And he called his ten servants, and delivered them ten pounds, and said unto them, Occupy till I come. But his citizens hated him, and sent a message after him, saying, We will not have this man to reign over us. And it came to pass, that when he was returned, having received the kingdom, then he commanded these servants to be called unto him, to whom he had given the money, that he might know how much every man had gained by trading. Then came the first, saying, <u>Lord, thy pound hath gained ten pounds. And he said unto him, Well, thou good servant: because thou hast been faithful in a very little, have thou authority over ten cities.</u> And the second came, saying, Lord, <u>thy pound hath gained five pounds. And he said likewise to him, Be thou also over five cities.</u> And another came, saying, Lord, behold, here is thy pound, which I have kept laid up in a napkin: For I feared thee, because thou art an austere man: thou takest up that thou layedst not down, and reapest that thou didst not sow. And he saith unto him, Out of thine own mouth will I judge thee, thou wicked servant. Thou knewest that I was an austere man, taking up that I laid not down, and reaping that I did not sow: <u>Wherefore then gavest not thou my money into the bank, that at my</u>

> coming I might have required mine own with usury? And he said unto
> them that stood by, Take from him the pound, and give it to him that
> hath ten pounds. (And they said unto him, Lord, he hath ten pounds.)
> For I say unto you, That unto every one which hath shall be given; and
> from him that hath not, even that he hath shall be taken away from
> him. But those mine enemies, which would not that I should reign over
> them, bring hither, and slay them before me.

The man who refused to work and produce according to that which the Lord
had given him was not the one slain. Rather, his reward was taken away from
him and given to the other servants who were willing to serve him. The only
men in this parable who ended up facing the wrath of the Lord are the
enemies who hate him and refuse to let him reign over them. This, the citizens
of the kingdom in this parable, is a perfect example of the unbelieving Jews
who did not believe that Jesus was the Christ, and therefore rejected his
authority as their king.

Therefore, we can conclude that in the New Testament, we serve God out of a
loving heart for him as our Father, and that this is made possible by the Holy
Ghost, which dwells inside us all as believers (John 7:38-38, 1 Cor. 3:16). If we
obey the Lord's commands and do good works, we will earn rewards in the
kingdom of heaven, while those who do not follow him will be disciplined, or
'taken away' by the Lord.

Serving God in the Spirit

Since we now have a "new spirit" which is put within us (Eze. 36:26-27), and
no longer "serve the law of sin (Rom. 7:25)" except with the unregenerate
flesh, we can see how there is a manifest difference between the Old and New
Testaments. The Hebrew Roots want to make both virtually the same,
blurring the lines between these covenants as if the only change is the
knowledge of the Messiah. The attitude is that the Messiah came to restore
obedience to every precept of the written Law of Moses. However, is this
true? The scriptures say,

> Hebrews 7:11-19 - If therefore perfection were by the Levitical
> priesthood, (for under it the people received the law,) what further
> need was there that another priest should rise after the order of
> Melchisedec, and not be called after the order of Aaron? For the

175

priesthood being changed, <u>there is made of necessity a change also of the law</u>. For he of whom these things are spoken pertaineth to another tribe, of which no man gave attendance at the altar. For it is evident that our Lord sprang out of Juda; of which tribe Moses spake nothing concerning priesthood. And it is yet far more evident: for that after the similitude of Melchisedec there ariseth another priest, Who is made, not after <u>the law of a carnal commandment</u>, but after the power of an endless life. For he testifieth, Thou art a priest for ever after the order of Melchisedec. For there is verily a disannulling of the commandment going before for the weakness and unprofitableness thereof. <u>For the law made nothing perfect,</u> but the bringing in of a better hope did; by the which we draw nigh unto God.

While it is clear that the law is "holy, and just, and good (Rom. 7:12)," the law is also spiritual (Rom. 7:14)." Therefore, with the law under the old covenant, nothing was made perfect due to the unprofitableness of the carnal commandments. Carnal means 'fleshly.' There were some commandments in the Torah which could only be obeyed in the flesh, and which do not have a spiritual application. These are referred to also as 'carnal ordinances (Heb. 9:10).

If then, these are called fleshly, then what use do they have to us today? Our spirit is born again, and it is the flesh which is weak, and which shall not inherit the kingdom of God (1 Cor. 15:50). Jesus told us that "they that worship him must worship in spirit and in truth (John 4:24)." We are those "which worship God in the spirit, and rejoice in Christ Jesus, and have <u>no confidence</u> in the flesh (Phil. 3:3)." We are made to "serve in the newness of the spirit, and not in the oldness of the letter (Rom. 6:6)."

What does it mean, that we serve in the spirit and not in the letter? The "letter" is mentioned several times in Scripture, and undoubtedly refers to the written law of God. Mere blind obedience to the law on the outside does not make us right in the eyes of God. This is why Jesus said that we "must" worship him in the spirit. The Bible says,

> 2 Corinthians 3:5-9 - Not that we are sufficient of ourselves to think any thing as of ourselves; but our sufficiency is of God; <u>Who also hath made us able ministers of the new testament; not of the letter, but of the spirit: for the letter killeth, but the spirit giveth life. But if the</u>

> ministration of death, written and engraven in stones, was glorious, so that the children of Israel could not stedfastly behold the face of Moses for the glory of his countenance; which glory was to be done away: How shall not the ministration of the spirit be rather glorious? For if the ministration of condemnation be glory, much more doth the ministration of righteousness exceed in glory.

The 'letter' is defined as that which was written and engraven in stones, and is called the "ministration of death." Remember, because of our fleshly nature, we cannot be subject to the law of God. The purpose of the law was to show us how sinful we were, to stop our mouths and bring us guilty before God (Rom. 3:19). It was our "schoolmaster, to bring us unto Christ (Gal. 3:24)." The law taught us our sinfulness and pointed us to Christ. This was its only purpose. Those who obey it religiously as if it's necessary for salvation will ultimately fail, and only bring death upon themselves.

This is why it is said that we are no longer under the law, because we serve God by the spirit and not by the letter. This means, we do not obey the commandments of God in a legalistic way; reading the Torah and observing every little precept and command. Rather, we serve God in the spirit, by the leading of the Spirit. For whosoever is born of God doth not commit sin (1 John 3:9), so it is the Spirit inside of us, or the inward man, which "delights in the law of God (Rom. 7:22)."

Is the Torah for Christians?

In the book of Hebrews, the changes between the covenants are expressed clearly, so that we can learn what the difference is now that we serve God in the spirit and not in the letter, which is after the flesh. One passage which deals with this especially is the following,

> Hebrews 8:4-13 - For if he were on earth, he should not be a priest, seeing that there are priests that offer gifts according to the law: Who serve unto the example and shadow of heavenly things, as Moses was admonished of God when he was about to make the tabernacle: for, See, saith he, that thou make all things according to the pattern shewed to thee in the mount. But now hath he obtained a more excellent ministry, by how much also he is the mediator of a better covenant, which was established upon better promises. For if that first covenant

had been faultless, then should no place have been sought for the second. For finding fault with them, he saith, Behold, the days come, saith the Lord, when I will make a new covenant with the house of Israel and with the house of Judah: Not according to the covenant that I made with their fathers in the day when I took them by the hand to lead them out of the land of Egypt; because they continued not in my covenant, and I regarded them not, saith the Lord. For this is the covenant that I will make with the house of Israel after those days, saith the Lord; I will put my laws into their mind, and write them in their hearts: and I will be to them a God, and they shall be to me a people: And they shall not teach every man his neighbour, and every man his brother, saying, Know the Lord: for all shall know me, from the least to the greatest. For I will be merciful to their unrighteousness, and their sins and their iniquities will I remember no more. In that he saith, A new covenant, he hath made the first old. Now that which decayeth and waxeth old is ready to vanish away.

There is evidently a change between the covenants; as it says in the previous chapter "there is of necessity a change also of the law (v. 12). The covenant which we now have with God through Jesus Christ is described as a "better covenant." If the precepts of the law were the same, how could it accurately be described as 'better?' God made it clear in Jeremiah 31, which is quoted from in this passage, that the new covenant is not according to the one made with the fathers at Mount Sinai. It is different, and established on better promises. Therefore, since Jesus is called the "mediator of a better covenant," which is the new testament in his blood (Matt. 26:28, Luke 22:20), that which is old has vanished away. We are no longer to under the old testament.

The covenant made at Sinai was, according to Exodus 19:5-7, that if the nation of Israel kept the commandments of God delivered to them on the mountain, they would be a kingdom of priests and a holy nation, and the people of God. If, then, the new covenant is not according to the first, and is described as 'better', how can one reasonably claim that the new covenant requires us also to keep the commandments of God to be the people of God? That would make the covenants the same.

Rather, as pointed out earlier in the section against the doctrine of Zionism, we as believers are now the people of God (1 Pet. 2:9), and we are counted as the children of Abraham and heirs of his promises (Gal. 3:29). We took a look also at Galatians 4 earlier, which compares the two women which represent the two covenants: Hagar the woman in bondage, is the covenant at Sinai (Gal. 4:24), while we who are born in the Spirit are free, and under the new covenant (Gal. 4:26-29). Therefore, since the covenant at Sinai is described as being bondage, and that we are not under bondage, but have liberty in Christ, we know that we are no longer bound by the law given at Sinai.

Recall again 2 Corinthians 3:6-7, which speaks of the new testament as being of the spirit and not of the letter. Since we have transferred from the old to the new, we no longer serve according to the letter, but the spirit. There is indeed a difference between the two covenants which go beyond the revelation of Jesus Christ as the son of God. The Hebrew Roots want to hold on to the old covenant, and view the two testaments as almost identical. This, as we've seen in scripture, is false. They will use various scriptures, like the following, in an attempt to prove that the law of Moses is still the same to us:

> Matthew 5:17-19 - Think not that I am come to destroy the law, or the prophets: I am not come to destroy, but to fulfil. For verily I say unto you, Till heaven and earth pass, one jot or one tittle shall in no wise pass from the law, till all be fulfilled. Whosoever therefore shall break one of these least commandments, and shall teach men so, he shall be called the least in the kingdom of heaven: but whosoever shall do and teach them, the same shall be called great in the kingdom of heaven.

This was perhaps my favorite set of verses when I was in the Hebrew Roots movement, because I believed that it established several of my beliefs quite well: firstly, that it allegedly shows that the law in its entirety is still in place; and secondly, I believed that one could only be saved by keeping the commandments, based on verse 19. However, as already shown, this cannot be the case, for it contradicts a multitude of other scriptures, including the words of Jesus Christ himself. Let's take a look at what Jesus say and *what he does not say*.

Firstly, it was erroneously assumed by me, and is by many in the Hebrew Roots movement, that Christians are antinomians (or anti-law), and believe that the law was entirely abolished in Christ. This is false, as we shall see later. Jesus said he did not come to destroy the law or the prophets; what those in the Hebrew Roots movement ignore is the phrase "or the prophets." The 'law and prophets' was a combined way of referring to the Old Testament

179

scriptures, based on the Law of Moses found in the Pentateuch, or Torah, and the remainder of the Tanakh, referred to as the prophets. We see this on several occasions (Matt. 7:12, 22:40, Luke 16:16, 24:44, John 1:45, Acts 13:15, Romans 3:21).

However, one might notice that in v. 18, Jesus just says the law, and in verse 19, mentions the commandments. Therefore, it is assumed that Jesus is simply talking about the instructions of God given in the Torah. However, seeing that Jesus begins identifying the subject as 'the law, or the prophets,' why would he change to only talking about the law? We see in the Bible that the phrase 'the law' is sometimes a shorthand way of saying 'the law and the prophets.' For example, Jesus said in John 10:34 "Is it not written in your law, I said, ye are gods?" This is a quote from Psalm 82:6, which is not part of the Torah, yet Jesus still calls it "your law."

 In John 12:34, the people say "We have heard out of the law that Christ abideth forever." Again, there is no direct mention of the Christ in the Torah, although many prophecies in the Old Testament prophets which talk of the Messiah ruling for ever (such as Eze. 37:25). Jesus does this same shorthand in Luke 16:16-17, beginning in v. 16 by saying "the law and the prophets," but then simply saying "the law" in v. 17. Jesus said also concerning the commandments "Thou shalt love the LORD God with all thy heart" and "Thou shalt love thy neighbor as thyself" that "upon these two commandments hang all the law and the prophets (Matthew 22:40)." Even though the commandments are not in the prophets, Jesus refers to these two sections of scriptures in union.

Therefore, Matthew 5 is not even talking about the law, as in, the commandments which the LORD gave to Moses for Israel to obey. Rather, he is saying that he did not come to destroy the scriptures, or that which is written in the Tanakh. This is made evident also by his statement that he came to 'fulfill' such. There were multitudes of prophecies which Christ fulfilled during his ministry, which were based on promises given from Judges to Malachi, and not from Genesis to Deuteronomy.

As 2 Timothy 3:16 says, "All scripture is given by inspiration of God, and is profitable for doctrine, for reproof, for correction, for instruction in righteousness..." Just because we as Christians believe that the letter of the law has been changed in the new testament, which is clearly taught by the

Bible, does not mean that we view these commandments as useless. Each ordinance of the Old Testament has important spiritual truths within them, which have been fulfilled or 'completed' by Christ. As it is written, they were "a shadow of good things to come (Hebrew 10:1)," but as the same verse says "and not the very image of things, can never with those sacrifices year by year continually make the comers thereunto perfect."

We are not made perfect by the images and shadows of the Old Testament. They simply pointed us to the future and showed to us beforehand the Gospel of Christ. Now that Christ has come, and we are under his covenant, there is a change to this law. If we move on in the book of Hebrews from chapter 8, which testifies that the new covenant is better than the old, and the old has vanished, it is written:

> Hebrews 9:6-10 - Now when these things were thus ordained, the priests went always into the first tabernacle, accomplishing the service of God. But into the second went the high priest alone once every year, not without blood, which he offered for himself, and for the errors of the people: The Holy Ghost this signifying, that the way into the holiest of all was not yet made manifest, while as the first tabernacle was yet standing: Which was a figure for the time then present, in which were offered both gifts and sacrifices, that could not make him that did the service perfect, as pertaining to the conscience; <u>Which stood only in meats and drinks, and divers washings, and carnal ordinances, imposed on them until the time of reformation.</u>

Here we see the change written clearly. There existed figures in the old testament, which could not make anybody perfect in their conscience (which can only be purged by the blood of Christ, v.14), but were signs by the Holy Ghost to picture "the way into the holiest of all." Verse 10 defines what these things are as "meats and drinks, and divers washings, and carnal ordinances." It says also that these were "imposed on them until the time of reformation." The word 'reformation' means "the act or process of making changes to something in order to improve it." As we already read in Hebrews 7 and 8, there is a "change of the law" in the new testament, and this new testament is described as a better covenant. Therefore, the 'time of reformation' refers to the beginning of the new testament.

Thus, these 'carnal' or fleshly ordinances, were only imposed on the people of

God until the time of the new testament. Since the old has vanished away, these ordinances are no longer in place. This is what is meant by "change in the law." That which was only meant for a picture of the future and that the offence might abound (Rom. 5:20) are no longer of a place to us as new testament Christians. If this isn't clear yet, consider some other scriptures on the doctrine:

> Ephesians 2:13-17 - But now in Christ Jesus ye who sometimes were far off are made nigh by the blood of Christ. For he is our peace, who hath made both one, and hath broken down the middle wall of partition between us; <u>Having abolished in his flesh the enmity, even the law of commandments contained in ordinances</u>; for to make in himself of twain one new man, so making peace; And that he might reconcile both unto God in one body by the cross, having slain the enmity thereby: And came and preached peace to you which were afar off, and to them that were nigh.

In Jesus Christ's flesh, when he was on the cross dying for our sins and shedding his own blood, he abolished "the law of commandments contained in ordinances." Again, we see that there were certain commandments which were "abolished." Although Jesus did not come to destroy 'the law and the prophets' in the sense that he was not eliminating that which is written in the Tanakh, it is simply a myth that he did not change and remove some commandments from the law of Moses. The word 'ordinance' means "a righteous decree." Those righteous decrees, or statutes, instituted by the LORD in the Old Testament which are 'carnal', again meaning "after the flesh" are no longer in place.

Although the Book of Hebrews already gives us a basic overview of these carnal ordinances, such as in meats, and drinks, and divers washings; other portions of scripture explain the abolition of certain commandments with more detail. For example, consider the following passage:

> Colossians 2:11-17 - In whom also ye are circumcised with the circumcision made without hands, in putting off the body of the sins of the flesh by the circumcision of Christ: Buried with him in baptism, wherein also ye are risen with him through the faith of the operation of God, who hath raised him from the dead. And you, being dead in your sins and the uncircumcision of your flesh, hath he quickened together

with him, having forgiven you all trespasses; <u>Blotting out the handwriting of ordinances that was against us,</u> which was contrary to us, and took it out of the way, nailing it to his cross; And having spoiled principalities and powers, he made a shew of them openly, triumphing over them in it. <u>Let no man therefore judge you in meat, or in drink, or in respect of an holyday, or of the new moon, or of the sabbath days: Which are a shadow of things to come; but the body is of Christ.</u>

Here is a passage which I knew about well during my time in the Hebrew Roots movement. I would explain this scripture away by ignoring the context and focusing on verse 16, reversing the verse on Christians and saying "It says not to judge concerning the sabbath day" and therefore, believing that one was allowed to obey the Sabbath day command without the doctrines and commandments of men attacking my belief. However, this does not fit in with the theme of the passage, nor does it fit with the larger context of scripture, such as the passages we've already seen.

Particularly, we should pay attention to the word 'therefore' in verse 16. The word 'therefore' means "for this reason." Reading the preceding verses is necessary to determine what that reason is. If we start in early parts of Colossians 2, we learn that Paul is writing concerning rooting yourself in Jesus Christ, in whom we are complete (v. 6-10). Following this, it is written that this same Jesus Christ, who makes us complete, circumcises us in the 'circumcision made without hands,' which is undoubtedly referring to the circumcision of the heart, mentioned in Romans 2:29, which is "inwardly."

In verse 14 we see another key phrase which cannot be overlooked: "Blotting out the handwriting of ordinances that was against us." If we do what the scriptures teach us to do and compare "spiritual things with spiritual (1 Cor. 2:13)," the meaning of this verse becomes abundantly clear. Comparing with Ephesians 2, we see very similar language used. In Ephesians 2, it is written that he "abolished in his flesh the enmity." Here we see that he has blotted out that which "was against us." In Ephesians 2, that which is abolished is specified as "the law of commandments contained in ordinances." Here in Colossians, it's "the handwriting of ordinances." This is speaking of the same thing.

When Jesus died on the cross, those commandments contained in ordinances were blotted out. Notice the use of the word 'handwriting.' Comparing this with 2 Corinthians 3:6-7 and other verses which mention the 'letter,' a picture begins to develop of what the subject is. The letter, being that which was "written and engraven in stones" is what "killeth (2 Cor. 3:6)." Likewise, this "handwriting of ordinances" is what was "against us." Finally, it was "the law of commandments" which is described as "the enmity."

The passage in Colossians 2 is clear. When Jesus Christ died, he abolished the carnal ordinances which are spoken of repeatedly in the new testament as being done away with. A simple comparison to these other scriptures, as well as Hebrews 9:10 - "imposed on them until the time of reformation" shows us that under the new testament, there exist some things, although commandments and righteous decrees of God, which have been done away with.

Thus, knowing the context of Colossians 2, it is written in v. 16, "Let no man THEREFORE." Recall that therefore is an adverb connecting the previous statements to the following. As a result of the fact that Jesus Christ, by his death on the cross, blotted out the letter, or the handwriting, of those carnal ordinances which were against us, we should not let any man judge us "In meat, or in drink, or in respect of an holyday, or of the new moon, or of the sabbath days."

The first part of the verse is already established by Hebrews 9:10 as having been done away with in Christ, now that the reformation has taken place. Thus, it is not difficult to see also that, just as the meats and drink only stood until the bringing in of a better covenant, so did these particular celebrations, which are nothing more than ordinances established by God in the Old Testament, "which are a shadow of things to come." This phrase in verse 17 is often emphasized by those in the Hebrew Roots movement (once again ignoring the context) in a vain attempt to defend their observance of the Sabbath and the appointed times.

However, what they ignore is the remaining half of the verse, "but the body is of Christ." Once again, we can't ignore even the smallest word in the scriptures. The conjunction 'but' signifies a contrast between the statement which comes after and that which comes before. It's the same as saying "nevertheless" or "however." Paul is writing that even though these ordinances are a shadow of things to come (as written also in Heb. 10:1), the body (which is the church, Col. 1:18) is of Christ. Essentially what we learn from this is that, just as Jesus said, he did not come to "destroy the law and the prophets." It is still true that "All scripture is given by inspiration of God." The handwriting in the Old Testament is still useful in a way; we can still gather important spiritual truths from these ordinances; however, because the church is of Christ, we do not need to observe them anymore.

Particularly, the claim that the Sabbath has been blotted out and is no longer to be observed in the New Testament is at odds with the Hebrew Roots movement. This is one of their major doctrines; defending the Sabbath because it's one of the Ten Commandments of God. This is why I and many others in the Hebrew Roots movement have had close connections with other Sabbatarian groups like the Seventh-Day Adventists, and why shortly after getting saved, when I still believed the Sabbath was in place, I considered myself a "Seventh-Day Baptist."

Those in the Hebrew Roots movement claim that the Sabbath was intended to be a commandment which would last forever, instituted by God on the seventh-day and given as a perpetual sign to all people who make a covenant with him, whether in the new or the old testaments. They attack Christians as replacing the Sabbath-day with Sunday, often lumping in false religions like Roman Catholicism with those who actually base their beliefs on the authority of scripture alone (like Baptists). Both of these claims are incorrect, as shall be shown.

Firstly, besides the clear testimony in the scriptures already given, the Bible shows us also that the Sabbath was not meant to be established forever, neither is it morally wrong to break the Sabbath day. First of all, as pointed out many times before in this book, the covenant made between God and the children of Israel at Mount Sinai was conditional. The Bible says,

> Exodus 19:5-6 - Now therefore, if ye will obey my voice indeed, and keep my covenant, then ye shall be a peculiar treasure unto me above all people: for all the earth is mine: And ye shall be unto me a kingdom of priests, and an holy nation. These are the words which thou shalt speak unto the children of Israel.

The condition was, that if the Israelites kept the covenant and commandments which God gave to them, they would be God's peculiar treasure, a kingdom of priests, and a holy nation. We have already seen in the

Bible that this covenant is done away with and replace by a better covenant, what the book of Hebrews calls the new testament. Therefore, this conditional covenant is not the basis for our own covenant; for the LORD said that it is " Not according to the covenant that I made with their fathers in the day that I took them by the hand to bring them out of the land of Egypt; which my covenant they brake (Jer. 31:32)." We see also that it is written that the Sabbath was a sign of this covenant:

> Ezekiel 20:11-21 - And I gave them my statutes, and shewed them my judgments, which if a man do, he shall even live in them. <u>Moreover also I gave them my sabbaths, to be a sign between me and them, that they might know that I am the Lord that sanctify them.</u> But the house of Israel rebelled against me in the wilderness: they walked not in my statutes, and they despised my judgments, which if a man do, he shall even live in them; <u>and my sabbaths they greatly polluted</u>: then I said, I would pour out my fury upon them in the wilderness, to consume them. But I wrought for my name's sake, that it should not be polluted before the heathen, in whose sight I brought them out. Yet also I lifted up my hand unto them in the wilderness, that I would not bring them into the land which I had given them, flowing with milk and honey, which is the glory of all lands; <u>Because they despised my judgments, and walked not in my statutes, but polluted my sabbaths</u>: for their heart went after their idols. Nevertheless mine eye spared them from destroying them, neither did I make an end of them in the wilderness. But I said unto their children in the wilderness, Walk ye not in the statutes of your fathers, neither observe their judgments, nor defile yourselves with their idols: I am the Lord your God; walk in my statutes, and keep my judgments, and do them; <u>And hallow my sabbaths; and they shall be a sign between me and you, that ye may know that I am the Lord your God.</u> Notwithstanding the children rebelled against me: they walked not in my statutes, neither kept my judgments to do them, which if a man do, he shall even live in them; <u>they polluted my sabbaths</u>: then I said, I would pour out my fury upon them, to accomplish my anger against them in the wilderness.

In this text, God acknowledges that the Sabbath was in place in order to be a sign between the nation of Israel and the LORD. This was quoted from the Torah, in Exodus 31:13, where God says the same thing: "it is a sign between me and you throughout your generations; that ye may know that I am the LORD that doth sanctify you." It was a decreed ordinance with this purpose: to show that the Israelites were called out of the Gentiles to be a holy nation to God, as said in Exodus 19. However, over and over again, it is written that they "polluted my sabbaths." Despite the sabbath being established as a sign of the covenant, and that they were God's holy people, they broke their end of the deal which they had promised by breaking the commandments of the Law.

Thus, the Israelites were kicked out of the land of Canaan for their disobedience; first the ten northern tribes for an indefinite amount of time by the Assyrians, and then the nation of Judah for 70 years by Babylon. Since Israel broke their end of the covenant, which was to keep the commandments of God, they were kicked out of the land. In the prophets, the LORD makes it clear what his attitude was toward the sabbath days:

> Isaiah 1:11-14 - To what purpose is the multitude of your sacrifices unto me? saith the Lord: I am full of the burnt offerings of rams, and the fat of fed beasts; and I delight not in the blood of bullocks, or of lambs, or of he goats. When ye come to appear before me, who hath required this at your hand, to tread my courts? Bring no more vain oblations; incense is an abomination unto me; the new moons and sabbaths, the calling of assemblies, I cannot away with; it is iniquity, even the solemn meeting. Your new moons and your appointed feasts my soul hateth: they are a trouble unto me; I am weary to bear them.

This scripture mentions not just the sabbaths, but also the appointed feasts. The LORD says, even in this time, that the observance of the sabbath is iniquity, and says that he hates such things. Why is this so? The answer is just as we find in the new testament: because they were carnal ordinances. These appointed days and times and feasts were only established as signs of the covenant. However, since the Israelites had sinned against God, God saw these signs as useless. In the following verses, it is written,

> Isaiah 1:16-17 - Wash you, make you clean; put away the evil of your doings from before mine eyes; cease to do evil; Learn to do well; seek judgment, relieve the oppressed, judge the fatherless, plead for the widow.

The LORD didn't care about Israel keeping the sabbaths as much as he cared about what Jesus later calls "the weightier matters of the law" which included "justice and mercy and faith (Matthew 23:28)." God criticized the Israelites for their wickedness, and told them that they were so wicked, he despised their feasts and sabbaths. If these feasts and sabbaths are absolutely necessary, then why would God say this? This is not the only time we find a passage of this nature in the Old Testament.

> Hosea 2:11 - I will also cause all her mirth to cease, her feast days, her new moons, and her sabbaths, and all her solemn feasts.

If breaking the sabbath is so bad, then why would God cause the sabbaths and the feast days to cease? The Hebrew Roots movement treats the Sabbath as if any defilement of the day is wicked and terrible in all circumstances. The Bible is clear that God does not tempt any man with evil (James 1:13). Why then, would God cause these days to cease out of the land of Israel if it's so evil? We indeed see that this does happen. Consider the following scripture:

> Lamentations 2:6 - And he hath violently taken away his tabernacle, as if it were of a garden: he hath destroyed his places of the assembly: the LORD hath caused the solemn feasts and sabbaths to be forgotten in Zion, and hath despised in the indignation of his anger the king and the priest.

The LORD caused these days to be forgotten in Zion, according to this verse. It wasn't just the wickedness of man, but the LORD's doing which eliminated the practice of these days among the Israelites. This isn't difficult to understand once somebody realizes what the scripture says about the Sabbath day, and as already shown, that this day stood only as a sign of the covenant at Sinai, between the Israelites and God (Exo. 31:13, Eze. 20:12). Since the Israelites had broken this covenant, which was conditional, the Sabbath day no longer had any effect for them. They were no longer the holy people of God, and therefore had no set-apart day in which to keep the sabbath.

Likewise, this is why in the new testament, now that we are no longer under the old testament, but in a better covenant, we do not keep the Sabbath. We understand that the sabbath was an ordinance established until the time of reformation, that it was one of those things blotted out at Jesus' crucifixion.

After all, we read in the new testament that Jesus had broken the sabbath day. Those in the Hebrew Roots movement may deny this, as I did, but it's clear in the Gospels that he did not rest, even on the day of rest. After healing a man who had an infirmity for 38 years, it is written:

> John 5:16-18 - And therefore did the Jews persecute Jesus, and sought to slay him, because he had done these things on the sabbath day. But Jesus answered them, My Father worketh hitherto, and I work.Therefore the Jews sought the more to kill him, because he not only had broken the sabbath, but said also that God was his Father, making himself equal with God.

Both John the writer of this gospel and Jesus himself testify to his non-observance of the sabbath day. In verse 17, Jesus says, "My Father worketh hitherto, and I work." The word 'hitherto' means "until this point." There's no doubt about why Jesus was saying this. In the context, the Jews seek to kill Jesus because he had healed a man on the sabbath day, and after attacking him verbally, this is Jesus' reply. He did not deny breaking the sabbath day at all, but rather directly confessed and said both he and his Father had continued to work until that time.

Later in the chapter, Jesus explained that all that he did was in accordance with the will and action of the Father, saying, "for what things soever he doeth, these doeth the Son likewise (v. 19)," and "for the works that the Father hath given me to finish, the same works that I do, bear witness of me, that the Father hath sent me (v. 36)." Jesus, in response to the Pharisees, is telling them that everything he has done, including the work of healing a man on the Sabbath day, was given to him of the Father, and he did such because the Father had sent him to do it.

Even John acknowledges also that Jesus had broken the sabbath day, as in verse 18, he writes, "he not only had broken the sabbath." This is not a quotation from the Pharisees, this is the narrator's comment. *John* is telling us that Jesus had broken the Sabbath day, and thus refusing to deny it just like Jesus did. Yet the Bible still tells us that Jesus was without sin (Heb. 4:15, 1 Pet. 2:22, 1 John 3:5). Christ broke the sabbath day despite there being no wickedness in him.

The Hebrew Roots movement misunderstands the attitudes associated with sin in the scripture. They view the law legalistically; that we should obey the commands simply because it says so. However, as already shown in places like Isaiah 1 and Hosea 2, even certain commandments which he had ordained at Sinai were despised and rejected by the LORD. Let's look at an example in the Old Testament of one breaking the sabbath day to show that when it came to observance of these ordinances, God was more concerned with where the heart was and not the breaking of the commandment itself.

> Numbers 15:30-36 - But the soul that doeth ought presumptuously, whether he be born in the land, or a stranger, the same reproacheth the Lord; and that soul shall be cut off from among his people. Because he hath despised the word of the Lord, and hath broken his commandment, that soul shall utterly be cut off; his iniquity shall be upon him. And while the children of Israel were in the wilderness, they found a man that gathered sticks upon the sabbath day. And they that found him gathering sticks brought him unto Moses and Aaron, and unto all the congregation. And they put him in ward, because it was not declared what should be done to him. And the Lord said unto Moses, The man shall be surely put to death: all the congregation shall stone him with stones without the camp. And all the congregation brought him without the camp, and stoned him with stones, and he died; as the Lord commanded Moses.

The story doesn't begin until verse 32; however, I included the preceding two verses for a reason. The LORD gives this command right before telling us about this man who gathered sticks for a reason. From verses 24 to 29, it's clear that if somebody sins out of ignorance, they could offer a sacrifice and have their sin forgiven, and in taking up that offering, they would not have to worry about the punishments associated with that sin. There is no indication that this does not include the sabbath day. Next, we learn that on the contrary to one who sins in ignorance, there are also those who sin presumptuously. Those who "despised the word of the Lord" and refuse to obey his commands and thus wilfully sin are those who God says to put to death. This follows with an example of a man who God tells Israel to certainly put to death.

The concern with this man was that he despised the word of the LORD, and despite knowing what he ought to do (since it was already commanded several times by God himself and by God through Moses throughout the Torah), he broke the sabbath anyway. He was executed because he had broken this sabbath day wilfully, going against the commandment of the LORD because his heart was wicked.

Putting this information together, we can see that the sabbath day was an ordinance established in the old testament, and stood for a sign between Israel and God. However, God himself did not keep the sabbath day, but continued to work after the first seventh-day of the creation week. Jesus did so as well, and in his death on the cross, blotted out the handwriting (or, letter) of these ordinances.

Those in the Hebrew Roots movement will have difficulty accepting this, still. However, there is indeed a passage which explains to us directly what the purpose of the sabbath day was. Hebrews 10:1 and Colossians 2:16 tell us that the sabbath was a shadow of things of come. They pictured the future of the Gospel in some way. What it pictured is written about earlier in the book of Hebrews. It says,

> Hebrews 3:17-19 - But with whom was he grieved forty years? was it not with them that had sinned, whose carcases fell in the wilderness? And to whom sware he that they should not enter into his rest, but to them that believed not? So we see that they could not enter in because of unbelief.

In Hebrews 3, it introduces the term 'rest.' Those who did not enter into this rest are those who did not believe, according to these verses. Since the congregation of Israel in the wilderness refused to believe God, they did not enter into the rest of God, which was undoubtedly the land of Canaan God had promised to give them. Since the Israelites did not believe in the word of the LORD, but feared the land because of the giants found therein, and sought to turn back to Egypt, God promised the Israelites that they would wander in the wilderness for forty years (Numbers 14:26-35).

The next chapter explains what this means even further:

> Hebrews 4:1-11 - Let us therefore fear, lest, a promise being left us of entering into his rest, any of you should seem to come short of it. For unto us was the gospel preached, as well as unto them: but the word preached did not profit them, not being mixed with faith in them that heard it. For we which have believed do enter into rest, as he said, As I have sworn in my wrath, if they shall enter into my rest: although the

works were finished from the foundation of the world. For he spake in a certain place of the seventh day on this wise, And God did rest the seventh day from all his works. And in this place again, If they shall enter into my rest. Seeing therefore it remaineth that some must enter therein, and they to whom it was first preached entered not in because of unbelief: Again, he limiteth a certain day, saying in David, To day, after so long a time; as it is said, To day if ye will hear his voice, harden not your hearts. For if Jesus had given them rest, then would he not afterward have spoken of another day. There remaineth therefore a rest to the people of God. For he that is entered into his rest, he also hath ceased from his own works, as God did from his. Let us labour therefore to enter into that rest, lest any man fall after the same example of unbelief.

In my Hebrew Roots day, I and many I knew quoted verse 9 out of context, assuming it to be some sort of proof that we should continue keeping the Sabbath day, especially since corrupted Messianic versions translated the word rest here as 'sabbath-keeping.' However, taking the whole passage with knowledge of the words written in the previous chapter and the broader context of the Bible, it becomes clear.

The passage opens up by continuing the point Paul had made in Hebrews 3. We looked at this chapter early when discussing the subject of eternal security, and how he admonishes the church as a whole to exhort one another and to make sure those among them truly believed. In the same way, he writes that we should fear, lest we come short of the promise of entering into his rest. . He makes clear that those who do not enter in are those who do not believe (Heb. 3:19, 4:6), while those who do enter in are those who do believe (Heb. 4:3).

Therefore, we who are Christians, who have everlasting life because we have believed on the Lord Jesus Christ, we have 'entered into his rest.' We didn't do so because we kept the Sabbath day or because we did anything else but believe on Christ. What this means is explained later in the chapter, particularly in verse 10. It says, "he that is entered into his rest, he also hath ceased from his own works." This is indeed true, for the scripture says, "Not by works of righteousness which we have done, but according to his mercy he saved us (Titus 3:5)," and as Paul writes at the beginning of chapter 6, the foundation of the doctrine of Christ is "repentance from dead works, and faith in Christ."

When we turn from dead works and acknowledge that Jesus alone is able to save us, and thus place our trust in him instead of trying to work our way to righteousness, we have entered into the rest of God, according to Hebrews 4. Since verse 3 states that those who believe enter into the rest, we thus know that those who believe have ceased from their works. This is what the Sabbath is. The Hebrew word shabbat means "rest," and on the day in which one rested in the Old Testament, they would cease from their works.

Why then, if we already cease from our works the moment we believe, do we need to continue in the Sabbath? Right now, because I believe, regardless of whether I'm keeping the sabbath day or not, I have entered into the rest of God, and thus ceased from my own works. Even if it's the middle of the week and not the seventh day, I have ceased from my own works, because I trust entirely upon God for the works that he does.

This is the fulfillment of the sabbath day, and the way in which it foretold and pictured the new testament, as Colossians 2:16-17 tells us it did. Nevertheless, the 'body is of Christ.' These ordinances have been blotted out, and therefore, the fact that I don't keep the sabbath day is not something the Hebrew Roots should judge me about.

Yet they do, and usually the issue goes back to the Hebrew Roots false idea that all of Christianity has been corrupted by paganism. One of the major mistakes of the Hebrew Roots movement is simply its ignornance of Christianity; I experienced this same ignorance when I followed the same teachings. I believed that the only reason why Christians didn't celebrate the seventh-day sabbath was not because they believed the sabbath was done away with, but because they believed it had been transferred to Sunday.

This indeed is true for the Roman Catholics. The 321 decree of Constantine did in fact command all men to rest on the day of the sun, and thus, they believe they continue to celebrate the sabbath day to this day, although it's on a different day of the week. Several denominations which came out of the Reformation, such as the Presbyterians, emphasize this same 'first-day sabbath' instead of the 'seventh-day sabbath.' However, I'll make it clear that I and other Baptists reject this entirely. Rather, we do not believe that any day is the sabbath for us, but the sabbath is entirely abolished in the new testament. There is no day of rest.

Paul criticized those who observed days, saying,

> Galatians 4:9-10 - But now, after that ye have known God, or rather
> are known of God, how turn ye again to the weak and beggarly
> elements, whereunto ye desire again to be in bondage? Ye observe days,
> and months, and times, and years.

Here observance of days, and months, and times, and years, are described as
turning to the "weak and beggarly elements," and says that doing so is as if
we have a desire to return to bondage. Is not the sabbath a day? Indeed, it is.
Therefore, if one desires to observe the sabbath day, they are again returning
to bondage, which is the main subject of what Paul is writing against in the
book of Galatians. A few chapters earlier, those who desire to bring the
churches into bondage again are called "false brethren unawares brought in
(Gal. 2:4)."

The Hebrew Roots movement who seeks to return us in the new testament to
observe these days are thus 'false brethren.' They're bringing us back into
bondage and trying to pull us away from the liberty which we now have in the
new testament to serve God in the spirit and not in the letter, which would be
the handwriting of ordinances that was against us. There is no difference with
the Roman Catholics and other denominations who observe Sunday as a new,
transferred sabbath.

Those in the Hebrew Roots movement misunderstand why we meet in church
on Sunday. We congregate as a church on the day of Sunday, but do not do so
in observance of a sabbath. We do so because it is specifically recorded in the
Bible that this is when believers met.

> Acts 20:7 - And upon the first day of the week, when the disciples came
> together to break bread, Paul preached unto them, ready to depart on
> the morrow; and continued his speech until midnight.

> 1 Corinthians 16:2 - Now concerning the collection for the saints, as I
> have given order to the churches of Galatia, even so do ye. Upon the
> first day of the week let every one of you lay by him in store, as God
> hath prospered him, that there be no gatherings when I come.

Firstly, we know that this is a day in which the disciples came together to break bread. The word church means 'congregation' (compare Psalm 22:22 to Hebrews 2:12). When we as believers congregate together for fellowship and preaching, this is church. 1 Corinthians 16 also lays out that when we give offerings and tithes, we do so when we come together on the first day of the week. So here we have written in the Bible that the disciples: 1) Came together, 2) broke bread, 3) listened to preaching, and 4) laid up what they had earned in store, all on the first day of the week.

We Christians do not go to church on Sunday because Rome told us to do so, but because the Bible tells us. The Hebrew Roots movement will often look at verses about the sabbath in the Book of Acts and misinterpet them to assume that this is the day we are to meet together (Acts 13:14, 42, 44, 17:1-2, 18:4). The problem is that even though they mention the sabbath day, every single reference says that this involved Paul preaching to the Jews! Of course Paul was going to preach to the Jews on the sabbath, because this is when Jews met in their synagogues. Assembling as the body of Christ in church is an activity for believers, not for unbelievers. Paul was preaching to unbelievers and trying to lead them to Christ, not preaching to those who were already Christians.

Therefore, all of the claims of the Hebrew Roots movement about the sabbath day do not stand when compared to scripture. There is simply no mention of believers observing the sabbath day, or of them meeting together on the sabbath, but there are plenty of scriptures which tell us that the sabbath has been blotted out and fulfilled.

Colossians 2:16, which we looked at earlier, mentions also the feast days. or as the Hebrew Roots will call them, the *moedim* or appointed times. This includes the Passover, feast of unleavened bread, day of firstfruits, Shavuot, the day of trumpets, the day of atonement (Yom Kippur), and the feast of tabernacles. I tried keeping these to the best of my ability with the resources that I had, resting on these days just as Leviticus 23 commands.

However, since these are carnal ordinances, they are also done away with in Christ. Remember, the feast days are another thing mentioned in Hosea 2:11 as something which God would make cease, along with the sabbaths. The appointed times are also included in the "days, months, times, and years" which bring us into bondage (Gal. 4:9-10)." Yet the Hebrew Roots have no problem understanding why these are fulfilled. In fact, a major part of

Hebrew Roots doctrine is emphasizing that Jesus has fulfilled these days, and believes that as a result, we should observe them as a reminder of the things that he's done.

There's only one memorial given in the New Testament, and that's the Lord's Supper. While the Lord's Supper is similar to and a fulfillment of the Passover, it is not the passover. The passover feast was a day of rest in which one would kill and eat a lamb without blemish (Exo. 12:3-7). The lamb itself was called 'the passover' (Exo. 12:21, 27, 2 Chr. 30:15, Mark 14:12-14). However, the Lord's Supper does not involve eating a lamb at all, but simply partaking of the bread and wine. Jesus' command concerning this is as follows:

> Matthew 26:26-28 - And as they were eating, Jesus took bread, and blessed it, and brake it, and gave it to the disciples, and said, Take, eat; this is my body. And he took the cup, and gave thanks, and gave it to them, saying, Drink ye all of it; For this is my blood of the new testament, which is shed for many for the remission of sins.

> Luke 22:17-20 - And he took the cup, and gave thanks, and said, Take this, and divide it among yourselves: For I say unto you, I will not drink of the fruit of the vine, until the kingdom of God shall come. And he took bread, and gave thanks, and brake it, and gave unto them, saying, This is my body which is given for you: this do in remembrance of me. Likewise also the cup after supper, saying, This cup is the new testament in my blood, which is shed for you.

Jesus gave two signs: the bread which was his broken body, and the wine which represented his shed blood. He commanded, "this do in remembrance of me." He didn't say, "Keep the passover in remembrance of me." Rather, we are instructed to partake in this new ordinance which Christ has commanded. A more detailed description of the Lord's Supper comes also later in the scriptures.

> 1 Corinthians 11:23-28 - For I have received of the Lord that which also I delivered unto you, that the Lord Jesus the same night in which he was betrayed took bread: And when he had given thanks, he brake it, and said, Take, eat: this is my body, which is broken for you: this do in remembrance of me. After the same manner also he took the cup,

when he had supped, saying, this cup is the new testament in my blood: this do ye, as oft as ye drink it, in remembrance of me. For as often as ye eat this bread, and drink this cup, ye do shew the Lord's death till he come. Wherefore whosoever shall eat this bread, and drink this cup of the Lord, unworthily, shall be guilty of the body and blood of the Lord. But let a man examine himself, and so let him eat of that bread, and drink of that cup.

It is written that the way in which we show the Lord's death is by eating the bread and drinking the cup of the fruit of the vine, not the Passover. It is certainly true that Christ's death was a fulfillment of the Passover, for he is called "Christ our passover (1 Cor. 5:7)," he died on the passover (Matt. 26:17-19, Luke 22:7-8, John 18:39, 19:14), and was called "the lamb of God (John 1:29), who was without blemish (1 Peter 1:19). Yet, despite his death being a fulfillment of the passover, we have received no commandment nor written example of the disciples concerning keeping the passover in the new testament. Rather, all we see is the commandments regarding the Lord's supper.

Since the Passover is fulfilled, and it is written that the feast days are no longer for the body of Christ, then we can conclude that the same story goes for the other appointed times. The day of firstfruits, commanded in Leviticus 23:10-12, which took place "on the morrow after the sabbath" was fulfilled in the resurrection of Christ. Christ rose from the dead on the first day of the week (Matt. 28:1, Luke 24:1, John 20:1). Christ is called "the firstfruits of them that slept" and "Christ the firstfruits" in 1 Corinthians 15:20-24. Since the resurrection is often compared to a harvest (Matt. 13:39), this makes sense. Just as the priests waved the firstfruits of the harvest before the LORD on the morrow after the sabbath following the Passover, the firstfruits from among the dead, Jesus Christ, rose to be presented before the Father on the same day.

The day of Shavuot was also fulfilled. This took place always in the third month, fifty days after the Passover, the day when the LORD descended in fire and smoke upon Mount Sinai (Exodus 19). This was fulfilled on the day of Pentecost (meaning, fiftieth in Greek, referring to the fiftieth day of Shavuot), when the Holy Ghost descended upon the believers in Jerusalem (Acts 2:1-4). This began the preaching of the new testament, just as the descent of God upon Mount Sinai began the preaching of the Torah, or the old testament.

Another day which was fulfilled in Christ was the day of atonement, also known in Hebrew as "Yom Kippur." This was a day in which the priest would make atonement for Israel. The Torah says,

> Leviticus 16:29-34 - And this shall be a statute for ever unto you: that in the seventh month, on the tenth day of the month, ye shall afflict your souls, and do no work at all, whether it be one of your own country, or a stranger that sojourneth among you: For on that day shall the priest make an atonement for you, to cleanse you, that ye may be clean from all your sins before the Lord. It shall be a sabbath of rest unto you, and ye shall afflict your souls, by a statute for ever. And the priest, whom he shall anoint, and whom he shall consecrate to minister in the priest's office in his father's stead, shall make the atonement, and shall put on the linen clothes, even the holy garments: And he shall make an atonement for the holy sanctuary, and he shall make an atonement for the tabernacle of the congregation, and for the altar, and he shall make an atonement for the priests, and for all the people of the congregation. And this shall be an everlasting statute unto you, to make an atonement for the children of Israel for all their sins once a year. And he did as the Lord commanded Moses.

On the tenth day of the seventh month, it was commanded that the high priest went in before the ark of the covenant to make atonement for the sins of himself and for the sins of Israel. The entirety of Leviticus 16 concerns this commandment, and goes into detail about the specifics of what the LORD wanted the priest to do. The scripture is clear that the high priest was to sprinkle blood on the mercy seat (v. 14) and come before the LORD himself inside of the holy place. This was of course, fulfilled in the sacrifice and intercession of Jesus Christ, who is called our "great high priest (Heb. 4:14)" and "an high priest for ever after the order of Melchisedec (Heb. 6:20)."

> Hebrews 9:1-14 - Then verily the first covenant had also ordinances of divine service, and a worldly sanctuary. For there was a tabernacle made; the first, wherein was the candlestick, and the table, and the shewbread; which is called the sanctuary. And after the second veil, the tabernacle which is called the Holiest of all; Which had the golden censer, and the ark of the covenant overlaid round about with gold, wherein was the golden pot that had manna, and Aaron's rod that budded, and the tables of the covenant; And over it the cherubims of

glory shadowing the mercyseat; of which we cannot now speak particularly. Now when these things were thus ordained, the priests went always into the first tabernacle, accomplishing the service of God. <u>But into the second went the high priest alone once every year, not without blood, which he offered for himself, and for the errors of the people:</u> The Holy Ghost this signifying, that the way into the holiest of all was not yet made manifest, while as the first tabernacle was yet standing: Which was a figure for the time then present, in which were offered both gifts and sacrifices, that could not make him that did the service perfect, as pertaining to the conscience; Which stood only in meats and drinks, and divers washings, and carnal ordinances, imposed on them until the time of reformation. <u>But Christ being come an high priest of good things to come, by a greater and more perfect tabernacle, not made with hands, that is to say, not of this building; Neither by the blood of goats and calves, but by his own blood he entered in once into the holy place, having obtained eternal redemption for us</u>. For if the blood of bulls and of goats, and the ashes of an heifer sprinkling the unclean, sanctifieth to the purifying of the flesh: <u>How much more shall the blood of Christ, who through the eternal Spirit offered himself without spot to God, purge your conscience from dead works to serve the living God</u>?

Here a description is made of how the day of atonement is fulfilled, directly describing the ordinance as it's described in the Old Testament. In that covenant, the high priest who was a son of Aaron would come before the mercy seat of God with the blood of a bullock (Lev. 16:14) and of a goat (Lev. 16:15), and in doing so, would atone for and cleanse the sins of the congregation (Lev. 16:27, 30). However, as pointed out, this was required once every year (v. 7). Jesus Christ, however, having ascended to heaven to enter into the heavenly tabernacle, offered up his own blood and obtained "eternal redemption for us."

Why then, would we continue to celebrate the day of atonement, if Christ has already died and paid for our sins eternally by his own blood, "once for all (Heb. 10:10)?" The only purpose of the day of atonement was for the priest to offer up a sacrifice for the sins of Israel. If an eternal sacrifice has already been made, why do the Hebrew Roots assume it necessary to continue to keep it? Not only is there no reason to, but it is impossible. The temple no longer exists, and we no longer have the tabernacle made with hands, nor a high priest on this earth. Jesus Christ is our high priest forever. He is the one mediator between God and man (1 Tim. 2:5).

The Hebrew Roots have no argument for defending the feast days. There's no commandment in the New Testament by Jesus or the apostles, but plenty which show that these are no longer in place, as demonstrated. We can still learn from these feasts, since they point to Christ, and "all scripture is given by inspiration of God, and is profitable (2 Tim. 3:16)." However, they, being shadows of good things to come, since the good things have already come, are no longer necessary. In Hebrews 10, the sacrifices are called "a shadow of good things to come," but makes it clear that they "can never with those sacrifices which they offered year by year make the comers thereunto perfect (v. 1)." Following these verses is the explanation that Christ "offered one sacrifice for sins for ever (Heb. 10:12)," and therefore, "there is no more offering for sin (Heb. 10:18)."

Just stop to think for a moment: if the sacrifices were only a shadow of things to come, but not perfect, and they are abolished when that which is perfect has come, then why should it be any different for the other ordinances? If Colossians 2:17 describes the sabbaths, new moons, and feast days as "a shadow of things to come," then why would this same principle not apply? They pictured Christ and things he would do; he already did them and brought in that which was perfect. Therefore, just as the sacrifices no longer remain, the feast days no longer remain. The Hebrew Roots claim that we should continue to observe the appointed times simply does not line up with any scripture.

While on the subject of the sabbath, before moving onto other commandments in the Torah, we should look at a subset of strange interpretations of the sabbath among some of the Hebrew Roots movement. Although the majority of those in this movement keep the Sabbath as the Jews do, from Friday evening to Saturday evening, there are some groups and ministries which believe differently. There are two particularly bizarre doctrines, the sunrise sabbath and the lunar sabbath.

As I said, these are not believed by all in the Hebrew Roots movement, but since it fits with the general trend of this faith of "restoration," and since there are a considerable number of ministries who hold to these interpretations of the sabbath days, I feel it worth mentioning, since the sabbath day was still in place in the old testament. The first of the 'other sabbaths' is the 'sunrise sabbath.' Those who hold to this doctrine attack the idea that the sabbath begins at sunset, and believe that the day of rest goes from sunrise to sunrise. We can easily show from the scriptures that the "Hebrew reckoning" of time which this movement adores so much is different from our own. Firstly, in the book of Genesis, it says:

> Genesis 1:5 - And God called the light Day, and the darkness he called Night. And the evening and the morning were the first day.

This verse uses the phrase "and the evening and the morning were" followed by the numbered day it was during the creation week. In this verse, we have the detail also that the light is day and the darkness is night. The evening by definition is the beginning of night, while the morning is the beginning of the day. Since evening comes first before morning, this is the beginning of the day. The 'first day' began in the evening, and ended after the morning. The reason for this makes sense when considering the context, that God created light on the first day. Since initially, "darkness was upon the face of the deep (v. 2)," then the world began in darkness, but light was created thereafter.

This can be demonstrated also by the commandments concerning the feast days in Leviticus 23. For example, concerning the day of atonement, it commands that the 'tenth day of this seventh month there shall be a day of atonement (Lev. 23:27)." However, later, it states that this high sabbath begins "in the ninth day of the month at even, from even to even (v. 32). The statement 'from even to even' shows that this holy day does not begin in the morning, but in the evening. The fact that it starts with "in the ninth day" also shows that the ninth day ends at evening. Since the day of atonement is on the tenth day, according to verse 27, the tenth day begins at evening, when the ninth transitions into the tenth.

This absurd interpretation of the sabbath can also be defeated with the description of Jesus' resurrection. For example, in Mark 16:1, the story says, "when the sabbath was past," and Luke 24:1 says "on the first day of the week," showing again that the seventh-day had already ended. However, in John 20:1, it specifies that when this happens "it was yet dark." The sun had not risen yet, but the sabbath was still over and the first day of the week had begun. Nehemiah 13:19 shows something similar, by saying, "when the gates of Jerusalem began to be dark before the sabbath." This is sunset, or evening, when darkness was just coming on a Friday night. Therefore, with all of this scriptural evidence, we can conclude that the practices of some of these men in the Hebrew Roots movement is completely foreign, even to the old testament.

The lunar sabbath is another bizarre corruption of the sabbath. Those who observe the lunar sabbath only abstain from work on certain days of the month. Their interpetation of 'seventh day' is that it's always intervals of seven days throughout every month. The first day is reserved for the "new moons", and then subsequently the 8th, 15th, 22nd, and 29th days are kept as the sabbath days. Therefore, the sabbath always falls on the same days of the month according to the lunar Hebrew calendar.

However, there's no scripture about this at all in the Bible. Rather, in Genesis 2, it clearly says "God blessed the seventh day." In his commandment to the Israelites in Exodus 20, he says, "Six days shalt thou labour, and do all thy work: but the seventh day is the sabbath of the LORD thy God (Exo. 20:9-10)." The 'seventh day' is meant to be taken literally as the day following a period of six days of work. However, if the lunar sabbath were biblical, there could be up to 8 days without a sabbath. For example, if a Hebrew month has 30 days (which is indeed possible on the lunar calendar), and the sabbath was kept on the 29th day of the month, then they would not keep it again until the 8th day. This is not "six days thou shalt labour" but eight days.

Another reason why this doesn't make any sense is because of the commandment of Pentecost. In Leviticus 23:15-16, it specifies that in order to come to the day of Shavuot, "seven sabbaths shall be complete" and "unto the morrow after the seventh sabbath ye shall number fifty days." With the traditional reckoning of the sabbath as being weekly, or literally every seven days, this makes sense; the 49 days for the seven weeks, followed by an extra day which makes fifty total days. However, as pointed out, under the lunar sabbath, there could be 8-9 days between sabbaths. This would throw off the calendar so that fifty days after the day of firstfruits could potentially come before the seventh sabbath, and not "unto the morrow" as it's commanded.

Therefore, both of these corruptions of the sabbath are unbiblical. The point being made is that many in the Hebrew Roots movement, although claiming to be following the 'original faith' of the people of God, do the same thing they criticize the Pharisees for, and add and subtract to, or completely change many of the commandments given in the Torah. This often ends up in detailed arguments about how the law is to be followed, despite scripture telling us to avoid "strivings about the law (Titus 3:9)." Yet, I often see many Hebrew Roots documentaries and articles which are designed to strive against their opponents and the specifics of the Torah's command. The attitude is "you're not doing it the way I'm doing it, therefore you're wrong," despite it being against the Bible to continue to do these things in the first place!

Another commandment the Hebrew Roots movement will hold onto (and hypocritically twist and not do according to what the scriptures actually say), is that of wearing tzizit. Tzitzit simply means 'tassel,' and refers to the fringes the Israelites were commanded to wear on the border of their garment.

> Numbers 15:38-40 - Speak unto the children of Israel, and bid them that they make them fringes in the borders of their garments throughout their generations, and that they put upon the fringe of the borders a ribband of blue: And it shall be unto you for a fringe, that ye may look upon it, and remember all the commandments of the Lord, and do them ; and that ye seek not after your own heart and your own eyes, after which ye use to go a whoring: That ye may remember, and do all my commandments, and be holy unto your God.

Another commandment concerning these fringes is Deuteronomy 22:12, which specifies that they are to be on the four quarters of one's garment. Many in the Hebrew Roots movement, such as myself, who do not own a tallit, or prayer shawl, own a product called "Tzitzit-in-a-snap" which was a snap-on tzitzit one could attach to their belt. As mentioned earlier, I wore these often when I was in the Hebrew Roots movement. After all, it's commanded in the Torah. However, as we see above in Numbers 15, the purpose of the tzitzit is clearly given: "that ye may look upon it, and remember all the commandmnets of the Lord, and do them."

Tzitzit were not given by God just to be some kind of special piece of clothing. They had a purpose, and that was to remind one of the commandments of God. However, in the New Testament, we have the Holy Ghost which does this for us. The Bible says,

> John 14:26 - But the Comforter, which is the Holy Ghost, whom the

Father will send in my name, he shall teach you all things, and bring all things to your remembrance, whatsoever I have said unto you.

1 Corinthians 2:10-13 - But God hath revealed them unto us by his Spirit: for the Spirit searcheth all things, yea, the deep things of God. For what man knoweth the things of a man, save the spirit of man which is in him? even so the things of God knoweth no man, but the Spirit of God. Now we have received, not the spirit of the world, but the spirit which is of God; that we might know the things that are freely given to us of God. Which things also we speak, not in the words which man's wisdom teacheth, but which the Holy Ghost teacheth; comparing spiritual things with spiritual.

The Bible tells us that the Holy Ghost which is given to us teaches us of all things and brings all things to our remembrance. This is the fulfillment of the promise in the Tanakh that God would put the law in our inward parts, and write it in our hearts (Jer. 31:33). Those who are born again and receive the spirit of God have the Spirit within them, who teaches them of spiritual things, including the commandments of God. For this reason, Paul said, "I delight in the law of God after the inward man (Rom. 7:23)."

Therefore, since we have the spirit of God inside of us which teaches us and brings to remembrance the commandments of God, what is the purpose of tzitzit? Answer: there is none. God didn't tell the Israelites to do this because not doing so would be in any way wicked. Like many of the commandments in the Torah, there's no punishment pronounced for not wearing these tzitzit. God is simply telling Israel to wear the tassels for the reason which is given in Numbers 15.

Another law of the Torah which the Hebrew Roots movement wants to hold onto are those concerning dietary laws. As a result of my adherence to the movement, I didn't willingly consume any unclean meats for nearly three years. I assumed that doing so was somehow wrong, and that these commandments given in the Torah were still in place. However, that's not what we see in the New Testament. As already shown, in both Colossians 2:16 and Hebrews 9:10 "meats and drinks" are mentioned.

If the commandments concerning meat and drinks were only imposed until the time of reformation, then why do we need to continue to follow these

204

laws? Why are Christians judged concerning what they eat, when it tells us not to judge concerning meats in Colossians 2:16? One of the errors of the Hebrew Roots is that they often misread and misquote the Torah's commands concerning the dietary laws. The word 'abomination' appears in Leviticus 11, which is a list of what is unclean. However, pay close attention to the language which is used in the chapter:

> Leviticus 11:2-20 - Speak unto the children of Israel, saying, These are the beasts which ye shall eat among all the beasts that are on the earth. Whatsoever parteth the hoof, and is clovenfooted, and cheweth the cud, among the beasts, that shall ye eat. Nevertheless these shall ye not eat of them that chew the cud, or of them that divide the hoof: as the camel, because he cheweth the cud, but divideth not the hoof; <u>he is unclean unto you</u>. And the coney, because he cheweth the cud, but divideth not the hoof; <u>he is unclean unto you</u>. And the hare, because he cheweth the cud, but divideth not the hoof; <u>he is unclean unto you.</u> And the swine, though he divide the hoof, and be clovenfooted, yet he cheweth not the cud; <u>he is unclean to you</u>. Of their flesh shall ye not eat, and their carcase shall ye not touch; <u>they are unclean to you</u>. These shall ye eat of all that are in the waters: whatsoever hath fins and scales in the waters, in the seas, and in the rivers, them shall ye eat. And all that have not fins and scales in the seas, and in the rivers, of all that move in the waters, and of any living thing which is in the waters, <u>they shall be an abomination unto you</u>: <u>They shall be even an abomination unto you</u>; ye shall not eat of their flesh, but <u>ye shall have their carcases in abomination</u>. Whatsoever hath no fins nor scales in the waters, that shall be <u>an abomination unto you</u>. And these are they which <u>ye shall have in abomination</u> among the fowls; they shall not be eaten, they are an abomination: the eagle, and the ossifrage, and the ospray, And the vulture, and the kite after his kind; Every raven after his kind; And the owl, and the night hawk, and the cuckow, and the hawk after his kind, And the little owl, and the cormorant, and the great owl, And the swan, and the pelican, and the gier eagle, And the stork, the heron after her kind, and the lapwing, and the bat. All fowls that creep, going upon all four, shall <u>be an abomination unto you</u>.

Do you notice something? Over and over again, it is repeated "he is unclean unto YOU" and "they shall be an abomination unto YOU." The word abomination means "something that causes hatred or disgust." God is telling the Israelites to treat these animals as something digusting so that they don't eat them. However, the phrase "It is an abomination unto the LORD thy God," which is found in many other commandments in the Torah is not found. This is what God says concerning certain things, like idolatry (Deut. 27:15) or cross-dressing (Deut. 22:5), but there's no indication that God holds these to be an abomination unto himself.

Claiming so wouldn't make any sense. Consider that there were some things spoken of in the Law of Moses which were not so from the beginning of the world. Jesus pointed this out about the commandments concerning divorce. Deuteronomy 24:1-4 clearly gives a law concerning bills of divorcement. However, Jesus said when the Pharisees questioned him about putting away one's wife, "Moses because of the hardness of your hearts suffered you to put away your wives: but from the beginning it was not so (Matthew 19:8)." This shows that some things even in the Torah were not allowed before the Torah, or vice versa.

Similarly, the commandments concerning meats and drinks were only established under the Torah. There's no prohibition against eating unclean meats prior to Moses, but rather the exact opposite. God said to Noah,

> Genesis 9:3 - Every moving thing that liveth shall be meat for you; even as the green herb have I given you all things.

If it were naturally a sin to eat unclean meats, then why does God specifically tell Noah to eat "every moving thing that liveth." Pigs and shellfish are alive and moving, therefore, if Noah or his sons were to eat these creatures, he would not be breaking God's command at all. The dietary laws were not established until the time of Moses. Therefore, it's absurd to presume that we, under the new testament, are sinners if we consume unclean meats. Not only does it say not to judge concerning meats and drinks and that these were carnal ordinances done away with at the time of reformation, but there are two examples of passages in the Bible which show that these commandments no longer place. First of all, in the words of Jesus,

> 7:15-23 - There is nothing from without a man, that entering into defile him: but the things which come out of him, those are defile the man. If any man have ears to hear, let him hear.

206

And when he was entered into the house from the people, his disciples asked him concerning the parable. And he saith unto them, Are ye so without understanding also? Do ye not perceive, <u>that whatsoever thing from without entereth into the man, it cannot defile him; Because it entereth not into his heart, but into the belly, and goeth out into the draught, purging all meats</u>? And he said, That which cometh out of the man, that defileth the man. For from within, out of the heart of men, proceed evil thoughts, adulteries, fornications, murders, Thefts, covetousness, wickedness, deceit, lasciviousness, an evil eye, blasphemy, pride, foolishness: All these evil things come from within, and defile the man.

Here Jesus makes it clear that something from without cannot defile a man. The point Jesus was making is that wickedness comes from the heart and not from the outside. One is wicked because of the evil intentions of their heart, and not from that which they take in. The word 'defilement' here is clearly talking about spiritual corruption. In the context, the Pharisees criticized the disciples for eating bread with unwashed hands (v. 2-5).

The issue in this passage is not physical, but spiritual. The Pharisees' criticism was that Jesus' disciples were not obeying the tradition of the elders. Jesus responds by telling them that whether they eat bread with unwashen hands or not, this has no effect on their heart. The subject is talking about sin. If we consume any meat, it does not cause us to sin. Since Christ uses absolutes in this passages, such as "whatsoever thing" and "all meats," we know this includes even the unclean meats prohibited in the Old Testament. Essentially, even if we eat the unclean meats in the Old Testament, we are not sinning, because it is something from without and not something from within. There is no spiritual application to it; and it is thus a 'carnal ordinance.'

Another passage shows exactly how the dietary laws were fulfilled, and what they pictured. Before Cornelius the centurion came to Simon the tanner's house to talk with Peter, Peter received a vision from heaven.

> Acts 10:10-16 - On the morrow, as they went on their journey, and drew nigh unto the city, Peter went up upon the housetop to pray about the sixth hour: And he <u>became very</u> hungry, and would have eaten: but while they made ready, he fell into a trance, And saw heaven opened, and a certain vessel descending upon him, as it had been a great sheet

(carnel
Ordenance)

knit at the four corners, and let down to the earth: Wherein were all manner of fourfooted beasts of the earth, and wild beasts, and creeping things, and fowls of the air. And there came a voice to him, Rise, Peter; kill, and eat. But Peter said, Not so, Lord; for I have never eaten any thing that is common or unclean. And the voice spake unto him again the second time, What God hath cleansed, that call not thou common. This was done thrice: and the vessel was received up again into heaven.

While in the Hebrew Roots movement, I greatly misunderstood this passage, looking at it from the wicked perspective of man. My idea was that since Peter refused, saying "I have never eaten any thing that is common or unclean," this was proof that the apostles continued to obey the dietary laws. However, we need to understand first of all that this would not have been the only time that Peter would have returned to Old Testament practices. Paul specifically criticized Peter at one point, saying, "Why compellest thou the Gentiles to live as do the Jews (Gal. 2:14)?" The Greek word used here is the root for the word 'Judaize', Ἰουδαΐζειν. This is a word which I heard Christians use, unaware that it was indeed used in the New Testament.

Another thing to be noted is that the Lord tells Peter to eat these unclean meats. The Bible tells us that God does not tempt any man with evil (James 1:13). If this was truly sinful in the new testament, then why would God specifically tell Peter to eat these unclean animals? He says "What God hath cleansed, that call not thou common," showing to us that these meats which were once considered unclean are now clean. Later in the chapter, it is explained what this distinction between clean and unclean meats was a picture of. Peter says,

> Acts 10:28 - And he said unto them, Ye know how that it is an unlawful thing for a man that is a Jew to keep company, or come unto one of another nation; but God hath shewed me that I should not call any man common or unclean.

> Acts 10:34-35 - Then Peter opened his mouth, and said, Of a truth I perceive that God is no respecter of persons: But in every nation he that feareth him, and worketh righteousness, is accepted with him.

The unclean and clean meats pictured the separation between the nation of Israel and the Gentiles. However, now that the gate has been opened up to the

Gentiles, to the other sheep to be brought into the fold, this distinction is abolished. Just as these other carnal ordinances spoken of in the scriptures were fulfilled in the new testament, so are the dietary laws. And thus, we see no example of the apostles obeying these commandments. The Bible says "the kingdom of God is not meat and drink (Rom. 14:17)." Yet the Hebrew Roots movement wants to make the kingdom about observance of these dietary laws.

Disobedience of the Messianics

Now that it's been shown that the Hebrew Roots are in error for holding onto these carnal ordinances which are done away with in the new testament, it should also be mentioned that many in this movement are hypocritical and disobedient to their own rules of faith. People like Michael Rood lift up the Torah while criticizing manmade tradition, often comparing the traditions of Christianity with that of the Pharisees. However, in the same way, many in the Hebrew Roots movement add to the commandments of God and stick with Judaic traditions, even if they're not in the Bible.

For example, many Hebrew Roots and Messianic teachers will use the title of "Rabbi." The most famous of these is the well-known author Jonathan Cahn, who styles himself as "Rabbi Jonathan Cahn." Another ministry, called Etz Chayim, is headed by "Rabbi Mordecai Silver." A Messianic congregation I attended once in my area called "Beth Mayim Chayim" was headed by a man who took the title of Rabbi. James Trimm, a well-known plagiarizer and liar in the community and the founder of 'Nazarene Judaism,' is another who takes the title of Rabbi. Although this is not the case with all in the 'Torah-observant' community, it is certainly common. However, Jesus commands explicitly:

> Matthew 23:8 - But be not ye called Rabbi: for one is your Master, even Christ; and all ye are brethren.

Jesus tells us not to be called Rabbi. Those who take titles like this are no different than the Roman Catholics who take the title of 'father,' which is also prohibited by Jesus in the very next verse. Rabbi is not a title used for anybody in the New Testament except for Jesus Christ himself. The only reason why the Messianics take this name is because of tradition, from Judaism. Thus they do the same thing Jesus rebuked the Pharisees for, making the commandment of God of none effect by their traditions (Matt. 15:6).

The clothing reflects their desire to follow Judaism as well. Besides the tzitziyot already mentioned, we would often see men (especially Michael Rood) wear long Middle-eastern style clothing and hats. There's no reason to do so, there being no commandment to do so. Nothing about Rood's fancy Hebraic clothing makes him any more holy than a man wearing a t-shirt and jeans. So why does he do it? To draw attention to himself. To make one look more "Jewish." This is something Michael Rood criticized other Messianics for doing, since many wear kippahs and yarmulkes, despite no such command existing in the Bible. Yet, he does the same thing, even if what he wears isn't exactly what is commanded in Ashkenazi Jewish tradition.

Despite what the Hebrew Roots heretics will tell you, Jewish customs and culture does not trump every other just because it's "Hebraic." Paul said,

> 1 Corinthians 9:19-22 - For though I be free from all men, yet have I made myself servant unto all, that I might gain the more. And unto the Jews I became as a Jew, that I might gain the Jews; to them that are under the law, as under the law, that I might gain them that are under the law; To them that are without law, as without law, (being not without law to God, but under the law to Christ,) that I might gain them that are without law. To the weak became I as weak, that I might gain the weak: I am made all things to all men, that I might by all means save some.

What is Paul saying here? That depending on who he was preaching to, he became as them, that he might be received easier among them. Of course, he's not saying that if a culture participates in sinful activities, that he would also do so, but rather, he was willing to adopt certain cultural aspects of a people while being among them. Even though Paul was a Hebrew, he did not continue in all aspects of the Hebrew culture wherever he went. This means that if Paul was alive today in the United States, he would probably learn the English language, wear American clothing, and eat American food, instead of trying to draw attention to himself as a foreigner. The Hebrew Roots movement, despite being mostly among English-speaking Americans, tries to act as if they're ethnically Jewish, and thus, their everyday speech will include words like 'shalom' instead of 'hello' and their garments would include long eastern-style robes rather than a simple pair of pants and a shirt.

Some of these Hebrew Roots will go overboard with what they wear. Jesus critcized the Pharisees in this manner:

> Luke 20:46 - Beware of the scribes, which desire to walk in long robes, and love greetings in the markets, and the highest seats in the synagogues, and the chief rooms at feasts;

Walking in long robes, or as Mark 12 puts it, "long clothing," is seen as prideful. Long clothing and robes are reserved for royalty, such as Jesus Christ, the king of kings, who according to the Bible, will one day come wearing a long robe (Rev. 1:13). However, sinful men and religious leaders have no place walking around in garments like this, such as what Michael Rood wears.

Another strange and unbiblical trend in the Hebrew Roots movement regarding clothing is the wearing of head-coverings on women. Again, this is not the case for all, but it isn't rare to find a woman in the Hebrew Roots movement who has begun to cover their head, especially among those who are married to Hebrew Roots teachers around the Internet. The reasoning for this comes from 1 Corinthians 11; however, it's evident that these didn't read the whole passage, for it says:

> 1 Corinthians 11:3-15 - But I would have you know, that the head of every man is Christ; and the head of the woman is the man; and the head of Christ is God. Every man praying or prophesying, having his head covered, dishonoureth his head. <u>But every woman that prayeth or prophesieth with her head uncovered dishonoureth her head: for that is even all one as if she were shaven.</u> For if the woman be not covered, let her also be shorn: but if it be a shame for a woman to be shorn or shaven, let her be covered. For a man indeed ought not to cover his head, forasmuch as he is the image and glory of God: but the woman is the glory of the man. For the man is not of the woman: but the woman of the man. Neither was the man created for the woman; but the woman for the man. For this cause ought the woman to have power on her head because of the angels. Nevertheless neither is the man without the woman, neither the woman without the man, in the Lord. For as the woman is of the man, even so is the man also by the woman; but all

things of God. Judge in yourselves: is it comely that a woman pray unto God uncovered? Doth not even nature itself teach you, that, if a man have long hair, it is a shame unto him? <u>But if a woman have long hair, it is a glory to her: for her hair is given her for a covering.</u>

In order to come to the conclusion that it is necessary for a woman to cover her head with an article of clothing in order to honour her husband, you'd have to stop reading at verse 6. However, if one reads the whole passage down to verse 14 and 15, it becomes evident what is being written about: hair. A man should not have long hair, because it would cover his head, and thus dishonour his head, which is Christ. In addition, it says concerning women, "her hair is given her for a covering." This shows us that a woman does not need to wear some kind of special garment around her head like a Muslim woman would, but rather simply needs to have long hair. If a woman has long hair, there is no purpose for having another head covering, for the hair is her covering.

Another way in which those in the Hebrew Roots movement go against the teachings of the Bible is by doing exactly what the scriptures say to avoid:

> Titus 3:9 - But avoid foolish questions, and genealogies, and contentions, <u>and strivings about the law;</u> for they are unprofitable and vain.

As could be demonstrated by the constant disagreement over certain commandments in the Torah, there is often striving, or fightings about the law. One ministry might argue that we are to follow the lunar sabbath, while another the seventh-day weekly sabbath. One ministry might teach that one needs to wear tzitzit as actual fringes, while another may teach that it's acceptable to wear them as tassels. One ministry may say that all barley needs to be aviv for the first month to come, while others may just say that some need to be aviv. One may claim that polyester is forbidden by the commandment not to wear linen and wool mixed together, while another believes that this literally means only linen and wool.

This is exactly what we see. There are so many different Hebrew Roots teachers and ministries who hold to different opinions about the law, and not only do they hold different opinions, but they argue about such. Most Hebrew Roots sites and online videos will go in-depth trying to refute the other teachings and defend their own position. Yet, the Bible tells us to avoid these strivings, and tells us the exact reason why: they are unprofitable and vain. The reason why is evident: because as we've already seen, these carnal ordinances are done away with. Other commandments like, "Thou shalt not kill" don't need to be argued about, because they're clear. The strivings almost always have to do with these carnal commandments that are done away with in the New Testament.

Therefore, we should avoid these arguments. They're unprofitable and vain. The specifics of these commandments do not matter because they're done away with. Although it of course is profitable to study these (since all scripture is profitable), it is worthless to mindlessly argue about how to follow them exactly, since we no longer have to follow these commands.

Another issue which seems to come up a lot with some Hebrew Roots teachers is their love for money, which is often how many people are drawn in. The only difference between people like Michael Rood and wealthy televangelists like Kenneth Copeland is that the latter is more popular. If Rood had millions of followers, it wouldn't be surprising to see him emphasize money more and more. Even now, on many of his livestreams, he constantly asks for donations and money. His programs have emotional commercials about donating to Israeli victims of Palestinian attacks. Nobody knows whether those donations actually go towards this cause, or towards any of the causes he claims to use the donations for.

Michael Rood's monetary shenanigans can also be demonstrated by his overpriced products which he constantly promotes. One such example is the Chronological Gospels, which sells for $70 on his website. He claims this book is the result of 40 years of careful study and promotes it as accurate and important for understanding the gospels. Yet one could buy the entire Bible (Gospels and everything else) for $5 everywhere else. The Chronological Gospels are a scam.

It's the same story with his so-called "love gifts." These are special monthly items, mainly Judaica like menorahs, mezuzot, and the like, which are sent to people if they 'donate.' Paying and receiving something for it is not a gift. Perhaps this is why Rood doesn't understand the gospel, since salvation is a free gift, meaning it costs nothing (Rom. 6:23, Eph. 2:8). If one has to earn it through giving something themselves, it's not longer a gift, it's a purchase.

Rood is nothing more than another money-driven preacher who is "greedy of filthy lucre (Titus 1:11)."

Heaven and Hell or Soul-Sleep and Annihilation?

One major Hebrew Roots false doctrine is that which is also held by groups like the Jehovah's Witnesses and Seventh-Day Adventists. This is the doctrine of soul-sleep, which is related to the doctrines of conditional mortality and annihilationism. Most Hebrew Roots do not believe in heaven or hell or any immediate afterlife, but hold to the concept that a person is unconscious from the moment they die until the resurrection, regardless of whether they are God's people or not. At the final judgment, those who end up in the lake of fire are destroyed there and do not burn forever. Thus, the Christian doctrine of living with God in eternity for the saved or burning in hell for the damned is rejected.

This was one of the things which I thought Christians had gotten from paganism. After all, I knew that several pagan religions believed in the concept of an underworld or an afterlife. My idea of heaven was that the saints would only be there for a short period of time between the rapture and the establishment of the millenial kingdom on earth, but I rejected all beliefs that the spirit existed there apart from the body. Concerning hell, I believed that the proper term used in the Bible was "Gehenna," which I believed always referred to the lake of fire spoken of in the book of Revelation, and never a temporary fiery place between one's death and the final judgment.

However, now as a Christian, I understand this to be biblically false. Both heaven and hell are real places where the spirits of the physically dead depart to. This can be shown easily by examination of the scriptures. Let's look at some passages which show us that upon the death of the body of the Christian, their spirit departs into heaven.

> Philippians 1:20-24 - According to my earnest expectation and my hope, that in nothing I shall be ashamed, but that with all boldness, as always, so now also Christ shall be magnified in my body, whether it be by life, or by death. For to me to live is Christ, and to die is gain. But if I live in the flesh, this is the fruit of my labour: yet what I shall choose I wot not. For I am in a strait betwixt two, having a desire to depart, and to be with Christ; which is far better: Nevertheless to abide in the flesh

is more needful for you.

In this paassage, Paul discusses the subject of magnifiying Christ, which he says he wishes to do so either in life or in death. Verse 21 particularly is of interest to us, because it is written, "to die is gain." Stop and contemplate why Paul wrote those words. What gain is there to death if death is just an unconscious state? Why does he say "to me" at the start of the sentence to distinguish between him and others? If every person faces the same state of soul-sleep, no matter what their spiritual state is, how does this make sense?

If we continue reading, Paul answers our questions by telling us that if he departs, he will be with Christ. In context, since the verse before he writes about living in the flesh, and the verse after talks about abiding in the flesh, we know that this is a departure from the body. If we, as a born-again child of God (born in the Spirit, John 3:6), depart from the body, then we will be with Christ. And according to the Bible, where is Christ? He is in heaven (Acts 1:11, Eph. 1:20), where we shall be if we depart from the flesh.

Thus, we have one clear passage telling us about going to heaven after death. We stay here now to do the work of God, our presence here being needful to the people of the world, but there will come a time, unless we are those who are alive and remain at the coming of the Lord (1 Thes. 4:15) that our bodies will die and our spirits will go to God. This is taught not just in these verses, but in other passages as well. Consider the following:

> 2 Corinthians 5:6-8 - Therefore we are always confident, knowing that, whilst we are at home in the body, we are absent from the Lord: (For we walk by faith, not by sight:) We are confident, I say, and willing rather to be <u>absent from the body, and to be present with the Lord</u>.

Here the absence from the body is once again defined. Just as Philippians used the language of departing from the flesh, which means that we are with Christ, here Paul writes that if we are absent from the body, we are present with the Lord. Once again, the Lord is in heaven (Psa. 115:3). Once our spirits depart from the body (which is, death), then we will be with God in heaven; it's not some future event we won't experience until the second coming of Christ. The scriptures teach that at the resurrection we are given a new, spiritual body (1 Cor. 15:44). We will examine the resurrection in more detail later.

The teaching of scriptures is that death occurs when the spirit departs from the body. This is why in many instances the Bible talks about 'giving up the ghost.' The first time is in Genesis 25:8, when it says "Abraham gave up the ghost, and died in a good old age." When Jesus died on the cross, it is written that "he bowed his head, and gave up the ghost (John 19:30)." In the book of Genesis, it is written that the only reason why Adam's life began is because God breathed the "breath of life" into him. Therefore, it's not a difficult concept to grasp that once this departs (or we expire, from the Latin word *exspiro*, from *spiro*, meaning breath, from where we get the English word spirit), we are dead. With this knowledge, the Bible says,

> Ecclesiastes 12:7 - Then shall the dust return to the earth as it was: and the spirit shall return unto God who gave it.

This verse tells us the same thing that the previous two verses we saw in the New Testament teach. If our spirit departs from the body, which returns to the dust, then it "shall return unto God who gave it." This is what Christians call 'going to heaven.' If the body ceases from life, since our inward man has been born again and we have eternal life (John 3:36, 6:47), our spirit continues to live, but now in the presence of God in heaven. It is written also,

> 1 Thessalonians 5:9-10 - For God hath not appointed us to wrath, but to obtain salvation by our Lord Jesus Christ, Who died for us, that, whether we wake or sleep, we should live together with him.

Again, it is written that no matter if we are awake or asleep (referring to life or death), that we should live together with him. If one is unconscious and unable to do anything until the resurrection day, this doesn't make any sense. However, applying the New Testament teaching in other places, we know that if we are absent from the body, we are present with the Lord. Therefore, if we die, we shall still live together with Christ, but this time in his presence in heaven. We remain alive even after the death of the body; this is why Paul said that "to die is gain."

The Hebrew Roots movement, as well as others who teach the doctrine of soul-sleep, indeed understand the meaning of 'sleep' (hence the name soul-sleep). The scriptures in many places compare the death of the body with sleep. For example, whenever a king of Israel or Judah died, it would say "he slept with his fathers (1 Kin. 2:10, 11:43, 14:20, 31, 15:8, 24, 16:6, 28, 22:40,

216

etc.)." When Stephen was stoned to death, the passage ends with the phrase "he fell asleep." This obviously isn't talking about taking a rest. Stephen was murdered by the Jews, and died at that moment after asking the Lord to forgive his persecutor's sin. Another clear instance of the word 'sleep' is when Jesus raised Lazarus from the dead:

> John 11:11-14 - These things said he: and after that he saith unto them, Our friend Lazarus sleepeth; but I go, that I may awake him out of sleep. Then said his disciples, Lord, if he sleep, he shall do well. Howbeit Jesus spake of his death: but they thought that he had spoken of taking of rest in sleep. Then said Jesus unto them plainly, Lazarus is dead.

At first, Jesus tells them that Lazarus is sleeping. They take this literally, as it says "they thought that he had spoken of taking of rest in sleep." However, Jesus was not speaking of a literal bodily rest, but rather, he was using the same term used to describe the death of so many Old Testament figures. Thus, Jesus says plainly "Lazarus is dead." With this knowledge, examining 1 Thessalonians 5 again, we again see, that no matter if we are awake (alive), or sleeping (dead), we should live together with him (Jesus). Once again, we have another clear reference to going to heaven.

Not only do we have clear descriptions of what happens at death for the Christian, but an actual example of believers in heaven. In the book of Revelation, it says,

> Revelation 6:9-11 - And when he had opened the fifth seal, I saw under the altar the souls of them that were slain for the word of God, and for the testimony which they held: And they cried with a loud voice, saying, How long, O Lord, holy and true, dost thou not judge and avenge our blood on them that dwell on the earth? And white robes were given unto every one of them; and it was said unto them, that they should rest yet for a little season, until their fellowservants also and their brethren, that should be killed as they were, should be fulfilled.

When the fifth seal breaks, before the return of Christ, while the great tribulation is still going on (or, has not yet begun, depending on different interpretations), the souls of the martyrs are in heaven with Christ, under the altar. Not only are the souls described as being in heaven, but the souls are able to cry out to the Lord. This doesn't sound like an unconscious state of 'soul-sleep.' The souls are very much awake, and not only awake, but living in heaven with God.

Therefore, if we just take the Bible for what it plainly says, it's not difficult to find the teaching that we go to heaven after death, a teaching which the Hebrew Roots movement denies. There is no soul-sleep. Our souls live in heaven with Christ; the only thing sleeping is the body. In Daniel 12:2, which talks about the resurrection of the dead, it is written that "many of them that sleep in the dust of the earth shall awake." Now, according to Eccl. 12:7, it's the body which sleeps in the dust, while the spirit returns to God in heaven. So, when the resurrection takes place, it will be the awakening of the body, not of the soul.

Some in the Hebrew Roots' movement's teaching of soul-sleep is understandable. The stated goal of some is to put the emphasis back on the resurrection. While I was in the movement, I had this false perception that Christians didn't know much about the resurrection, and focused more on going to heaven immediately than the kingdom of heaven at the future return of Christ. This is once again, a false perception of what Christians believe (unless one does what the Hebrew Roots does, and assumes all Christians believe like Roman Catholics do). Rather, many, especially Baptists, understand the importance of the resurrection.

There's one key detail which is missed by the Hebrew Roots movement concerning this event, known as the return of Christ, the resurrection, and the rapture, which once again shows the truth that those who are dead in Christ are in heaven after death. As it's been already shown, when the body dies, the body sleeps in the dust, and the spirit departs to live in heaven with Christ. We remain in this state until the day of the Lord comes. Notice the details in the following passage, which describes the rapture in detail:

> 1 Thessalonians 4:14-17 - For if we believe that Jesus died and rose again, even so them also which sleep in Jesus will God bring with him. For this we say unto you by the word of the Lord, that we which are alive and remain unto the coming of the Lord shall not prevent them which are asleep. For the Lord himself shall descend from heaven with a shout, with the voice of the archangel, and with the trump of God: and the dead in Christ shall rise first: Then we which are alive and

remain shall be caught up together with them in the clouds, to meet the Lord in the air: and so shall we ever be with the Lord.

Remember that this is in the context of the passage we read earlier, that "whether we wake or sleep, we should live together with him." With that information, we know that those who sleep in Christ, despite being dead, live together with Christ. In 1 Thessalonians 4, therefore, we see in verse 14 that when Christ descends from heaven, he brings them which sleep in him with him. How could God bring the dead in Christ with him if they were not with him? With the soul-sleep doctrine, this makes no sense. If a believer is just unconscious and their spirit is just in 'the grave' and not in heaven, then how could Christ, who descends from heaven, bring the dead with him?

At the rapture, when Christ descends from heaven, he brings the spirits of those who sleep in Christ with him from heaven, since they "live together with him," or as 2 Corinthians puts it, are "present with the Lord." Simultaneously, the bodies of the dead rise from the graves, as we see in verse 16: these are the dead in Christ, who rise first. This is what is described also in 1 Corinthians 15, a passage which talks about the resurrection in detail. It is stated,

> 1 Corinthians 15:51-53 - Behold, I shew you a mystery; We shall not all sleep, but we shall all be changed, In a moment, in the twinkling of an eye, at the last trump: for the trumpet shall sound, and the dead shall be raised incorruptible, and we shall be changed. For this corruptible must put on incorruption, and this mortal must put on immortality.

Those which do not sleep are those written of in 1 Thessalonians 4, "we which are alive and remain." They will be given a new body, an incorruptible and immortal body. This is the same fate of the dead in Christ as well; as it is written several verses earlier, "So is the resurrection of the dead: It is sown in corruption, it is raised in incorruption (v. 42)." The Bible thus shows us a picture of what happens when the dead are resurrected: it is the bodies which are raised and transformed, while the spirits (those in heaven who Christ brings with him), unite with the body. Since the body without the spirit is dead (James 2:26), then this is the only way in which the bodies can be truly raised and given life, if the spirit unites with the body.

The scriptures tell us exactly what the fate of the spirit is after death, as we've already seen. It returns to God who gave it, and there dwells until the day of resurrection. The Hebrew Roots movement err by attacking Christians and claiming that we diminish the resurrection by teaching that the spirit is in heaven. Our spirit's presence in heaven is not the same as the kingdom of heaven, nor is it a belief that one exists there forever with no resurrection. Rather, we understand that the Bible teaches that our spirit already has eternal life (John 3:36, 6:47), but that the body does not, but it is this mortal body which shall be quickened (Rom. 8:11) one day. This truth is shown also by the prophecy of the dry bones in Ezekiel:

> Ezekiel 37:1-14 - The hand of the Lord was upon me, and carried me out in the spirit of the Lord, and set me down in the midst of the valley which was full of bones, And caused me to pass by them round about: and, behold, there were very many in the open valley; and, lo, they were very dry. And he said unto me, Son of man, can these bones live? And I answered, O Lord God, thou knowest. Again he said unto me, Prophesy upon these bones, and say unto them, O ye dry bones, hear the word of the Lord. Thus saith the Lord God unto these bones; Behold, I will cause breath to enter into you, and ye shall live: And I will lay sinews upon you, and will bring up flesh upon you, and cover you with skin, and put breath in you, and ye shall live; and ye shall know that I am the Lord. So I prophesied as I was commanded: and as I prophesied, there was a noise, and behold a shaking, and the bones came together, bone to his bone. And when I beheld, lo, the sinews and the flesh came up upon them, and the skin covered them above: but there was no breath in them. Then said he unto me, Prophesy unto the wind, prophesy, son of man, and say to the wind, Thus saith the Lord God; Come from the four winds, O breath, and breathe upon these slain, that they may live. So I prophesied as he commanded me, and the breath came into them, and they lived, and stood up upon their feet, an exceeding great army. Then he said unto me, Son of man, these bones are the whole house of Israel: behold, they say, Our bones are dried, and our hope is lost: we are cut off for our parts. Therefore prophesy and say unto them, Thus saith the Lord God; Behold, O my people, I will open your graves, and cause you to come up out of your graves, and bring you into the land of Israel. And ye shall know that I am the Lord, when I have opened your graves, O my people, and brought you up out of your graves, And shall put my spirit in you, and ye shall live,

and I shall place you in your own land: then shall ye know that I the Lord have spoken it, and performed it, saith the Lord.

When comparing this passage to 1 Thessalonians 4, we see very similar imagery. These bodies are raised up and restored, having the bones come together, and receiving sinews and skin upon them, but they are not yet alive, until breath comes into them, or as the LORD puts it later in the chapter, his spirit comes into them to cause them to live. Understanding once again based on the revelation of the New Testament that the spirit is with Christ after death, and that the spirit comes with Christ at his coming and the resurrection, this makes sense. Only after the breath, or spirit, enters into the dead do their bodies revive.

The Hebrew Roots doctrine of soul-sleep, at least for the believers, is false and unbiblical. There are only a few verses which they have to back up their own doctrine, which as we will see, are twisted and based on a misunderstanding of scripture. We'll look at three passages used by the Hebrew Roots movement to support this doctrine that one does not go to heaven after death. The first, written in the book of Job, says,

> Job 14:10-14 - But man dieth, and wasteth away: yea, man giveth up the ghost, and where is he? As the waters fail from the sea, and the flood decayeth and drieth up: So man lieth down, and riseth not: till the heavens be no more, they shall not awake, nor be raised out of their sleep. O that thou wouldest hide me in the grave, that thou wouldest keep me secret, until thy wrath be past, that thou wouldest appoint me a set time, and remember me! If a man die, shall he live again? all the days of my appointed time will I wait, till my change come.

Taking this passage at just what it says, we do not even see the Hebrew Roots doctrine. As we should with all the Bible, let us examine what the text actually does say, and what it does not say. In verse 10, Job says, "man giveth up the ghost, and where is he?" This rhetorical question is neither a clear statement of any belief, nor does it receive an answer. The assumption by deniers of the afterlife is that this question is meant to cast doubt upon the existence of a person's soul after death, yet this is reading into the text. Nowhere does it say or hint at such. Rather, Job does say "man giveth up the ghost." Comparing with other scriptures, such as Ecclesiastes 12:7, we know that giving up the ghost is equivalent to the spirit departing to the Lord, if one is saved.

221

The following verses tell us that until the heavens are no more, one will not awake out of their sleep or rise from the grave. This is consistent with the teaching of the New Testament, that the resurrection of the dead will take place in the time of the end. However, once again, using this verse to defend soul-sleep is based on the assumption that it is the soul which is sleeping, and not the body, which the Bible teaches (Daniel 12:2). Therefore, there is no indication that this teaches an unconscious state. Another verse used is the following:

> Psalm 115:17 - The dead praise not the Lord, neither any that go down into silence.

Those who use this verse ignore the very next one, which says, "But we will bless the LORD from this time forth and for evermore. Praise the LORD." There is a contrast between those who are called 'the dead' and 'we.' These dead spoken of in verse 17 will not praise the LORD, while it says that "we will bless the LORD from this time forth and for evermore." This is once again, consistent with the teaching of Christianity and the New Testament. Those who are saved have eternal life, and thus will never cease praising the LORD. Even after we die, we will still "live together with him (1 Thes. 5:10)."

So, the 'dead' spoken of in verse 17 cannot be those whose bodies are dead, but those who are dead in spirit. The Bible says that we were dead in trespasses and sins (Eph. 2:1). Before salvation, before we are given eternal life, we are dead. This is why in Revelation 20:10, when speaking of the final judgment, it defines the dead as those in hell. These are those who perished without Christ, and thus faced true death. Jesus promised to believers that we will never die (John 11:26), and never perish (John 10:28). This is how we are able to praise the LORD forever, while those who are dead, who do not have eternal life, do not.

A final verse used which is twisted by the Hebrew Roots movement to teach this doctrine of soul sleep is the following:

> Ecclesiastes 9:5 - For the living know that they shall die: but the dead know not any thing, neither have they any more a reward; for the memory of them is forgotten.

The book of Ecclesiastes itself is told in the theme of the vanity of this life. Thus, looking in the context, in the verse next verse, it says, "either have they

222

any more a portion for ever in any thing that is done under the sun." The key phrase is "under the sun." This is referring to our earthly lives. Thus, the verse before it is not talking about our deaths from a spiritual perspective, but an earthly one. The point the Preacher is trying to make is that those who are dead have no more part in this world; they don't know the things of this world, they don't have any more reward in this world, and people in this world forget about them.

When one fails to compare scripture and scripture, it is easy to get confused about what the Bible says. Yet, we see that the testimony of scripture is that those who die in Christ shall live with him, and pass from this world into heaven. We Christians are not in error, but those in the Hebrew Roots movement are.

This is not just the case for the teaching on heaven. Like the Seventh Day Adventists and Jehovah's Witnesses, most in the Hebrew Roots movement deny the concept of an eternal hell, and believe that the Lake of Fire is temporary. Their arguments range from assuming what Hebrew and Greek words and phrases mean (despite most certainly not knowing either of these languages), to the unscriptural emotional argument, "Why would God torture people for eternity?" Regardless of whether or not we like it from a foolish human perspective, the Bible is our final authority, and we should see what the scriptures say.

It's already been established that there is no basis for the idea that those who die remain in an unconscious state of soul-sleep. We know that those who die in Christ go to heaven, but what about those who are unsaved? What happens to them? It is once again taught by the Hebrew Roots movement that there is no judgment for them until the final judgment at the Great White Throne. Yet the Bible says,

> Hebrews 9:27 - And as it is appointed unto men once to die, but after this the judgment:

After the death of man comes the judgment. There is no indication that one needs to wait in a state of sleep until the final condemnation to the lake of fire. Rather, Jesus said, "he that believeth not is condemned already, because he hath not believed on the name of the only-begotten Son of God (John 3:18)." Those who reject Christ, based on God's foreknowledge, have already been

223

condemned. The LORD declares the end from the beginning (Isa. 46:10). He already knows who will reject him or not believe. Therefore, even at the point of death, those who shall be judged at the final judgment have already received the condemnation.)

The existence of hell is very real in the Bible, both with references in the Old and New Testaments. Since much of the Hebrew Roots movement use modern corrupt Bibles, they claim that these mentions of 'hell' do not actually refer to what we Christians say hell is. To them, hell is just a state of death and unconsciousness, which they will also refer to as 'the grave.' However, even in the Tanakh, the word hell is often used in the context of fire, destruction, and death of the wicked (see Deut. 32:22, Job 26:6, 55:15, Prov. 5:5, 7:27, 9:18, 27:20, Isa. 14:15, 28:15, Ezek. 31:16, Hab. 2:5).

Of particular interest in these verses are Isaiah 14:15 and Ezekiel 31:16, which give a synonym for hell as 'the pit.' Both are in the context of one who has exalted themselves above God, especially Isaiah 14, which identifies the subject as Lucifer in verse 12. This phrase is used repeatedly throughout the Old Testament in the phrase "them that go down into the pit" or "them that descend into the pit" (Psa. 28:1, 88:4, 143:7, Prov. 1:12, Isa. 38:18, Ezek. 26:20, 28:8, 31:14, 32:18, 24, 32:25, 29-30). Comparing this with the New Testament, we see that some of the devils besought Jesus that he would not send him down to 'the deep (Luke 8:31)', and in the parallel passage, the same devils plead to not be tormented before the time (Matt. 8:29).

It doesn't take much more reading to figure out what the deep is that the devils will be tormented in. Jesus said to the unsaved, "Depart from me, ye cursed, into everlasting fire, prepared for the devil and his angels (Matt. 25:41)." In this verse, the place in which the devils are to one day go to be tormented is "everlasting fire." Interestingly, the only place the New Testament uses the term 'the pit' is in Revelation 9, also called the "bottomless pit," where it says, "there arose a smoke out of the pit, as the smoke of a great furnace (Rev. 9:2)." Therefore, with comparison, we see that the pit, a synonym for hell in the Old Testament, is an everlasting fire, from which comes a great smoke, and which was created for the devil and his angels.

Continuing in reading the New Testament, it becomes clear that this is the overwhelming teaching of the Bible. Hell is indeed a place of fire in which the dead are tormented. Jesus spake of hell many times during his ministry, and clearly described it as being a place of fire, ⍳

> Matthew 5:22 - But I say unto you, That whosoever is angry with his brother without a cause shall be in danger of the judgment: and whosoever shall say to his brother, Raca, shall be in danger of the council: but whosoever shall say, Thou fool, shall be in danger of hell fire.

> Matthew 18:8-9 - Wherefore if thy hand or thy foot offend thee, cut them off, and cast them from thee: it is better for thee to enter into life halt or maimed, rather than having two hands or two feet to be cast into everlasting fire. And if thine eye offend thee, pluck it out, and cast it from thee: it is better for thee to enter into life with one eye, rather than having two eyes to be cast into hell fire.

Notice in Matthew 18 that 'everlasting fire' and 'hell fire' are interchangeable terms. This again shows that just that hell is a place of fire, but that this fire is everlasting. This is consistent with the comparison of hell with the pit of the angels, also called the "everlasting fire prepared for the devil and his angels." Jesus also said in the parallel passage in Mark,

> Mark 9:43-48 - And if thy hand offend thee, cut it off: it is better for thee to enter into life maimed, than having two hands to go into hell, into the fire that never shall be quenched: Where their worm dieth not, and the fire is not quenched. And if thy foot offend thee, cut it off: it is better for thee to enter halt into life, than having two feet to be cast into hell, into the fire that never shall be quenched: Where their worm dieth not, and the fire is not quenched. And if thine eye offend thee, pluck it out: it is better for thee to enter into the kingdom of God with one eye, than having two eyes to be cast into hell fire: Where their worm dieth not, and the fire is not quenched.

The imagery here is consistent with the concept of eternal fire. Here Jesus, as if "everlasting fire" is not clear enough, says "the fire that never shall be quenched." It's not difficult to understand what 'never' means. Just as pointed out before in regards to salvation, if one has everlasting life, that means they shall never die (John 11:26). Likewise, if there is an everlasting fire, that means the fire will never go out. The concept of everlasting seems to just go over the head of many in the Hebrew Roots movement. Yet, Jesus repeats the same phrase five times in this one passage, and says over and over again that the fires of hell will never be quenched.

Some (such as myself when I was in the Hebrew Roots movement) will claim that this isn't even talking about an immediate hell, but that this refers to the final lake of fire which the dead are sent to after the Great White Throne judgment. Evidence for this is usually based on the Greek word γέεννα (also called Gehenna), which comes from the Hebrew term 'Gehinnom' meaning 'valley of Hinnom.' This is a valley outside the city of Jerusalem which was used by pagans for burnt offerings (2 Kings 23:10, 2 Chr. 28:3, 33:6, Jer. 32:35). The assumption is that because the etymology of the word refers to a physical place on earth where men were burned, that this must refer to the lake of fire.

There are obviously problems with this. Firstly, there's no verse in the Bible which calls Gehenna the place of final judgment in which the wicked will be completely annihilated. They usually have to appeal to unbelievers to support this idea (which is common for many doctrines). Yet the Bible shows us something entirely different. Not only do these verses we've already looked at reveal to us that hell is a place of eternal fire, but there are others which show us that this is where the sinners go immediately after death. Remember, the Bible says "it is appointed unto men once to die, and after this the judgment." Jesus said,

> Luke 16:19-31 - There was a certain rich man, which was clothed in purple and fine linen, and fared sumptuously every day: And there was a certain beggar named Lazarus, which was laid at his gate, full of sores, And desiring to be fed with the crumbs which fell from the rich man's table: moreover the dogs came and licked his sores. And it came to pass, that the beggar died, and was carried by the angels into Abraham's bosom: the rich man also died, and was buried; And in hell he lift up his eyes, being in torments, and seeth Abraham afar off, and Lazarus in his bosom. And he cried and said, Father Abraham, have mercy on me, and send Lazarus, that he may dip the tip of his finger in water, and cool my tongue; for I am tormented in this flame. But Abraham said, Son, remember that thou in thy lifetime receivedst thy good things, and likewise Lazarus evil things: but now he is comforted, and thou art tormented. And beside all this, between us and you there

is a great gulf fixed: so that they which would pass from hence to you cannot; neither can they pass to us, that would come from thence. Then he said, I pray thee therefore, father, that thou wouldest send him to my father's house: <u>For I have five brethren; that he may testify unto them, lest they also come into this place of torment</u>. Abraham saith unto him, They have Moses and the prophets; let them hear them. And he said, Nay, father Abraham: but if one went unto them from the dead, they will repent. And he said unto him, If they hear not Moses and the prophets, neither will they be persuaded, though one rose from the dead.

Here we have a very clear description of hell. Some will erroneously claim that this story told by Jesus is just a parable. However, this interpretation makes no sense for several reasons: firstly, no other parable of Christ uses actual names like this story does; secondly, parables usually always began with statements like "The kingdom of heaven is like unto ____," and thirdly, the purpose of a parable was to compare a spiritual thing to an earthly concept. There is no lesson learned from this story in the sense that one would gain a spiritual meaning from an earthly parable. There is thus no reason to claim this is a parable, when all the evidence and the language used in the text shows that Jesus is telling a real story of a man named Lazarus.

From the imagery of the story we see that hell is described just like it is in the rest of the Bible. One of the important details is that hell is shown to be a place the wicked go immediately after death, and not a future description of hell. We see this first in verses 22 and 23, in which it describes the rich man lifting up his eyes in hell immediately after death. This does not say that he slept for thousands of years and then woke out of his sleep to be judged and thrown into the lake of fire. No, he immediately descended into hell. The end of the story shows us this truth even further: the rich man begs for Abraham to release him back into the world to plead for his brethren, that they do not end up in the same place. Abraham refuses because "They have Moses and the prophets." This shows that this is not referring to a future time, because his brethren remain on earth and are in danger of going to hell if they do not repent.

Therefore, from this passage we see that hell is an immediate place for the dead. The same story reveals to us what we've seen already from the other words of Jesus: that this hell is a place of fire and torment. The rich man says,

"I am tormented in this flame." The Hebrew Roots deny this truth, believing that one is not tormented in flame. Hell is not a state of separation, it is not an unconscious state of the dead or a future temporary punishment, but a place of torment (v. 28). Another scripture which shows the imminence of hell is the following,

> Revelation 20:11-15 - And I saw a great white throne, and him that sat on it, from whose face the earth and the heaven fled away; and there was found no place for them. And I saw the dead, small and great, stand before God; and the books were opened: and another book was opened, which is the book of life: and the dead were judged out of those things which were written in the books, according to their works. And the sea gave up the dead which were in it; <u>and death and hell delivered up the dead which were in them:</u> and they were judged every man according to their works. And death and hell were cast into the lake of fire. This is the second death. And whosoever was not found written in the book of life <u>was cast into the lake of fire.</u>

Read what is written carefully here in the book of Revelation. This is talking about the final judgment. The Hebrew Roots claims that this lake of fire mentioned in verse 15 is the same as the place of fire Jesus speaks of during his ministry. However, if this is true, then how can it be said that "death and hell delivered up the dead which where in them"? If the dead do not go down to hell before the great white throne judgment, how could they be delivered up at the final judgment out of hell? In order to be delivered up and then cast into the lake of fire they would need to have been there in the first place.

The word translated as 'hell' in verse 13 is ᾅδης (or as some say, Hades). This is the same exact word used in Luke 16:23, where it says "in hell he lift up his eyes." Therefore, Revelation and Luke 16 both agree: when one dies without Christ, they descend into hell. The rich man is included in those who were delivered out of hell to stand before the throne of God. They could only be delivered up from there if they were there in the first place. Therefore, based on these clear scriptures, we can conclude that hell, a place of fiery torment, is the abode of all those who are currently dead without Christ.

But what about the lake of fire? Is this also an eternal torment? The book of Revelation teaches us that those who were in hell are judged a final time, and then are cast into the lake of fire. This lake of fire is called the second death (see also Rev. 21:8). The first death is when those who die without Christ descend into hell (and thus why the dead are in hell), while the second death is being cast into the lake of fire. The Hebrew Roots claim that since it's called "the second death," this must mean that they are destroyed or burnt up in the lake of fire.

However, this is demonstrably false for the reason that the scriptures repeatedly show us that even after this final judgment, unbelievers will still suffer in eternal fire. There are several passages in scripture which show this clearly. One is earlier in the book of Revelation, where it says:

> Revelation 14:9-11 - And the third angel followed them, saying with a loud voice, If any man worship the beast and his image, and receive his mark in his forehead, or in his hand, The same shall drink of the wine of the wrath of God, which is poured out without mixture into the cup of his indignation; and he shall be tormented with fire and brimstone in the presence of the holy angels, and in the presence of the Lamb: And the smoke of their torment ascendeth up for ever and ever: and they have no rest day nor night, who worship the beast and his image, and whosoever receiveth the mark of his name.

Here we have an example of the assured punishment of those wicked during the time of tribulation who worship the beast: in verse 10, it's clear that they will be tormented with fire and brimstone, which no doubt refers to the lake which burneth with fire and brimstone (Rev. 21:8), and in verse 11, it's clear that the smoke of their torment will ascend eternally. There's no rest for them, but they are tormented in this lake of fire and brimstone forevermore. Jesus said also,

> Matthew 25:41 - Then shall he say also unto them on the left hand, Depart from me, ye cursed, into everlasting fire, prepared for the devil and his angels.

> Matthew 25:46 - And these shall go away into everlasting punishment: but the righteous into life eternal.

According to verse 31 and 32 of this chapter, this is when the Son of man comes in his glory. This is the judgment of the end times, and Jesus says to the wicked, to depart into everlasting fire. Again, everlasting means "lasts forever." If Jesus calls it everlasting fire, that means the fire will not stop burning, and is thus consistent with Revelation 14. Later, Jesus makes it clear that these wicked will go into everlasting punishment. Again, everlasting means it lasts forever. Since the punishment for the wicked is the lake of fire (Rev. 20), then they will be here everlastingly. It's absurd to claim that they will only be there temporarily if the Bible says both 'everlasting fire' and 'everlasting punishment.' The book of Jude says,

> Jude 1:6-7 - And the angels which kept not their first estate, but left their own habitation, he hath reserved in everlasting chains under darkness unto the judgment of the great day. Even as Sodom and Gomorrha, and the cities about them in like manner, giving themselves over to fornication, and going after strange flesh, are set forth for an example, suffering the vengeance of eternal fire.

Again, the Bible teaches us that the judgment which God brought upon Sodom and Gomorrah are an example of the vengeance of eternal fire. Just like everlasting life is also called eternal life in the scriptures, everlasting fire is also called 'eternal fire', in case you didn't understand the meaning.

These verses show undoubtedly that both hell and the lake of fire are places of eternal torment in fire, something which the Hebrew Roots movement often flat-out denies. Despite what the Bible clearly says, they defend their position with a false understanding of several scriptures which use words like 'death', 'perish' and 'destruction.' Their reasoning is that because these terms are usually associated with complete elimination of something, that means that one's soul is completely eliminated. For example, the Bible says,

> 2 Thessalonians 1:7-10 - And to you who are troubled rest with us, when the Lord Jesus shall be revealed from heaven with his mighty angels, In flaming fire taking vengeance on them that know not God, and that obey not the gospel of our Lord Jesus Christ: Who shall be punished <u>with everlasting destruction</u> from the presence of the Lord, and from the glory of his power; When he shall come to be glorified in his saints, and to be admired in all them that believe (because our testimony among you was believed) in that day.

The phrase 'everlasting destruction' is emphasized by annihilationists to teach that the lake of fire is a temporal punishment which simply destroys the wicked and does not torment them eternally. However, this doesn't make any sense when you actually read the whole passage instead of singling out two words. This passage is about the return of Christ in Revelation 19 to destroy the wicked nations of the earth (Rev. 19:19-21). This is before the millenium, when "he shall come to be glorified in his saints." So, is this talking about the lake of fire? No, but rather we see, that a thousand years later is when the dead are delivered up to be judged once again.

So what is meant by "punished with everlasting destruction?" Since this is talking about Jesus Christ coming to earth to destroy the wicked with flaming fire, it's evident this is talking about the destruction of the flesh. It's not saying that their souls will be annihilated forever in the lake of fire, but that their flesh will be annihilated forever from the presence of Jesus. This is exactly what is described in the next chapter, where it says "then shall that Wicked be revealed, whom the Lord shall consume with the spirit of his mouth, and <u>destroy</u> with the brightness of his coming (2 Thes. 2:9)."

Just as the Antichrist will be destroyed with the brightness of Christ's coming, so will the remnant be "slain with the sword of him that sat on the horse (Rev. 19:21)." Thus, 2 Thes. 1 is speaking of the everlasting destruction of the body, not of the spirit in the lake of fire. Yet the annihilationists still teach their everlasting destruction of the soul doctrine using other scriptures, such as the following:

> Matthew 10:28 - And fear not them which kill the body, but are not able to kill the soul: but rather fear him which is able to destroy both soul and body in hell.

Again, the assumption that this means that the wicked will not continue to exist is based on reading things into the text. What Jesus is teaching to his disciples is a comparison between mere men and God: men can only kill the body, while God can 'destroy both soul and body in hell.' The latter phrase is assumed to mean that one's soul ceases to exist. However, as already shown by what the Bible says; the lake of fire is called the 'second death.' Here in Jesus' statement the words 'kill' and 'destroy' are used interchangeably.

There are many uses of the word destruction in the Bible which do not mean "everlasting nonexistence" but rather as a synonym for death. For example, in Matthew 2:13, it is written that "Herod will seek the young child to destroy him." From the context we know that this simply means that Herod sought to kill Jesus. It's written also that the Pharisees sought to destroy Jesus (Matt. 12:14, 27:20, Mark 11:18, etc.) Jesus even said, "Destroy this temple, and in three days I will raise it up (John 2:19)," referring to the temple of his body. The fact that he follows it up with 'in three days I will raise it up' shows that the word 'destroy' in the Bible does not mean "come into a state of nonexistence." Just because Jesus' body was destroyed does not mean his body ceased to exist.

Likewise, God destroying the soul and body in hell is not about God eliminating both of these into a state of nonexistence. Rather, by 'destroy' he simply means "kill, or put to death." Since the lake of fire is called the second death, this makes sense. Yet, the scriptures also show us that this second death is a place of everlasting torment in fire and brimstone. The annihiliationists simply read their own doctrine into the idea of death, because they see death from an earthly perspective rather than how the Bible defines it.

Thus, the Hebrew Roots' common view of the afterlife and the dead is completely unbiblical and unsupported by anything in the scriptures. The truth is, there is no soul-sleep. The dead in Christ's spirits departs into heaven at death to be with Christ. At the second coming, the body is raised and reunited with the spirit, and thus those in Christ shall live forever with a new, spiritual body. The wicked who die without Christ immediately descend into a place of fiery torment called Hell, where they remain until after the millenium, when they are delivered up before the throne of God, judged a final time, and then cast into the lake of fire, where they are tormented eternally.

Trinity

Another false doctrine and heresy of the Hebrew Roots movement is their false understanding of who Jesus and God are. Again, this ranges from person to person. People like Michael Rood deny the divinity of Christ but hold to an Arian position similar to the Jehovah's Witnesses. Some completely deny that Jesus Christ pre-existed his birth and believe he was simply an exalted man. Some teach the heresy of Modalism, believing that Jesus was simply a manifestation or other form of the Father, such as Norman Willis from Nazarene Israel and Daniel John Lee. Others, although this is not common, do believe in the divinity of Christ and the Trinity.

I was in the camp which held to the Arian doctrine. My belief about Yeshua was that he was the Son of Elohim, but was not Elohim, and only held the title of a lesser god, just as judges are referred to as gods in Psalm 82:6. I believed that Jesus was the first creation of God, brought into the world at the beginning of time, and that he was incarnated into the world, but was not himself God Almighty, and was not by nature fully divine. Regarding the Spirit, I believed that this was not a person, but just a description of the Father's presence and power in this world. Yet now I reject this false belief, and with studying the scriptures, it should be abundantly clear that the Trinity doctrine is the truth.

Firstly, let's just see what the Bible teaches, and then address the claims made by the Hebrew Roots movement saying that the Trinity is false, which ranges from twisting of scripture to analysis of history and pagan religions. Firstly, something which the Hebrew Roots movement can agree on, that there is only one God. This truth can be argued from logic and necessity, but also clearly from the holy scriptures. The Bible repeats over and over again that there is only one God:

Deuteronomy 6:4 - Hear, O Israel: The Lord our God is one Lord

Deuteronomy 32:39 - See now that I, even I, am he, and there is no god with me: I kill, and I make alive; I wound, and I heal: neither is there any that can deliver out of my hand.

2 Samuel 7:22 - Therefore thou art great, O Lord God: for there is none like thee, neither is there any God beside thee, according to all that we have heard with our ears.

1 Kings 8:60 - That all the people of the earth may know that the Lord is God, and that there is none else.

2 Kings 19:15 - And Hezekiah prayed before the Lord, and said, O Lord God of Israel, which dwellest between the cherubims, thou art the God, even thou alone, of all the kingdoms of the earth; thou hast made heaven and earth.

Psalm 18:31 - For who is God save the Lord? or who is a rock save our God?

Isaiah 43:10-11 - Ye are my witnesses, saith the Lord, and my servant

233

whom I have chosen: that ye may know and believe me, and understand that I am he: before me there was no God formed, neither shall there be after me. I, even I, am the Lord; and beside me there is no saviour.

Isaiah 44:6-8 - Thus saith the Lord the King of Israel, and his redeemer the Lord of hosts; I am the first, and I am the last; and beside me there is no God. And who, as I, shall call, and shall declare it, and set it in order for me, since I appointed the ancient people? and the things that are coming, and shall come, let them shew unto them. Fear ye not, neither be afraid: have not I told thee from that time, and have declared it? ye are even my witnesses. Is there a God beside me? yea, there is no God; I know not any.

Joel 2:27 - And ye shall know that I am in the midst of Israel, and that I am the Lord your God, and none else: and my people shall never be ashamed.

1 Corinthians 8:6 - For though there be that are called gods, whether in heaven or in earth, (as there be gods many, and lords many,) But to us there is but one God, the Father, of whom are all things, and we in him; and one Lord Jesus Christ, by whom are all things, and we by him.

1 Timothy 2:5 - For there is one God, and one mediator between God and men, the man Christ Jesus;

James 2:19a - Thou believest that there is one God; thou doest well

The testimony of scripture is abundantly clear that there is only one God; and that God is the LORD, also known as Jehovah. The Hebrew Roots movement agrees with this concept, and this is their objection to the Trinity doctrine, erroneously supposing that such is equivalent to polytheism. However, as shall be shown you, the Trinity, which is indeed Biblical, is not the doctrine that there is more than one God, but only one God who exists as three persons. There are many objections to this which vary in nature, but by the end of this section, the only way for one to deny this truth is just to completely deny what the Bible says.

The first piece of evidence that the One God is more than one person is that God occasionally speaks using plural pronouns, especially in the book of

Genesis. The Bible says,

> Genesis 1:26 - And God said, Let us make man in our image, after our likeness: and let them have dominion over the fish of the sea, and over the fowl of the air, and over the cattle, and over all the earth, and over every creeping thing that creepeth upon the earth.

> Genesis 3:22 - And the Lord God said, Behold, the man is become as one of us, to know good and evil: and now, lest he put forth his hand, and take also of the tree of life, and eat, and live for ever:

> Genesis 11:7 - And the Lord said, Behold, the people is one, and they have all one language; and this they begin to do: and now nothing will be restrained from them, which they have imagined to do. Go to, let us go down, and there confound their language, that they may not understand one another's speech.

> Isaiah 6:8 - Also I heard the voice of the Lord, saying, Whom shall I send, and who will go for us? Then said I, Here am I; send me.

In several instances God says 'us', and 'our.' There are two common objections to this by Trinity-deniers: the first is utterly absurd and blasphemous, and supposes that God is speaking to the angels. Genesis 1:26 does not allow for this interpretation at all: because God says "Let us make man in our image." Are the angels in the image of God, and did the angels create anything? The Bible teaches that "in six days the LORD made the heaven and earth, the sea, and all that in them is (Exo. 20:11)." God is the creator of man, not any angels.

The second interpretation is equally absurd, and is the same lame argument used by the Muslims and Jews to attack the teachings of the New Testament: claiming that this is a use of the plural majesty, also known as the 'royal we.' The idea is that this is just an expression of God's power, and that the use of these plural pronouns emphasize that God is greater than all. There are several issues with this interpretation: firstly, this claim is based on the tendency of certain monarchs throughout history to do the same. However, there's no evidence that this was practiced before the Middle Ages. It began in Europe shortly after the fall of the Roman Empire among bishops and then among kings; but there's no evidence of this practice existing in the ancient Near East.

Another issue with this interpretation is that it creates the question: why didn't God always speak with plural pronouns? Why is it limited to only a few times, most of which involve the creation and great miracles of distant past? In fact, one of these instances, Genesis 3:22, seems to indicate that indeed God was speaking to another person: the LORD says "the man is become as one of us." It makes no sense to say 'one of us,' if there's only a single person. For example, if I were to say, "one of us has to go to the store," this would only make sense if there were two or more people. Claiming otherwise is grammatically impossible.

The word used for God constantly in the Old Testament is Elohim, who used the pronoun 'us' while in Hebrew, the verbs remained conjugated in the singular. The fact that the subject and pronoun are plural but the verb is singular demonstrates that there is more than one person, but they act collectively. Some will turn this on its head by claiming that since there's only a singular verb in this case, this means that 'Elohim' despite being plural, is again just a title of respect. However, there are several examples in the scriptures of there being plural pronouns when referring to the one God. For example, in Genesis 35:7, it says "there God appeared unto him." In Hebrew, the verb appeared, is נִגְלוּ (niglu), which is plural and not singular.

Again, in 2 Samuel 7:23, it's written, "God went to redeem a people for himself", and in Hebrew, the verb *halakh* is conjugated as *halakhu* (הָלְכוּ). This letter 'vav' on the end, which appears also in Gen. 35:7, and other places, such as Psa. 58:12, indicate a verb which is plural. If you don't believe me, go and search for other verses which use the same exact Hebrew words, and you'll see that the subject is plural.

Therefore, the fact that Elohim is called Elohim and not the singular "Eloah" shows that God is not just one. This is again, bolstered by the fact that the LORD uses plural pronouns in the Old Testament. Even in one case, as we read earlier in Isaiah 6:8, the LORD switches between a singular and plural pronoun in the same sentence. If this was just meant to be a plural majesty, then why was it not consistently plural? There's no explanation; the deniers of the Trinity just want to read an interpretation into the text instead of accepting the crystal-clear statements which show the plurality of the LORD.

Additional proof which can be found in the Old Testament is by the abundance of appearances of God which point us to a revelation of who the

LORD is. Firstly, let's start with a simple claim by God, and analyze this in the light of many other scriptures:

> Exodus 33:20 - And he said, Thou canst not see my face: for there shall no man see me, and live.

God says to Moses that no man can see him and live. This is a simple statement, and is quite difficult to misinterpret. This truth is repeated in the New Testament. Jesus said this several times about God the Father, and so did the apostles, that nobody had seen him:

> John 1:18 - No man hath seen God at any time, the only begotten Son, which is in the bosom of the Father, he hath declared him.

> John 5:37 - And the Father himself, which hath sent me, hath borne witness of me. Ye have neither heard his voice at any time, nor seen his shape.

> John 6:46 - Not that any man hath seen the Father, save he which is of God, he hath seen the Father.

> 1 Timothy 6:16 - Who only hath immortality, dwelling in the light which no man can approach unto; whom no man hath seen, nor can see: to whom be honour and power everlasting. Amen.

> 1 John 4:12 - No man hath seen God at any time. If we love one another, God dwelleth in us, and his love is perfected in us.

The majority of the Hebrew Roots movement which holds to either a Socinian (denying any divinity) or Arian view (believing Jesus was the first creation, but not God) believe that only the Father is God. I used verses like this when I denied the Trinity myself; the argument is that since there's no doubt that the Father is God, and since the Bible says nobody had seen the Father, and nobody had seen God, and since Jesus was indeed seen, this meant that Jesus was not God. It is indeed true that no man has ever seen God the Father. However, there are numerous times in which God appears and is seen. For example, in the very same chapter that God says to Moses, "for there shall no man see me, and live," it also says,

> Exodus 33:11 - And it came to pass, as Moses entered into the tabernacle, the cloudy pillar descended, and stood at the door of the

> tabernacle, and the Lord talked with Moses. And all the people saw the cloudy pillar stand at the tabernacle door: and all the people rose up and worshipped, every man in his tent door. <u>And the Lord spake unto Moses face to face,</u> as a man speaketh unto his friend. And he turned again into the camp: but his servant Joshua, the son of Nun, a young man, departed not out of the tabernacle.

Some key details here include that after the LORD descended in this pillar of cloud, it says that "the LORD spake unto Moses face to face." How can the LORD speak to Moses 'face to face' if Moses is not able to see the LORD's face? If unitarianism were indeed true, there would be here a contradiction in scripture. However, in light of the Trinity doctrine, this makes perfect sense. Consider the following story in which a very similar thing occurs, and notice what God says:

> Numbers 12:5-8 - And the Lord came down <u>in the pillar of the cloud, and stood in the door of the tabernacle,</u> and called Aaron and Miriam: and they both came forth. And he said, Hear now my words: If there be a prophet among you, I the Lord will make myself known unto him in a vision, and will speak unto him in a dream. My servant Moses is not so, who is faithful in all mine house. With him will <u>I speak mouth to mouth, even apparently, and not in dark speeches; and the similitude of the Lord shall he behold</u>: wherefore then were ye not afraid to speak against my servant Moses?

Here the LORD descends in a pillar of cloud, just as in Exodus 33, and it says that he 'stood in the door of the tabernacle.' This shows that there is an actual person standing before the tabernacle. Miriam and Aaron approach him, and he speaks to them, telling them that he will speak to Moses, "mouth to mouth," and that Moses will behold "the similitude of the LORD." Pay close attention to the language used here. Firstly, 'mouth to mouth' is very similar to the phrase 'face to face.' We know that this refers to a literal, direct interaction between God and Moses, since he says in the next breath that Moses will behold the similitude of the LORD. The word 'similitude' means "form" or "likeness." Essentially, God is telling Miriam and Aaron that Moses will see what he looks like. Notice that the LORD speaks in the third person here: he doesn't say "my similtude," but rather, "the similitude of the LORD," despite speaking in the first person several times in this passage.

So the question is, what does God mean by "the similitude of the LORD?" Well, if we understand the consistency between the Old and New Testaments, it's not difficult to figure out what the LORD is talking about. Jesus Christ is called "the image of the invisible God (Col. 1:15)," and it is written that he is "the brightness of his glory, and the express image of his person (Heb. 1:3)." Jesus Christ the Son is certainly the similitude, or express image, of God the Father. This is evidently why it is written, "No man hath seen God at any time; the only-begotten Son, which is in the bosom of the Father, he hath declared him (John 1:18)."

Understanding the two persons mentioned in John 1:18, we see a contrast between the Father and the Son Jesus Christ: the Father has not been seen, but the Son was the one who declared him. This means that in the Old Testament, all figures which are seen by the prophets and others are Jesus Christ the Son of God, and not the Father. This makes sense, considering that God said to Moses that "no man shall see me, and live." Yet, we saw an example of God speaking to Moses face to face, and another example in which the LORD says that he will speak to Moses directly. Not only that, but back in Exodus 24:10, it is written that the elders of Israel "saw the God of Israel." The only logical explanation of this, from the verses we've already seen, is not that they saw the Father (since nobody can see him and live), but that they saw the Son: and thus, we know that the Son is God.

This of course, may still not be enough to convince the hard-hearted deniers of the Bible's teachings. Yet this does not just appear in the book of Exodus, but is a recurring theme in the Bible, especially even in the Torah which the Hebrew Roots movement will lift up. After God speaks in his plural pronouns at the beginning of the book, we see an example of the Son's personhood as the LORD in Genesis 18-19. Consider the following passage:

> Genesis 18:1-3 - And the Lord appeared unto him in the plains of Mamre: and he sat in the tent door in the heat of the day; And he lift up his eyes and looked, and, lo, three men stood by him: and when he saw them, he ran to meet them from the tent door, and bowed himself toward the ground, And said, My Lord, if now I have found favour in thy sight, pass not away, I pray thee, from thy servant:

Again, pay attention to what the text says. In verse 1, the subject is identified as the LORD. It says "the LORD appeared unto him in the plains of

Mamre." In the very next verse, it describes three men approaching Abraham. Who are these three men? If we read the remainder of the story, it becomes clear. In verse 22 and 19:1, the Bible says,

> Genesis 18:22 - And the men turned their faces from thence, and went toward Sodom: but Abraham stood yet before the Lord.

> Genesis 19:1 - And there came two angels to Sodom at even; and Lot sat in the gate of Sodom: and Lot seeing them rose up to meet them; and he bowed himself with his face toward the ground;

Basic math is needed to understand this concept: in verse 2 of Genesis 18, it says that there are three men which appear to Abraham; this follows the revelation that the LORD appeared to Abraham. In verse 22, it says that the men left toward Sodom, and in the beginning of chapter 19, it specifies that these men are two angels. Therefore, it says again in verse 22 that "Abraham stood yet before the LORD." So, in the beginning, there were three men, two were angels that went to Sodom, and therefore left one person, who is clearly called the LORD.

This once again fits with what we saw in Exodus 33: a person called the LORD does indeed appear before Abraham, and Abraham speaks with him, despite not being able to see the Father. The story of Sodom and Gomorrah goes on to say in verse 24: "The LORD rained upon Sodom and upon Gomorrah brimstone and fire from the LORD out of heaven." Here the LORD is clearly referred to as two persons: one is on earth with Abraham, as we've already seen, while the LORD remains in heaven, the source of the fire and brimstone. The former is the Son, while the latter is the Father.

Later in the book of Genesis, we see another Old Testament appearance of Christ. This one is very similar with a later appearance in the book of Judges, both of which we will analyze:

> Genesis 32:24-30 - And Jacob was left alone; and there wrestled a man with him until the breaking of the day. And when he saw that he prevailed not against him, he touched the hollow of his thigh; and the hollow of Jacob's thigh was out of joint, as he wrestled with him. And he said, Let me go, for the day breaketh. And he said, I will not let thee go, except thou bless me. And he said unto him, What is thy name? And he said, Jacob. And he said, Thy name shall be called no more Jacob,

but Israel: for as a prince hast thou power with God and with men, and hast prevailed. And Jacob asked him, and said, Tell me, I pray thee, thy name. And he said, Wherefore is it that thou dost ask after my name? And he blessed him there. And Jacob called the name of the place Peniel: for I have seen God face to face, and my life is preserved.

This story has several similarities to that which happened to Jacob's grandfather Abraham. First, it tells us that there was a man, but as we continue to read on, several key details show us that this was more than a mere man. This 'man' which appeared to Jacob now gives him the name of Israel. Why is he named Israel? Because he hast power with God and with men, and hast prevailed. This makes sense, because the name Israel simply means "struggle with God." Now, it would be completely absurd to just ignore the context and the fact that Jacob was literally just wrestling and struggling with this figure. Why would this 'man' appear to Jacob, wrestle with him, and then give him a name which means 'struggle with God' if he were not God? If this isn't clear enough, the prophet Hosea refers back to this event:

> Hosea 12:3-4 - He took his brother by the heel in the womb, and by his strength he had power with God: Yea, he had power over the angel, and prevailed: he wept, and made supplication unto him: he found him in Bethel, and there he spake with us;

Notice in verse 3 that Hosea first says that Jacob had 'power with God,' the meaning of Israel, and in the very next verse, says that he 'had power over the angel.' Therefore, the figure which appeared to Jacob is referred to as an angel, meaning messenger, as well, despite being clearly called God. Even Jacob got the picture, and for this reason, calls the place Peniel, "For I have seen God face to face." Notice that this is the same language used in the book of Exodus to describe how Moses spake to God. Both the elders of Israel and Moses talked directly to and saw the God of Israel, and they were not the first. Jacob had experienced the same thing. In addition, just a few chapters later in the book of Genesis, the Bible says,

> Genesis 35:9-10 - And God appeared unto Jacob again, when he came out of Padanaram, and blessed him. And God said unto him, Thy name is Jacob: thy name shall not be called any more Jacob, but Israel shall be thy name: and he called his name Israel.

Notice that it says that God appeared unto Jacob again; and this time, when God appears to him, he says the same thing that the 'man' which appeared to him said, and gave him the name of Israel. After blessing Jacob, the scriptures say "God went up from him in the place where he talked with him (Gen. 35:13)," which shows us that God was literally there, standing before Jacob and speaking to him. Therefore, we can conclude that the person who wrestled with Jacob was indeed God, and yet Jacob saw him. Again, if God is only one person, how can this be so, since God said, "no man shall see my face and live?"

There is a very similar parallel passage in the Bible where the same exact figure appears, to another person, named Manoah, the father of Samson, and to his wife. The Bible records in the book of Judges,

> Judges 13:3-6 - And the angel of the Lord appeared unto the woman, and said unto her, Behold now, thou art barren, and bearest not: but thou shalt conceive, and bear a son. Now therefore beware, I pray thee, and drink not wine nor strong drink, and eat not any unclean thing: For, lo, thou shalt conceive, and bear a son; and no razor shall come on his head: for the child shall be a Nazarite unto God from the womb: and he shall begin to deliver Israel out of the hand of the Philistines. Then the woman came and told her husband, saying, A man of God came unto me, and his countenance was like the countenance of an angel of God, very terrible: but I asked him not whence he was, neither told he me his name:

> Judges 13:9-22 - And God hearkened to the voice of Manoah; and the angel of God came again unto the woman as she sat in the field: but Manoah her husband was not with her. And the woman made haste, and ran, and shewed her husband, and said unto him, Behold, the man hath appeared unto me, that came unto me the other day. And Manoah arose, and went after his wife, and came to the man, and said unto him, Art thou the man that spakest unto the woman? And he said, I am. And Manoah said, Now let thy words come to pass. How shall we order the child, and how shall we do unto him? And the angel of the Lord said unto Manoah, Of all that I said unto the woman let her beware. She may not eat of any thing that cometh of the vine, neither let her drink wine or strong drink, nor eat any unclean thing: all that I commanded her let her observe. And Manoah said unto the angel of the Lord, I

pray thee, let us detain thee, until we shall have made ready a kid for thee. And the angel of the Lord said unto Manoah, Though thou detain me, I will not eat of thy bread: and if thou wilt offer a burnt offering, thou must offer it unto the Lord. For Manoah knew not that he was an angel of the Lord. And Manoah said unto the angel of the Lord, What is thy name, that when thy sayings come to pass we may do thee honour? And the angel of the Lord said unto him, <u>Why askest thou thus after my name, seeing it is secret</u>? So Manoah took a kid with a meat offering, and offered it upon a rock unto the Lord: and the angel did wonderously; and Manoah and his wife looked on. For it came to pass, when the flame went up toward heaven from off the altar, that the angel of the Lord ascended in the flame of the altar. And Manoah and his wife looked on it, and fell on their faces to the ground. But the angel of the Lord did no more appear to Manoah and to his wife. Then Manoah knew that he was an angel of the Lord. And Manoah said unto his wife, <u>We shall surely die, because we have seen God.</u>

A very similar story is shown in this passage to what we see in Genesis 32. Firstly, this figure that appears to Manoah and his wife is called both 'a man' and 'the angel of the LORD.' Note that these identifications are not just given by Manoah, but by the author of the text as well. The writer says that Manoah "came to the man." So, just like with Jacob, this person is called both a man and the angel of the LORD. However, there are several clues in this text about the identity of this man. Firstly, in verse 18, after Manoah asks the name of the angel, he replies by saying, "Why askest thou thus after my name, seeing it is secret?" which is almost exactly the same reply the man who wrestled with Jacob gave.

Thus, we've determined from the scriptural evidence that God appeared to Jacob and wrestled with him. Here in Judges 13, the same person appears, and again, Manoah recognizes that they have seen God, and are afraid that they will die because they had seen him; just as God had told Moses, that "no man shall see me and live." Yet they do not die. Why is this? Because this is God the Son, not God the Father.

What does the angel's refusal to reveal his name show to us? The New Testament tells us that the name of Jesus was given to Mary and Joseph before Christ's conception (Matt. 1:21, Luke 1:31). We see also that it is written "there is none other name under heaven given among men whereby we must be saved (Acts 4:12)," and that "God also hath highly exalted him, and given him a name which is above every name (Phil. 2:9)." Prior to Christ's incarnation, the name Jesus was not yet given to us. Rather, under the old testament people referred to God as the LORD or Jehovah. Therefore, it makes sense that this person is Jesus Christ.

Other Old Testament appearances of Christ show to us his amazing glory. We've already seen from numerous scriptures that there is a man which appears to Old Testament men, and who is called God and the LORD in several instances. We already know that men have seen God, despite the Bible telling us repeatedly that no man can see the Father. Instead, as was told to Miriam and Moses, they saw the 'similitude of the LORD.' Since the New Testament tells us clearly that Jesus is the "brightness of his glory, and the express image of his person (Heb. 1:3)," there should be no doubt about who this is that Moses and others spake face to face with. Ezekiel also saw the Son:

> Ezekiel 1:26-28 - And above the firmament that was over their heads was the likeness of a throne, as the appearance of a sapphire stone: and upon the likeness of the throne was the likeness as the appearance of a man above upon it. And I saw as the colour of amber, as the appearance of fire round about within it, from the appearance of his loins even upward, and from the appearance of his loins even downward, I saw as it were the appearance of fire, and it had brightness round about. As the appearance of the bow that is in the cloud in the day of rain, so was the appearance of the brightness round about. This was the appearance of the likeness of the glory of the Lord. And when I saw it, I fell upon my face, and I heard a voice of one that spake.

In the beginning of the book of Ezekiel, he sees this amazing vision, and in the vision, he sees "the appearance of a man" sitting in a throne above him. So far, we have two details: first of all, the one sitting in a throne looks like a man, and second, Ezekiel is able to see him. We already can see that this cannot be God the Father. The passages continues with a description of this man in the throne, and the description includes the details that surrounding him is fire and brightness. Ezekiel then writes in verse 28, "this was the appearance of the likeness of the glory of the Lord." Remember, likeness is a synonym for similitude. Essentially, Ezekiel is writing that he is beholding himself the similitude of the LORD, and describing his glory. This same person appears several additional times in the book of Ezekiel:

Ezekiel 3:23 - Then I arose, and went forth into the plain: and, behold, the glory of the LORD stood there, as the glory which I saw by the river of Chebar: and I fell on my face.

Ezekiel 8:2-5 - Then I beheld, and lo a likeness as the appearance of fire: from the appearance of his loins even downward, fire; and from his loins even upward, as the appearance of brightness, as the colour of amber. And he put forth the form of an hand, and took me by a lock of mine head; and the spirit lifted me up between the earth and the heaven, and brought me in the visions of God to Jerusalem, to the door of the inner gate that looketh toward the north; where was the seat of the image of jealousy, which provoketh to jealousy. And, behold, the glory of the God of Israel was there, according to the vision that I saw in the plain. Then said he unto me, Son of man, lift up thine eyes now the way toward the north. So I lifted up mine eyes the way toward the north, and behold northward at the gate of the altar this image of jealousy in the entry.

Ezekiel 10:4 - Then the glory of the LORD went up from the cherub, and stood over the threshold of the house; and the house was filled with the cloud, and the court was full of the brightness of the LORD'S glory.

Ezekiel 43:2-5 - And, behold, the glory of the God of Israel came from the way of the east: and his voice was like a noise of many waters: and the earth shined with his glory. And it was according to the appearance of the vision which I saw, even according to the vision that I saw when I came to destroy the city: and the visions were like the vision that I saw by the river Chebar; and I fell upon my face. 4nd the glory of the LORD came into the house by the way of the gate whose prospect is toward the east. So the spirit took me up, and brought me into the inner court; and, behold, the glory of the LORD filled the house.

Notice the details written throughout the book. The person who appeared in the throne above Ezekiel is constantly called "the glory of the God of Israel" or "the glory of the LORD." In Ezekiel 8, the same description is given as in chapter 1: that there is fire and brightness around this man, and that this glory which proceeded outward from this man, the one who sat in the throne, filled the whole house of God. Now, notice the details used to describe this man, including in Ezek. 43:2, where it says, "his voice was like a noise of many waters." Now, compare to the following two passages:

> Daniel 10:5-6 - Then I lifted up mine eyes, and looked, and behold a certain man clothed in linen, whose loins were girded with fine gold of Uphaz: His body also was like the beryl, <u>and his face as the appearance of lightning, and his eyes as lamps of fire, and his arms and his feet like in colour to polished brass</u>, and the voice of his words like the voice of a multitude.

> Revelation 1:13-18 - And in the midst of the seven candlesticks one like unto the Son of man, clothed with a garment down to the foot, and girt about the paps with a golden girdle. His head and his hairs were white like wool, as white as snow; and his eyes were as a flame of fire; And his feet like unto fine brass, as if they burned in a furnace; and <u>his voice as the sound of many waters.</u> And he had in his right hand seven stars: and out of his mouth went a sharp twoedged sword: and <u>his countenance was as the sun shineth in his strength</u>. And when I saw him, I fell at his feet as dead. And he laid his right hand upon me, saying unto me, Fear not; I am the first and the last: I am he that liveth, and was dead; and, behold, I am alive for evermore, Amen; and have the keys of hell and of death.

In Ezekiel 1, the prophet see a man who sits in a throne, called the glory of the LORD, whose body is like the appearance of amber, and who is surrounded with brightness and fire. In Daniel, we see again, a man who appears with a body shining like a precious stone, who's countenance is bright, and whose arms and legs look like polished metal. Now, in Revelation, we see almost the exact same description. This time, we know undoubtedly who the subject is: Jesus Christ. In verse 13 he is called the Son of man, and in verse 18, he says "I am he that liveth, and was dead." We of course know that this refers to Jesus' resurrection.

The other detail is that when Jesus Christ appears to John in Revelation 1, it says "his voice as the sound of many waters." This is the exact same description used in Ezekiel 1 to described 'the glory of the God of Israel.' This makes sense when one considers the Biblical truth that Jesus is the brightness of God's glory (Heb. 1:3). Therefore, we know that the person Ezekiel saw by the river Chebar, who is called "the likeness of the glory of the LORD," is none other than Jesus Christ, and we thus understand that this is the same similitude of God which appeared to Moses, and who is still called by the name of the LORD.

The book of Isaiah, which is filled with proofs of the Trinity, reveals another Old Testament appearance of Christ quite early in the book. In Isaiah 6, it says,

> Isaiah 6:1-10 - In the year that king Uzziah died I saw also the Lord sitting upon a throne, high and lifted up, and his train filled the temple. Above it stood the seraphims: each one had six wings; with twain he covered his face, and with twain he covered his feet, and with twain he did fly. And one cried unto another, and said, Holy, holy, holy, is the Lord of hosts: the whole earth is full of his glory. And the posts of the door moved at the voice of him that cried, and the house was filled with smoke. Then said I, Woe is me! for I am undone; because I am a man of unclean lips, and I dwell in the midst of a people of unclean lips: for mine eyes have seen the King, the Lord of hosts. Then flew one of the seraphims unto me, having a live coal in his hand, which he had taken with the tongs from off the altar: And he laid it upon my mouth, and said, Lo, this hath touched thy lips; and thine iniquity is taken away, and thy sin purged. Also I heard the voice of the Lord, saying, Whom shall I send, and who will go for us? Then said I, Here am I; send me. And he said, Go, and tell this people, Hear ye indeed, but understand not; and see ye indeed, but perceive not. Make the heart of this people fat, and make their ears heavy, and shut their eyes; lest they see with their eyes, and hear with their ears, and understand with their heart, and convert, and be healed.

The reason why this scripture is so important is because John specifically declares that this person sitting on the throne, called the Lord, and around whom the seraphim say, "Holy, holy, holy, is the LORD of hosts: the whole earth is full of his glory", is Jesus. After the Pharisees rejected Christ and refused to believe on him, it is written,

> John 12:39-41 - Therefore they could not believe, because that Esaias said again, He hath blinded their eyes, and hardened their heart; that they should not see with their eyes, nor understand with their heart,

and be converted, and I should heal them. These things said Esaias, when he saw his glory, and spake of him.

Here it quotes from Isaiah 6, and John says, "These things said Esaias, when he saw his glory, and spake of him." Jesus Christ was seen by the prophet Isaiah, and it was him who sat upon the throne above all, full of glory, just as Ezekiel and Daniel saw. There's no doubt that Jesus is God. Yet this may still not convince those in the Hebrew Roots movement. However, as we continue to go through the book of Isaiah, it should be abundantly clear that Jesus is divine. Consider the next passage,

> Isaiah 9:6-7 For unto us a child is born, unto us a son is given: and the government shall be upon his shoulder: and his name shall be called Wonderful, Counsellor, The mighty God, The everlasting Father, The Prince of Peace. Of the increase of his government and peace there shall be no end, upon the throne of David, and upon his kingdom, to order it, and to establish it with judgment and with justice from henceforth even for ever. The zeal of the Lord of hosts will perform this.

Here is a prophecy of Jesus Christ; this is evident by the fact that this refers to a child being born into the world, who, according to verse 7, is going to sit upon the throne of David and establish his kingdom forever. The angel said to Mary of Jesus, "He shall be great, and shall be called the Son of the Highest: and the Lord God shall give unto him the throne of his father David: And he shall reign over the house of Jacob for ever; and of his kingdom there shall be no end (Luke 1:32-33)." There's no doubt who the subject of this prophecy is.

Here the Messiah is clearly called 'the Mighty God.' In the Hebrew Roots movement I attempted to make all kinds of excuses for why this did not identify Jesus as God, and I hear all kinds of excuses from unitarians even now. However, if one continues to read the book of Isaiah, there should be no confusion about what God is saying. In the very next chapter, it is written,

> Isaiah 10:20-21 - And it shall come to pass in that day, that the remnant of Israel, and such as are escaped of the house of Jacob, shall no more again stay upon him that smote them; but shall stay upon the Lord, the Holy One of Israel, in truth. The remnant shall return, even the remnant of Jacob, unto the mighty God.

Here it is clear, "the mighty God" is the LORD, the Holy One of Israel. This verse uses the same Hebrew phrase, El Gibbor, as in Isaiah 9:6. Therefore, Isaiah 9:6 tells us that a child would be born into the world who is called by a name which is given to the LORD. God didn't want us to mistake what he was saying: that He would be born into the world, that is, Jesus, who is God, who is the LORD, the Holy One of Israel. We're not done yet, however. The book of Isaiah is still jam-packed with other references to the Trinity. Consider the next passage:

> Isaiah 35:4-5 - Say to them that are of a fearful heart, Be strong, fear not: behold, your God will come with vengeance, even God with a recompence; he will come and save you. Then the eyes of the blind shall be opened, and the ears of the deaf shall be unstopped.

Here is a prophecy that God will come, "and save you." Is not Jesus Christ the one who saves, according to the New Testament? Not only that, but if Jesus Christ is not God in the flesh, how could it be said that God will come and save us? Indeed, we did see this to happen, as shall be shown later when we examine the New Testament. This particular prophecy is expounded upon later,

> Isaiah 40:3-5 - The voice of him that crieth in the wilderness, Prepare ye the way of the Lord, make straight in the desert a highway for our God. Every valley shall be exalted, and every mountain and hill shall be made low: and the crooked shall be made straight, and the rough places plain: And the glory of the Lord shall be revealed, and all flesh shall see it together: for the mouth of the Lord hath spoken it.

This is interesting because this passage is quoted both by John the Baptist himself and the gospel writers, in all four of the gospel records (Matt. 3:3, Mark 1:3, Luke 3:4). John even said when the Jews asked him "Who art thou?," "I am the voice of one crying in the wilderness, Make straight the way of the Lord, as said the prophet Esaias (John 1:23)." Now, in the Old Testament reference here in Isaiah 40, 'the LORD' is written in Hebrew as Jehovah. Therefore, John the Baptist, who fulfilled this, was the one preparing the way for Jehovah, and the way "for our God."

Yet if one reads the New Testament, it's evident that John the Baptist was the one preparing the way for Jesus Christ, who literally came after him, and who John pointed to. Therefore, if we just read the scriptures and what they say of the Lord, we see that Jesus Christ is God. Verse 5 in this passage even says that all flesh shall see the glory of the LORD. As we've already seen in many passages, the only way men have ever seen the glory of God is in the person of Jesus Christ, who is "the brightness of his glory (Heb. 1:3)." Consider the next passage:

> Isaiah 48:16-17 - Come ye near unto me, hear ye this; I have not spoken in secret from the beginning; from the time that it was, there am I: and now the Lord God, and his Spirit, hath sent me. Thus saith the Lord, thy Redeemer, the Holy One of Israel; I am the Lord thy God which teacheth thee to profit, which leadeth thee by the way that thou shouldest go.

Here, it is evident that the LORD is speaking, as shown by verses 12 and 13, where the speaker says, "I am he; I am the first, I am also the last," which is the same thing God had said repeatedly in the previous chapters (Isa. 41:4, 44:6). The LORD is the one who is the first and the last, and it is the LORD here who says, "the LORD God, and his Spirit, hath sent me." How can God and his Spirit send God, unless there is more than one person? In the context of the New Testament, we know that Jesus said in several instances that the Father had sent him (John 5:30, 36-37, 6:39, 44, 57, 8:16, 18, 42, 12:49, 14:24, 17:21). Understanding this and the multitudes of scriptures we've already seen, it becomes evident that when the LORD speaks here, this is the Son, Jesus Christ, and that the LORD God who sends him is the Father.

Now take the most famous messianic prophecy in the book of Isaiah, in Isaiah 53, which describes the crucifixion and resurrection of the Messiah, called the righteous servant, who shall "justify many (v. 11)." The details given in this chapter and the surrounding chapters show us exactly who this is speaking of. For example, in verse 1, it says, "To whom is the arm of the LORD revealed?" Several verses in the book of Isaiah reveal the arm of the LORD to be the Messiah. For example, in Isaiah 51:5, it says "on mine arm shall they trust." In Isaiah 59:16 it says, "there was no intercessor: therefore his arm brought salvation unto him; and his righteousness, it sustained him."

In Isaiah 52, the previous chapter, it says, " The Lord hath made bare his holy arm in the eyes of all the nations; and all the ends of the earth shall see the salvation of our God (Isa. 52:10)." We see here that the holy arm of God is associated with the salvation of God (and of course, the Hebrew Roots movement is abundantly aware that Yeshua means salvation). So, by taking into account all these scriptures, we see that it is the holy arm of the LORD which brings salvation, and that this of course refers to the servant written of in Isaiah 53. Of this same servant the Bible says that he shall "justify many (Isa. 53:11)."

However, in the very same book where we read about this, the Bible says, "I am the LORD thy God, the Holy One of Israel, thy Saviour (Isaiah 43:4)," "I, even I, am the LORD; and beside me there is no saviour (Isa. 43:11), "Israel shall be saved in the LORD with an everlasting salvation (Isa. 45:17), "Look unto me, and be ye saved, all the ends of the earth: for I am God, and there is none else (Isa. 45:21)." In Isaiah 59, just before talking about Israel's iniquities and transgressions, God says, "Behold, the LORD's hand is not shortened, that it cannot save (Isaiah 59:1)." In Psalm 38:22 David calls the LORD 'my salvation.' In Psalm 62, it says "He only is my rock and my salvation."

In Isaiah 45:25, it says also "In the LORD shall all the seed of Israel be justified." In Isaiah 50:10, God says, "let him trust in the name of the LORD." In Psalm 37:40 it says, "And the LORD shall help them, and deliver them: he shall deliver them from the wicked, and save them, because they trust in him." Just as the New Testament constantly shows us that we are to believe on the Lord Jesus Christ for our salvation, the Old Testament uses that same principle, but always refers to the subject of our belief as the LORD. Thus, analyzing the latter section of the book of Isaiah, we see here that both the LORD and the righteous servant of God are said to bring salvation and be a saviour, both justify, and both we are to trust on.

Why is this? Because the righteous servant is God. That's exactly why in Isaiah 48 the LORD said that the LORD sent him; the former is the Christ, and the latter is the Father. Jesus Christ has always been God, and this is the truth which the Bible shows us repeatedly. So far all we've looked at is the Old Testament, at the repeated references to the second person of the Trinity. Even when the Old Testmant prophecies the birth of Jesus Christ in Bethlehem, it is written that "his goings forth have been of old, from everlasting (Micah 5:2)." Christ has always been begotten of God, he has existed from eternity past with God the Father. This is why the book of John begins with the statement,

John 1:1 - In the beginning was the Word, and the Word was with God, and the Word was God.

Then, as we see later in the chapter: "The Word was made flesh, and dwelt among us (and we beheld his glory, the glory as of the only begotten of the Father), full of grace and truth (John 1:14)." This is Jesus, the only-begotten Son of God. He existed in the beginning, and according to verse 3, "All things were made by him; and without him was not any thing made that was made." This is the same testimony we have in the book of Colossians, where it again says of Jesus, that "by him were all things created, that are in heaven, and that are in earth, visible and invisible (Colossians 1:16)." Hebrews 1:2 tells us that the worlds were made through Jesus. Jesus Christ existed long before he came into this world, and he himself created the world. That's exactly why, as we've seen in the book of Genesis, God says, "Let US make man in OUR image." Not just one person was active in the creation of the world, but it was the Father, the Word, and the spirit (Psalm 33:6).

From eternity past, Jesus Christ has ruled as the LORD, and this is why the scriptures say of him, that "who, being in the form of God, thought it not robbery to be equal with God (Philippians 2:6)." The very next verse tells us that Jesus humbled himself and took the form of a servant, and was made in the likeness of men. This is the incarnation, the act in which the Mighty God, the Word, became flesh. The Bible says of this also:

1 Timothy 3:16 - And without controversy great is the mystery of godliness: God was manifest in the flesh, justified in the Spirit, seen of angels, preached unto the Gentiles, believed on in the world, received up into glory.

This is again probably one of the clearest verses which reveals to us the deity of Jesus Christ. I knew about this during my time in the Hebrew Roots movement, however, because of my objections to the Trinity, I couldn't help but make up excuses for why this wasn't true. My explanation came from an appeal to the corrupt manuscripts. The Alexandrian manuscripts (of which there are only 3 out of 5000+) write "He was manifest in the flesh" rather than "God was manifest in the flesh." The fact of the matter is that at least two of the manuscripts, the Codex Sinaiticus and Alexandrinus, originated in Alexandria, a place where Arianism (the heresy originating in the 4th century which denied the divinity of Jesus) was common. And, as already spoken of, there's abundant evidence that all of these manuscripts are garbage, since they not only contradict themselves and each other, but are filled with erasures and re-writings, have entire verses and sections missing, and have only been discovered recently, despite God's promise to preserve his word for all generations (Psalm 12:6-7).

Therefore, the argument that this shouldn't say God is impossible without appealing to corrupted manuscripts. If one sticks with the majority of manuscripts, not just in Greek but in all other languages the Bible had been translated into, one will find the word for God (*Theos* in Greek, for example). Therefore, this verse clearly references God being manifested in the flesh, which of course, is consistent with what we've already seen. The promise was made back in the book of Isaiah that a child would be born, who would be called the Mighty God, the same title applied to the LORD, the Holy One of Israel. And then John 1 tells us that the Word, which "was God" was made flesh. It makes perfect sense therefore, to say that God was revealed in the flesh, in the person of Jesus Christ. Consider the next verse as well:

> Romans 9:5 - Whose are the fathers, and of whom as concerning the flesh Christ came, who is over all, God blessed for ever. Amen.

Here again we have a clear reference to Christ being God. The verse calls Christ, "over all, God blessed for ever." This is once again, a difficult verse to argue with. In the Hebrew Roots movement, I simply put this off while attempting to look for an explanation, but could never find a satisfactory one. Another verse which shows the divinity of Jesus directly tells us that Jesus is not just God, but that the fulness of the Godhead dwells in him:

> Colossians 2:8-9 - Beware lest any man spoil you through philosophy and vain deceit, after the tradition of men, after the rudiments of the world, and not after Christ. For in him dwelleth all the fulness of the Godhead bodily.

The problem with understanding verse 9 is that many do not understand what the word "Godhead" means. For some odd reason, the assumption is that Godhead is some special term to refer to who God is. This is not true. The suffix '-head' is simply an older English way of saying "hood." Compare with the German suffix -heit and the Dutch suffix -heid. Head refers to a quality or nature. In saying that all of the fulness of the Godhead bodily dwells in Christ, Paul is literally telling us that the entirety of that which makes God 'divine' exists within Jesus Christ. Thus, from this verse, we know that it is not just a fact that Jesus is God, but that he is fully God. Another passage which interestingly refers to Jesus as God is not as clear, but upon looking closely to what it says, it should be clear. The Bible says in Hebrews 3,

> Hebrews 3:1-4 - Wherefore, holy brethren, partakers of the heavenly calling, consider the Apostle and High Priest of our profession, <u>Christ Jesus</u>; Who was faithful to him that appointed him, as also Moses was faithful in all his house. <u>For this man was counted worthy of more glory than Moses, inasmuch as he who hath builded the house hath more honour than the house. For every house is builded by some man; but he that built all things is God.</u>

Here we have two subjects: Christ Jesus and Moses. In verse 1, Christ Jesus is identified as the subject, and next, that "this man was counted worthy of more glory than Moses." Just by reading the context, the only man it could possibly be talking about is Christ Jesus, the only person mentioned in the preceding verses. Thus, we know that Jesus is counted worthy of more glory. It tells us why directly after this: "he who hath builded the house hath more honour than the house." So, why does Jesus have more glory than Moses? Because more honour should be given to the one who built the house than the house itself.

Verse 4 reveals the truth: that "every house is builded by some man; but he that built all things is God." So, here we have a progression; that Jesus is worthy of more glory than Moses, because the one who builds the house receives more glory than the house. In the next breath, Paul tells us that the one who builds all things is God. If we just take what the verse says, it's obvious that Christ Jesus is being called God, since God built all things, which would include the house of Moses. This was one of the verses which convinced me that Jesus was indeed Almighty God.

These evidences from both the Old and New Testament should be enough, but for some reason, some of those in the Hebrew Roots movement will raise the same objections that Muslims do (showing their lack of belief in the holy scriptures) by simply ignoring these passages and asking the question: What did Jesus teach? Did Jesus ever claim to be God? After all, none of what we've looked at so far came directly from the mouth of Jesus during his earthly ministry. So, did Jesus ever claim to be God while on this earth? The answer is absolutely, since he said,

> John 8:58 - Jesus said unto them, Verily, verily, I say unto you, Before Abraham was, I am.

This is perhaps one of the clearest remarks by Jesus identifying himself to be God, and is perhaps one of the most attacked verses. However, if we just take what Jesus said clearly and compare it with other scriptures, we know that Jesus is claiming to be Jehovah. First he starts off in the past tense, "Before Abraham was." Despite speaking of that which was past, he declares "I am." This Greek phrase, ἐγώ εἰμι (ego eimi) means exactly what it says in English.

Heretics who don't know anything about Greek, like the Jehovah's Witnesses, will erroneously translate this sometimes as "I have been." This simply doesn't make sense when you look at other instances of the term *ego eimi*. For example, in John 9:9, after the man who was born blind is healed, the people say "He is like him: but he said, I am he." It would simply make no sense for him to respond, "I have been," just like it doesn't make any sense in John 18:5, or the multiple other I am statements of Jesus (John 4:26, 6:20, 8:24, 8:28, 13:19, 15:1). However, these all differ from John 8:58 in that in this verse, Jesus declares "I am" right after telling the Jews "Before Abraham was."

Ego eimi, again, meaning I Am, is the same phrase used in the Greek translation of the Old Testament, the Septuagint, in Exodus 3:14. When Moses asks God his name, God replies, "I AM THAT I AM; and he said, Thus shalt thou say unto the children of Israel, I AM hath sent me to you." This is right before revealing the third-person form of the same name, Jehovah, to Moses, at the burning bush. By Jesus declaring "I am," he is directly declaring himself to be the God of the Old Testament. That's exactly why the Jews took up stones to stone him in the very next verse, because they knew exactly what he was saying.

Another evidence for Jesus' Godhead is the fact that only God can forgive sins. It is stated in the Gospels, "who can forgive sins but God alone (Mark 2:7)?" However, critics of this concept point to the fact that this question is raised by the scribes and Pharisees, and therefore is not true. However, their objection was entirely valid, since the scriptures tell us that only God forgives sins.

> Isaiah 43:25 - I, even I, am he that blotteth out thy transgressions for mine own sake, and will not remember thy sins.

It is stated in the Book of Isaiah that it is God who blots out transgressions. It tells us also in chapter 45 that it is in the LORD that Israel shall be justified. Yet we see Jesus forgiving sins and justifying men, and in the New Testament, that the remission of sins come through him. This would make no sense if Jesus were not God, if the scriptures show us that only God can remove sin. Another piece of evidence which shows the deity of Christ is the following:

> John 5:17-18 - But Jesus answered them, My Father worketh hitherto, and I work. Therefore the Jews sought the more to kill him, because he not only had broken the sabbath, but said also that God was his Father, making himself equal with God.

Notice that verse 18 is not the words of the Jews themselves, but the explanation given by the author of the book, which is John. John is saying that Jesus made himself equal with God by calling God his Father. This same thing happened when Jesus said, "I and my Father are one (John 10:30)." The Jews took up stones to stone him, and accused him of making himself equal with God, and Jesus never denied it. Rather, he quoted from Psalm 82:6, which calls human judges 'gods', and then compares these sinful men to whom the word of God came, to him, "whom the Father hath sanctified, and sent into the world (John 10:36)." This passage is exactly what the scriptures tell us: that Jesus was in the form of God, and thought it not robbery to be equal with God (Philippians 2:6).

Therefore, from all of these scriptures, we can see that Jesus Christ the Son is indeed equal with God, meaning that he is fully God himself. Both the Old and New Testaments show this, that there is more than one person; that besides the Father, there is the similitude of the LORD, the likeness of the glory of the LORD, who existed in the beginning with God, who is from everlasting and equal with God. This is what the Bible says about him; and this is just scratching the surface of the scriptures which delve into the deity of Christ. This isn't even to mention the abundance of Old Testament references which use the name of Jehovah, which are quoted in the New Testament as "Lord" in reference to Jesus Christ. For example, compare Joel

2:32 to Romans 10:13 - "Whosoever shall came upon the name of the Lord shall be saved."

The Holy Ghost is also God, a divine person just like the Father and Jesus Christ. This is another thing which Trinity deniers have trouble with, especially those in the Hebrew Roots movement who exalt the Father only. To them, the Ruach Ha-Kodesh is described similar to how the Jehovah's Witnesses describe the Spirit: as nothing more than an acting force or power of God, an emanation of the Father rather than a distinct person. This can be disproven easily by the scriptures. Consider the next scripture;

> Acts 5:3-4 - But Peter said, Ananias, why hath Satan filled thine heart to lie to the Holy Ghost, and to keep back part of the price of the land? Whiles it remained, was it not thine own? and after it was sold, was it not in thine own power? why hast thou conceived this thing in thine heart? thou hast not lied unto men, but unto God.

Here, when Peter rebukes Ananias, he first says that he has lied to the Holy Ghost, and then in the next verse, says "thou hast not lied unto men, but unto God." Therefore, we know that the Holy Ghost himself is God. However, some will still claim that the Holy Ghost is simply a part of a God. They scoff at the doctrine that the Holy Ghost is a person, despite the fact that the Bible uses male pronouns to refer to the Holy Ghost. Consider the following,

> John 14:16-17 - And I will pray the Father, and he shall give you another Comforter, that he may abide with you for ever; Even the Spirit of truth; whom the world cannot receive, because it seeth him not, neither knoweth him: but ye know him; for he dwelleth with you, and shall be in you.

> John 14:26 - But the Comforter, which is the Holy Ghost, whom the Father will send in my name, he shall teach you all things, and bring all things to your remembrance, whatsoever I have said unto you.

> John 15:26 - But when the Comforter is come, whom I will send unto you from the Father, even the Spirit of truth, which proceedeth from the Father, he shall testify of me.

> John 16:7-8 - Nevertheless I tell you the truth; It is expedient for you that I go away: for if I go not away, the Comforter will not come unto

you; but if I depart, I will send <u>him</u> unto you. And when <u>he</u> is come, <u>he</u> will reprove the world of sin, and of righteousness, and of judgment:

John 16:13-14 - Howbeit when he, the Spirit of truth, is come, <u>he</u> will guide you into all truth: for <u>he</u> shall not speak of himself; but whatsoever <u>he</u> shall hear, that shall <u>he</u> speak: and <u>he</u> will shew you things to come. <u>He</u> shall glorify me: for <u>he</u> shall receive of mine, and shall shew it unto you.

Over and over again Jesus refers to the Holy Ghost as 'he' and 'him.' These personal pronouns thus show us that the Holy Ghost, just as Peter shows in Acts 5, is a person, and is God. Further proof of this is in the descriptions of the attributes of the Spirit, which show us that the Holy Ghost has certain personal characteristics. We've already seen some in the above verses: that the Holy Ghost teaches, speaks, glorifies, and shows. These things are all examples of personal traits which demonstrate his personhood. Examine these other verses:

Acts 8:29 - Then the Spirit said unto Philip, Go near, and join thyself to this chariot.

Acts 10:19 - While Peter thought on the vision, the Spirit said unto him, Behold, three men seek thee.

Acts 13:2 - As they ministered to the Lord, and fasted, the Holy Ghost said, Separate me Barnabas and Saul for the work whereunto I have called them.

Acts 16:6-7 - Now when they had gone throughout Phrygia and the region of Galatia, and were forbidden of the Holy Ghost to preach the word in Asia, After they were come to Mysia, they assayed to go into Bithynia: but the Spirit suffered them not.

Romans 8:26-27 - Likewise the Spirit also helpeth our infirmities: for we know not what we should pray for as we ought: but the Spirit itself maketh intercession for us with groanings which cannot be uttered. And he that searcheth the hearts knoweth what is the mind of the Spirit, because he maketh intercession for the saints according to the will of God.

1 Corinthians 2:10 - But God hath revealed them unto us by his Spirit:

for the Spirit searcheth all things, yea, the deep things of God.

Here we see numerous examples of personal traits ascribed to the Holy Ghost. The things which the Holy Ghost does shows to us indeed that He is a person and not just some mystical force. The Holy Ghost speaks, he commands, he forbids, he searches the mind, he makes intercession for us, he teaches us, and has emotion. This is exactly what a person is.

Therefore, we come to the doctrine of the Trinity that the majority of those in the Hebrew Roots movement deny. The Bible teaches that there is one God, but that the Father, the Son, and the Holy Ghost are all separate persons, who are all called God. That is exactly what the Trinity is: some like to descibe it as a 'tri-unity.' However, we haven't even addressed the most obvious verse which teaches the Trinity, which summarizes all of the evidence in the scriptures we've already looked at:

> 1 John 5:7 - For there are three that bear record in heaven, the Father, the Word, and the Holy Ghost: and these three are one.

Here we have a clear reference to the Biblical fact that the Father, the Word (which is Christ, John 1:1, 14, Rev. 19:13), and the Holy Ghost, despite being three, are also one. They are three persons, but one God. There are two problems with understanding this verse: The first is an objection to what it teaches. Instead of just having the faith that the Word of God is true, deniers of the Trinity will object using man's wisdom. How can three be one? For me as a Hebrew Rootist, I scoffed at this doctrine because it didn't make sense to me.

The issue is that the Hebrew Roots movement and other Arians can't get past the traditional, pagan definition of God. Since the Bible declares that there's only one God, we should get our definition of what "God" is based on what the scriptures say, not what the world teaches. The Trinity is a unique doctrine to Christianity, while the heathen religions of this world hold to a different understanding of what the word 'god' means. For this reason the Hebrew Roots will accuse the Trinity of being paganism in disguise, claiming that it teaches tritheism; this argument comes from the inability to comprehend or accept that three persons can be one God, so they immediately jump to the faulty conclusion that we believe in three separate gods.

However, consider for a moment the beliefs of the polytheists and their triads of gods. Gods are considered to be different from each other not just based on the fact that they are different persons, but based on numerous other qualifications. For example, consider in Hinduism, that there is a triad known as the Trimurti, made up of Vishnu, Brahma, and Shiva. These, despite being a triad like the Trinity, are all different. They are depicted differently, are considered to have different origins, and have different roles: Brahma as creator, Vishnu as preserver, and Shiva as destroyer. In Greek religion, Zeus, Poseidon, and Hades are often grouped together. These are three brothers, but again, they have different origins and ages, they appear differently, have different roles and oversee different things.

However, based on the Biblical definition of the one God, the LORD, all things which make the Father God make the Son God as well. All three persons partake of the same Godhead, all three persons have existed from eternity and will exist for eternity, all three persons created the world, all three persons are omnipotent, all three persons are holy, and loving, and merciful, but also express justice, judgment, and wrath against wickedness. The three have an inter-relationship with each other; for example, Jesus said, "I am in the Father, and the Father in me (John 14:11)," and we know that the Holy Ghost dwelled in Christ as well (Acts 10:38)." Jesus said that he proceeded forth and came from God (John 8:42)," (which we know to be an eternal begetting (Micah 5:2)), and that the Holy Ghost proceeds from the Father (John 15:26)." The Son also is described as the express image of the person of the Father (Heb. 1:3).

Thus, the Trinity is not a teaching that there are three separate gods, but that there are three persons, and these three are one God: meaning they are all united in purpose, in creation, in divinity, in holiness, in omnipotence, in omniscience, in omnipresence, in power, in glory, and are in each other and proceed from each other, although they are in reality, all separate persons. This may be difficult to wrap our mind around, but understand, you in the Hebrew Roots movement, that this is not the only time the Bible says that more than one is one. Even in the second chapter of the Bible, it is written that a man and a wife are one flesh (Genesis 2:24), which Christ quotes as being "they twain shall be one flesh." A man and a wife remain separate persons at marriage, yet they are considered to be one flesh; likewise, God is three persons, but one God.

Besides this simple misunderstanding about what the Bible says, some will still fight against 1 John 5:7, one of the most powerful testaments to the Trinity doctrine, on the basis that they don't believe that this phrase, "the Father, the Word, and the Spirit: and these three are one" is authentic. This phrase is referred to as the Comma Johanneum, and is one of the most controversial verses in textual criticism. Many Greek manuscripts do not contain the Comma, which creates the claim that it was a later addition from the Middle Ages. However, I believe, for good reason, that the Comma is authentic, and it was mistakenly removed from many Greek manuscripts, an error which was perpetuated, although it remained intact in some writings.

The Textus Receptus of Stephanus, from which the King James Bible is translated, contains the Comma Johanneum because Erasmus, after careful study of the manuscript evidence, found that there was an abundance of evidence that the verse was not just a later invention, but had been in Bibles since antiquity. The oldest Greek manuscripts which we now have that contain the Comma are the Codex Ottbonianus, also known as miniscule 629, which is dated to the 14th century, and the Codex Montfortianus, from the early 16th century. However, when examining other language texts, it becomes clear that the verse existed in Greek long before, and was translated into Latin.

Several manuscripts from long before show the Comma Johanneum. One of these is the Latin manuscript known as the Leon Pampliset, from the 7th century. Examination of this text shows that in the 1st epistle of John, it follows the reading of the Old Latin text, known as the Vetus Latina, which was first translated from Greek as early as the 2nd or 3rd centuries. Another text, which is considered as older, is the Codex Frisengensis, dated from the 6th century, and which also follows the Old Latin reading. There are numerous other Latin manuscripts which contain 1 John 5:7, showing that this was not just a minority addition, but appeared in many ancient manuscripts.

The verse is also quoted by many ancient church theologians and "church fathers." Tertullian, writing at the beginning of the 3rd century, references the text is his work *De Pudicita*, 21:16. Cyprian of Carthage, who wrote in the middle of the 3rd century, quotes from the verse in his work *Unity of the Church*, Treatise I, section 6. Athanasius of Alexandria, writing in the mid-4th century, quoted from the verse in his *Disputation against Arius*. Priscillian of

Avila's *Liber Apologeticus*, written in 380 AD, directly quotes from the verse as well. There are numerous other examples, but the point is that the manuscript evidence and early witnesses shows that this verse wasn't just a later invention as many claim. Even before the Trinity doctrine was directly formulated and argued over during the Arian controversy, authors had quoted from it.

Therefore, from the evidence, 1 John 5:7 was a known verse, and was definitely part of the original text of the epistle of John. It is authentic, and gives us great evidence that the Trinity is indeed the teaching of the New Testament. Many attack the Comma Johanneum, attempting to use 'history' to prove it's not supposed to be in the Bible, but when you turn this tactic against them, it's abundantly clear they're picking and choosing what to quote from (more on this in chapter 4). The Hebrew Roots err because they do not know the scriptures and the clear witness of an abundance of passages which show the deity of the three persons; the Father, Son, and the Holy Ghost. Yet despite the abundance of evidence, since this is such a controversial and important doctrine, some continue to argue because of their own proof texts. Some of the following were objections that I myself often raised. However, none of these objections are valid.

One of the objections is the Jesus is clearly called a man in the New Testament (such as in Acts 2:22). How could God be called a man if it is said in the scriptures, "God is not a man (Numbers 23:19)," and "I am God, and not man (Hosea 11:9)?" This was one of my major arguments against the Trinity doctrine when I was in the Hebrew Roots movement. However, as explained in several instances, this just shows ignorance of the claim being made. We've already seen by several clear scriptures (and we'll see from even more) that God is more than one person; we know from the New Testament that indeed the Father is not a man. But what about the Son?

It should be noted first of all that the Son of God, Jesus Christ did not become a man until the incarnation (being made flesh). The book of Philippians tells us,

> Philippians 2:6-8 - Who, being in the form of God, thought it not robbery to be equal with God: But made himself of no reputation, and took upon him the form of a servant, and was made in the likeness of men: And being found in fashion as a man, he humbled himself, and

262

became obedient unto death, even the death of the cross.

Here we see that Jesus was in the form of God, but that he "was made in the likeness of men" and was "found in fashion as a man." Until the day that he was conceived of the Holy Ghost in Mary's womb, Jesus Christ was not a man in our sense of the term. This is why also the scriptures say that "he was made of the seed of David according to the flesh (Romans 1:3)" and "the Word became flesh (John 1:14)." So yes, Jesus was a man when he walked upon this earth, but prior to that, he was not actually a man.

However, it should be noted that as we've seen, many appearances which we've identified to be of Christ in the Old Testament refer to him as a man, such as in Genesis 18 and 32, Judges 13, and Ezekiel 1. The latter chapter clears the question up: Ezekiel does not just call this person a man, but "as the appearance of a man." The scriptures tell us that Jesus is the "image of the invisible God (Colossians 1:15)." It also tells us that by him were all things created (John 1:3, Colossians 1:16)," and therefore, applying that truth to the book of Genesis, we see God say, "Let us make man in our image, after our likeness." Mankind is created in the image of God. Therefore, it's no surprise that Jesus, despite being God, but being visible unlike the Father, has the appearance of a man.

Another objection to the Trinity is based on Deuteronomy 6:4, where the Bible declares "The LORD our God is one LORD." The issue is that this Hebrew phrase, which is a well-known declaration among the Hebrew Roots movement, *YeHoVaH Eloheinu, YeHoVaH echad*, is often translated as "YHVH is our God, YHVH is one." The assumption is that since it says that YHVH is one, this must mean that YHVH is only one person. However, the word *echad* means one in unity, and not in number. It is the same word used in Genesis 2:24 to describe the relationship between a man and his wife, as one (*echad*) flesh. If this verse were declaring God as solely one person, it would use the word *yachid*, which is often translated as "only" in the Bible. Thus, the one here is exactly a 1 John 5:7 declares: there are three persons, but it is one LORD, or one God.

Another objection to the Trinity, particularly regarding the deity of Christ, is that Jesus calls the Father his God, or calls him the only true God. This again is based on a misunderstanding of the incarnation and what the Trinity is about. Let's look at some of these verses:

> John 17:3 - And this is life eternal, that they might know thee the only true God, and Jesus Christ, whom thou hast sent.

> John 20:17 - Jesus saith unto her, Touch me not; for I am not yet ascended to my Father: but go to my brethren, and say unto them, I ascend unto my Father, and your Father; and to my God, and your God.

> Revelation 3:12 - Him that overcometh will I make a pillar in the temple of my God, and he shall go no more out: and I will write upon him the name of my God, and the name of the city of my God, which is new Jerusalem, which cometh down out of heaven from my God: and I will write upon him my new name.

The point of the objection is that Jesus, when praying to the Father, calls him "the only true God," and also tells Mary, "I ascend unto... my God, and your God," and repeatedly calls the Father "my God" to the church of Philadelphia. To unitarians, this supposedly proves that only the Father is God. This is a ridiculous conclusion for several reasons: Firstly, as shown by verses like 1 John 5:7, the Father, the Word, and the Holy Ghost, though being three, are all one. Nobody claims that the Father is a separate God than Jesus; the Bible repeatedly declares that there is only one God, but it also happens to call both the Father and the Son by the title of God. Thus, in him calling the Father "the only true God," this does not conflict with the doctrine that Jesus is God, since they are the same God.

Regarding Jesus' identification of the Father as "my God," unitarians evidently ignore the comment by Thomas several verses later, where he says to Jesus, "My Lord and my God! (John 20:28)." Jesus does not rebuke him for saying this, but rather replies with, "Thomas, because thou hast seen me, thou hast believed." Thomas' expression, which is directed toward Christ, is acknowledged as an expression of faith by Jesus. Consider also the following two passages:

> Psalm 45:6-7 - Thy throne, O God, is for ever and ever: the sceptre of thy kingdom is a right sceptre. Thou lovest righteousness, and hatest wickedness: therefore God, thy God, hath anointed thee with the oil of gladness above thy fellows.

> Hebrews 1:8-9 - But unto the Son he saith, Thy throne, O God, is for

ever and ever: a sceptre of righteousness is the sceptre of thy kingdom. Thou hast loved righteousness, and hated iniquity; therefore God, even thy God, hath anointed thee with the oil of gladness above thy fellows.

Here we have a passage from a Psalm, and the New Testament quotes from it, in which Paul identifies the person called "O God" as the Son. To the Son the Father has said, "Thy throne, O God, is for ever and ever." Notice the very next verse, in which it says, also to the same subject, "God, even thy God, hath anointed thee..." Here we have a clear statement of both the deity of Christ and his subordination to the Father. Therefore, it does not contradict the Trinity doctrine for Jesus to say, "my God," when it says also in the Scriptures, in the very passage where the Son is called God, that the Father is his God.

One of the issues with accepting the Trinity doctrine is the assumption that being equal with God means being equal in rank and power with the Father. We've already looked at chapters like Philippians 2, which tell us that he took the form of a servant and humbled himself despite "being in the form of God." The Bible tells us also that on the last day, after the Son subdues all things, he will be subject to the Father (1 Cor. 5:28). Jesus declared "My Father is greater than I (John 14:28)." Just because the Son has subjected himself to the will and authority of God the Father does not make him by nature any less God.

It took me a bit to understand the Trinity after I got saved because of this troubling issue. In essence, by that time I believed that Jesus was indeed the divine Son of God who was in the beginning with God, but I couldn't wrap my mind around the idea that he was equal with God. Whenever I heard this, to me it sounded like those who believed this doctrine were making Jesus the same as the Father. Therefore, for a few months I decided to focus instead on other doctrines, and for the most part avoided scriptures on Christology; it was a few months after I got saved that I listened to sermons which fully explained the doctrine. Upon searching the scriptures, I understood that the Bible does indeed teach this. There is one God, and that God eternally exists as three persons who are equally divine: the Father, the Son, and the Holy Ghost.

For the most part, that sums up the false doctrines of the Hebrew Roots movement. When held up to scrutiny, the beliefs held by the majority of these

Messianics fail in light of the scriptures. The Jews are not God's chosen people and the physical nation of Israel is not the center of God's focus; the Bible has been preserved for all people; the name of Jesus is indeed the name of the Messiah; we are saved by grace through faith and eternally secure by God; the carnal ordinances of the Torah are abolished for New Testament Christians; the fate of believers is heaven and the unbelievers is hell; and Jesus is God in the flesh.

CHAPTER 5: HEBREW ROOTS MOVEMENT ANSWERED FURTHER (WICKED FRUITS AND HISTORICAL BLUNDERS)

False Prophets of the Hebrew Roots

A recurring theme among some of those in the Hebrew Roots movement is their twisting of Bible prophecy and heavy use of predictions of the future which turn out to be false. Like many others, when the predictions fail to come to pass, they try to claim that they never said anything of the sort, try to cover up their past failures, or simply make a new prediction which still fails to come to pass. This is the same thing that many like William Miller and Harold Camping did. The Bible says concerning false prophets,

> Deuteronomy 18:21-22 - And if thou say in thine heart, How shall we know the word which the Lord hath not spoken? When a prophet speaketh in the name of the Lord, if the thing follow not, nor come to pass, that is the thing which the Lord hath not spoken, but the prophet hath spoken it presumptuously: thou shalt not be afraid of him.

If a person speaks in the name of the LORD, and they make a prediction, but this thing does not come to pass, then they are not a prophet of God, they speak these words presumptuously. The intensity in which one claims to speak for God varies among the Hebrew Roots: some flat-out say "Thus saith the LORD" and some are more cautious, using words like "maybe" or "I'm pretty sure" to make it seem like they're only guessing. Yet, the Bible says concerning the coming of Jesus Christ, "of that day and hour knoweth no man, no, not the angels of heaven, but my Father only (Matt. 24:36)." Yet despite this, they pridefully assume that they can figure out when events in the book of Revelation will take place.

One of the most infamous is of course, Michael Rood, who is also one of the most well-known teachers of the Hebrew Roots movement. He has made numerous predictions in the past which did not come to pass; predictions which he says with certainty. Rood said the following words in 2017: "This is what is about to transpire, ladies and gentlemen. At the end of this war, which has been prepared; you voted for it, you wanted change, you're getting change sweetheart... Get cleaned up, it is time to get ready, because the beginning of the Messianic age, the end time Messianic Age, is upon us. The confirmation of the covenant, watch, this fall, sundown, September 23rd, will be the day of trumpets."

"The upcoming day of trumpets will not be the gathering together, or rapture, so much anticipated by the dispensational theologians of American Gentile Churchianity; but rather, the initiation of the intermediate fulfillment of the fall feasts of the LORD. Nuclear war will level Damascus, and bring the nation of Israel to its knees; right where Almighty God wants them, before the revealing of the ark of the covenant on Yom Kippur. Millions of Israelis will be dead before the smoke clears. Global economic collapse will precipitate the gathering of the lost tribes of Israel from the ends of the earth, and will bring them into the smoldering ruins of the land of Israel. This will lead up to the feast of tabernacles on the temple mount in Jerusalem, soon to be purged of its gold-domed abomination. On the last great day, the latter rain, the double portion outpouring of the Holy Spirit, and the sealing of the 144,000 of all the tribes of Israel will equip the righteous for the final 7-year dash to the finish line, and the reward ceremony on the sea of fire and glass. It was a privilege to serve you, an honor to serve with you, and it will be an honour to die by your side in the service of the King of Kings, the prophet Yeshua HaMashiach. God have mercy on those who love him, and who are the called to his kingdom. I will see you on the sea of fire and glass, when the smoke clears."

All of this was spoken in his series, done in 2017, called "10 Jubilees to the End Time Messianic Age," a prophecy series he did on his show, Shabbat Night Live. In the last video, before he spoke the words above, he said this: "I have some help that comes from heaven, and it comes from another country, to someone who has never met me, and this is how it works: He, the Almighty, gives him a message, a clear message that is then brought to me, but it has to be translated, because we don't speak each other's languages; and he gives me specific information, knows things that I, that no one knows, and that is the one thing that I ask of the Almighty. If you send someone a message, then they have to immediately start out by telling me something that they can't possibly know. This person gave specific revelation and information concerning what I was to do, and so, in the spring of this last year, I went back there up on the Golan Heights; I prayed, I read the scriptures he said to read, and I was told to pray and ask about the hidden things; the dark things, the hidden things. And, I prayed for them. I prayed.

And then I was given more information to go back and what to put in order, in August. And then, when everything was done, finally the last piece came. Everything was done, and I'm not going to specify what was done, except that everything was accomplished. I had gone through one of the hardest periods of my life, and at that moment of time, that was when a person who had gone through great trouble and tribulation: a Messianic Jew there in the Galilee, came to me with this: There's a Rabbi, in the 13th century, early in the 1200s, and he wrote three books, but, only one still exists; the other two, there are just brief quotations in other books. His name, is Judah. He was called Judah the Pious, Judah the righteous. He was a German rabbi. And what he was known for was calling people to live a righteous and a godly life; calling people back to the Torah, to be obedient to the Torah. That was his message. That was his life."

As the video goes on, Michael explains why he believes that September 23rd is the date when what he calls "Zechariah's Thermonuclear War" will occur. This Jewish rabbi (who of course, was not a man of God, but a Christ-denying Shekhinah-worshipping heretic), predicted that there would be a certain number of Jubilees before the end of the world. Michael puts together his framework of end-times prophecy. According to him, since General Allenby took Jerusalem in 1917, and since 50 years later, after the Six-Days War, Israel regained full control of the city, he concluded that these were jubilee years, and that 2017 would again be a Jubilee, in which Israel would gain full control of the land and cast out the Muslims. Of course, this prophecy is based on the faulty assumption that the Jews are God's chosen people, which I've already shown to be entirely unbiblical.

As seen in the quotes above, Michael Rood did not simply mention this as just a "maybe." He spoke with authority, that this will happen on September 23rd, 2017. He was confident. He claimed that the information revealed to him about Judah the Pious was revelation from God, that this unknown person from a foreign country had led Michael to uncover these "hidden things, the dark things." However, despite claiming that he had "help from heaven," as we know, this prediction did not come to pass, and is one of the greatest blunders of the Hebrew Roots movement, since many caught onto this prediction. In fact, a documentary called "The Sign" which discussed the total eclipse in August of 2017, featured Michael Rood, in which he talked about this prophecy. He said, "When we come to the end of September, that is when we are expecting the full-scale invasion and the war against Israel."

This documentary featured many who shared the same ideas as Rood. I personally was deceived into thinking this would come to pass, and listened to many Messianics claim that 2017 would be the year that the 70th week of Daniel began.

Yet it did not. The full-scale invasion of Israel did not occur, the Ark of the Covenant was not revealed, Damascus was not levelled, there was no global economic crash, and the lost tribes of Israel did not return to the land. All of the predictions which Michael Rood made, speaking with authority and claiming it was based on being led by God, were false. Therefore, Michael Rood is a false prophet; and just like many false prophets in the past, despite his foolish date-setting and inaccuracies and twisting of Bible prophecy, some insist that he's still a man of God.

His false prophecies concerning Israel are based on his ignorance of scripture. A student of the Bible; one who has actually read both the Old and New Testaments in full knows the following: that many of the 'return to the land' prophecies of the Tanakh were already fulfilled thousands of years ago because they concerned the Babylonian captivity; that the nation of Israel in the New Testament is a spiritual nation made up of all believers, both Jews and Gentiles, and has nothing to do with the physical descendants of Jacob; and that the modern-day Jews have nothing to do with Bible prophecy. We've already looked at some of this, but let's examine some of the particular prophecies that Rood twists to teach his lies. Here's one:

> Isaiah 66:8 - Who hath heard such a thing? who hath seen such things? Shall the earth be made to bring forth in one day? or shall a nation be born at once? for as soon as Zion travailed, she brought forth her children.

The question "shall a nation be born at once?" is something which Michael just takes and runs with. He often misquotes it and claims that it was prophesied that Israel would become a nation again in one day, and claims that was fulfilled in 1948. Of course, this is wrong on many levels. Firstly, there's no clear statement that says that in the far future the state of Israel would be established in one day. Michael is just reading his interpretation into this verse. The definition of a nation in the Bible is not our concept of a 'nation-state.' Israel is still a nation regardless of whether the children of Israel live in a defined geographic area or are run by Jews or not.

If you read the context, it has nothing to do with the modern day (which is true of many Old Testament prophecies that are forced into modern events). Consider what the Bible says,

> Isaiah 66:5-10 - Hear the word of the Lord, ye that tremble at his word; Your brethren that hated you, that cast you out for my name's sake, said, Let the Lord be glorified: but he shall appear to your joy, and they shall be ashamed. A voice of noise from the city, a voice from the temple, a voice of the Lord that rendereth recompence to his enemies. Before she travailed, she brought forth; before her pain came, she was delivered of a man child. Who hath heard such a thing? who hath seen such things? Shall the earth be made to bring forth in one day? or shall a nation be born at once? for as soon as Zion travailed, she brought forth her children. Shall I bring to the birth, and not cause to bring forth? saith the Lord: shall I cause to bring forth, and shut the womb? saith thy God. Rejoice ye with Jerusalem, and be glad with her, all ye that love her: rejoice for joy with her, all ye that mourn for her:

Notice how in verse 8, it asks the question, "Who hath heard such a thing?" What thing is it talking about? The whole passage is about Zion, or Jerusalem, bringing forth "her children." First we start in verse 5 and 6, the LORD talks about causing shame to those who oppose the fearers of God, and bringing recompense on his enemies. In verse 7, it says "before she travailed, she brought forth." Who is she? According to the context, it is "the city," mentioned in the previous verse, which would be Zion and Jerusalem, personified femininely in verses 8 and 10. Therefore, before the pain and travail of Jerusalem, the city brought forth. What was brought forth? According to verse 8, "a man child." Then, in verse 8, it talks about a different birth, in which Zion brings forth "her children" at the time of her travail. The next verse tells us that the LORD is the one who brings these forth.

So, what is the passage talking about? Michael Rood claims that this refers to what happened in 1948: about the modern-day state of Israel supposedly being born in one day. However, as already pointed out, this is just reading things into the text. There's no indication this has anything to do with the prophecy. There are two births mentioned here: the birth of a man child before the travail comes, and the birth of the children of Jerusalem (the nation spoken of in verse 8), "as soon as Zion travailled." The problem with

Rood's interpretation is that he claims the 1948 restoration of the nation of Israel was a forerunner to the year 2000, which he claims was the beginning of the 'time of Jacob's trouble.' Yet the text tells us that the children of Zion were born at the time of the trouble and pain of Jerusalem, not before. The only one born before the pain was 'the man child.'

I believe that this interpretation is referring to both Christ and the spiritual nation of Israel under the new covenant, which would be all believers in Christ. This is because the context in the surrounding chapters concerns the coming of the Messiah, and even later in the chapter, Isaiah 66, is about Christ returning to judge the earth in his wrath. Notice that the children spoken of here are referred to as the children of Jerusalem. The New Testament tells us in Galatians 4:26 that the "Jerusalem which is above is free, which is the mother of us all." This is the New Jerusalem, the Zion of God, being the mother of the nation of believers, which is the Israel of God (Gal. 6:16). We as New Testament believers are certainly a nation (1 Pet. 2:9), and that nation was indeed brought forth at once, when Christ "by his own blood he entered in once into the holy place, having obtained eternal redemption for us (Heb. 9:12)."

There is no indication in the context that this has anything to do with a state being established in one day in the far future. In fact, it's stupid to say that the modern-day state of Israel was created in one day. The passage in Isaiah 66 asks the question "shall a nation be born to once?" to illustrate that this isn't just a normal occurence. Israel was founded on May 14th, 1948, but it was a work which had been in place for decades and which continued on for years. It wasn't just like it miraculously appeared in the Middle East with no prior plan. The British had to first declare their support for the state in the Balfour Declaration 30 years earlier, take the land of Palestine from the Arabs by the direction of Baron Lionel Rothschild, then millions of Jews had to be moved to the land by the process of aliyah, then the United Nations had to create their partition plan for the state, and the Jewish Agency and Arab League had to accept the plan, before the state declared itself a nation, and subsequently spent the next couple years fighting against Palestinians to secure itself as an independent state.

By no means was Israel established in just one day. Just because they declared the state of Israel on one day doesn't mean that a nation was created "at once." With that logic, one could say that the United States and many other nations fit the bill as well, since many nations throughout history have officially declared themselves a state, or declared independence from another in one day. The prophecy has nothing to do with this. No wonder Michael Rood has such a skewed view of prophecy, and why he so readily makes false predictions.

Michael Rood is also known for an idolatrous mockery of Jesus Christ he made one year during a celebration of the passover. In 2014, during a passover event, four of Michael's assistants led a roasted lamb nailed to a cross with a crown of throwns wrapped around the top. I encourage you to look up this video. It's a mockery of the Messiah; to take a beast and nail it to a cross representing the one in which our saviour died. However, this is not surprising behaviour from a false prophet.

Another false prophet of the Hebrew Roots movement, a person who has gained much more popularity recently and drawn many in because of his political videos attempting to "expose pedophiles" in the US government is a man named Daniel John Lee. It is blatantly obvious that this man is a false prophet, and he's been called out by many, yet he has a following of 90,000 on Youtube. At first, he just seems like your average Hebrew Roots teacher, but once one delves into his preaching activities and prophecies, it's clear he's a false prophet. Daniel John Lee has been married and divorced 6 times, has been convicted of abuse both to his wives and children, is notorious for threatening people who disagree with him, and is a self-claimed prophet.

Lee was one of the many who made false 2017 predictions, but unlike Michael Rood, he was much more clear about claiming to be a prophet, and even asserted that Christ would return in this year. I pointed this out in my video on my Youtube channel, called "Daniel John Lee Exposed", beginning around the 27-minute mark, where I play a video of him claiming to be under the inspiration of God (the actual video I played on Youtube has since been deleted). Lee said the following words: "Proof Yahshua returns for his Bride in 2017, by Daniel John Lee. I am not writing a theory, I am not writing my ideas. I am not writing what I think or guess happens. I am writing under the authority of Yahshua of Nazareth, by his blood, and under his Ruach Ha-Kadosh, and this is 100% certain, so take heed: Yah speaks now." He said later, "I am writing this under the inspiration and anointing of the Ruach Ha-Kadosh, and under the authority of the blood of Yahshua of Nazareth. This is not a theory, this is a fact."

Blatantly Daniel John Lee claims to speak under the authority of Jesus, and the inspiration of the Holy Ghost. Daniel John Lee claimed that his words and the prophecy which he made in this video, claiming that Christ will return in 2017, was a fact, and the word of God. Yet, as we know, none of this happened, and was entirely untrue. What we know, from using Deuteronomy 18, is that he is a false prophet, and therefore we should not fear him. He has spoken presumptuously, and no matter how much he claims to be a prophet of God, he is nothing but a deceiver and a devil. He predicted also, saying, "Thus saith Yahweh, the US Dollar will completely collapse by March 23rd, 2012." Of course, eight years later, that still has not happened.

There are many things which could be said about Daniel John Lee that it's not even worth writing about. I encourage you, if you are a follower of Daniel, if you think he's a "prophet" or believe that he is a true follower of "Yahshua HaMashiach" as he claims, just look into his numerous false prophecies, his threats against people who call him out or question him, his violence, his stalking, and his perversion, and you be the judge of whether or not this is a man of God.

These are just a few short examples of false prophets in the Hebrew Roots movement. I chose these two in particular because it represents both the subtle and less-obvious as well as the extreme. Michael Rood is very popular, and there are several other well-known teachers who are false prophets because they lead people astray in false doctrine and claim they are speaking the truth, and claim they are serving Yehovah by teaching lies that are not in the Bible (lies which have been addressed already in this book).

Historical Lies

Another tendency of the Hebrew Roots movement is making up fake history, or being completely incompetent in historical research in an attempt to attack Christianity and defend their doctrines. The historical lies I will be discussing in this section include the claim that true followers of God haven't existed until this modern movement, to show the impossibility of proving anything by their appeal to historical sects like theirs, and to show that their claims that everything in Christianity comes from paganism is false.

Firstly, to briefly discuss something which has already been addressed in part about the Bible. The Hebrew Roots movement often likes to pick up books which are not God's word and attempt to add them into the Bible, or, in order to defend their false doctrines, they appeal to recent discoveries and manuscripts that have been buried for hundreds of years, particularly the Alexandrian manuscripts.

However, the Bible promises both the preservation of God's word and the preservation of the people of God. Consider the following passages:

> Psalm 12:6-7 - The words of the Lord are pure words: as silver tried in a furnace of earth, purified seven times. Thou shalt keep them, O Lord, thou shalt preserve them from this generation for ever.

> Matthew 24:35 - Heaven and earth shall pass away, but my words shall not pass away.

> Ephesians 3:21 - Unto him be glory in the church by Christ Jesus throughout all ages, world without end. Amen.

In all ages, and all generations, the word of God prevails, and the churches give glory to God. Verses like these have led the Hebrew Roots movement to conclude that their movement, which they believe to be correct, is not new, but that people have kept the Sabbath, and obeyed the laws of the Torah, and denied the Trinity since the time of Christ. While there have been numerous sects which have arose with similar beliefs to the modern Hebrew Roots movement (which I will discuss a bit later), there's a big problem with using this as proof that their beliefs are valid.

Here we will talk about the uselessness of historical research to determine what true believers of the Bible believe. This tactic, which includes out-of-context quotations by the so-called "Church Fathers," and by secular historians of the past, particularly before the council of Nicaea, is the same tactic the Roman Catholics and other cults use. They claim to be authentic because "the early church said the same things we say." The assumption is that the closer we get to the first century, the closer we get to what the apostles and the early followers of Jesus believed.

This is a faulty methodology of investigation for several reasons. First of all, undoubtedly there are many texts which have not survived. Only a handful of writings survived from the 1st and 2nd centuries outside of the Bible itself, despite there being thousands of Christians throughout the world. I seriously doubt only a dozen people in the period of a century wrote anything about what Christians believed at this time. If texts were not copied or stored to prevent decay, then the likelihood of their survival is much smaller. The only reason we know what people like Justin Martyr or Irenaeus among others said is because their texts were quoted by later authors, and their writings were copied and preserved through the following centuries. Therefore, there's no way to know the whole picture, because unlike the word of God itself, there was no divine preservation at work with these writings.

The improbability that these "church fathers" represent an accurate depiction of what the apostles believed is further bolstered by the fact that there many heretics at this time. For some odd reason, textual critics believed that the older the manuscript is, the more right it must be. In the same way, cults and religious movements which claim to restore ancient teachings have this idea that the older the church father, the more right they are. The attitude is seemingly that churches and the Bible evolved through time. This is ridiculous. Change over time did not have to take place in order for heresies to creep in. Only one copy of the Bible was necessary to change what the Bible says, and only one church had to go off the rails to create a new religious movement which preached false doctrine.

The scriptures tell us that even in the days of the apostles, heresies were widespread and common. Consider the following passages and verses:

> Acts 20:28-31 - Take heed therefore unto yourselves, and to all the flock, over the which the Holy Ghost hath made you overseers, to feed the church of God, which he hath purchased with his own blood. For I know this, that after my departing shall grievous wolves enter in among you, not sparing the flock. Also of your own selves shall men arise, speaking perverse things, to draw away disciples after them. Therefore watch, and remember, that by the space of three years I ceased not to warn every one night and day with tears.

> 2 Corinthians 2:17 - For we are not as many, which corrupt the word of God: but as of sincerity, but as of God, in the sight of God speak we in Christ.

> Galatians 1:6-7 - I marvel that ye are so soon removed from him that called you into the grace of Christ unto another gospel: Which is not

another; but there be some that trouble you, and would pervert the gospel of Christ.

Galatians 2:4 - And that because of false brethren unawares brought in, who came in privily to spy out our liberty which we have in Christ Jesus, that they might bring us into bondage.

2 Peter 2:1 - But there were false prophets also among the people, even as there shall be false teachers among you, who privily shall bring in damnable heresies, even denying the Lord that bought them, and bring upon themselves swift destruction.

1 John 4:1 - Beloved, believe not every spirit, but try the spirits whether they are of God: because many false prophets are gone out into the world.

Jude 1:3-4 - Beloved, when I gave all diligence to write unto you of the common salvation, it was needful for me to write unto you, and exhort you that ye should earnestly contend for the faith which was once delivered unto the saints. For there are certain men crept in unawares, who were before of old ordained to this condemnation, ungodly men, turning the grace of our God into lasciviousness, and denying the only Lord God, and our Lord Jesus Christ.

There are many scriptures in the New Testament which warn churches and believers of false prophets. It's not like there's just a minority of false teachers; but rather, even in the 1st century apostolic age there were many false teachers. Paul, Peter, John, and Jude all write about these false teachers and warn the brethren of them. It is written, "many false prophets are gone out into the world," and "we are not as many, which corrupt the word of God." The simple fact is that heretics and false prophets were more common than those who adhered to the truth, even in the time of the 1st century.

Notice that these verses also state these ungodly men and false brethren have "crept in unawares" or are "unawares brought in." In 2 Peter 2, it says they "privily shall bring in damnable heresies." Privily means 'in secret.' This was not an open practice. False prophets conceal themselves and come in as wolves in sheep's clothing. The false doctrine and heresies brought into the churches was done so in secret, and deceived many, so that the gospel of Christ was perverted, the word of God corrupted, and people learned false doctrine. Jesus taught, when speaking of false prophets, that a corrupt tree bringeth forth evil fruit (Matt. 7:17)." These false prophets only created more false prophets. They did not lead anybody to the LORD, but only multiplied and led more people astray.

Therefore, if even in the 1st century there were warnings about many false teachers and heretics creeping into churches, what use is it to quote from something a hundred or two hundred years later to prove that early Christians believe like these modern groups do? Just because somebody believed the same false doctrine 1900 years ago doesn't make it any more correct, but just proves the point being made in the verses above. The Hebrew Roots movement likes to search for ancient mentions of keeping the Sabbath day or doing similar things. There was indeed a sect known as the Nazarenes which prevailed into the 4th century that looks very similar to the modern Messianics. However, there were also other churches which believed different things. There were Gnostics since at least the late 1st century, and records of false teachers like Dositheos, Cerinthus, Menander, and Ebion from the time of the apostles. Just because they're old doesn't mean they're right.

In fact, there's no doubt that the "Hebrew Roots movement" existed at the time of Paul. They were the subjects of the book of Galatians! As already shown throughout this book, the book of Galatians is one of the greatest testimonies against their Hebraic Roots false doctrine. Chapter 1 deals with false teachers corrupting the Gospel of Christ; chapter 2 deals with false brethren seeking to bring us back into bondage (which is defined later in chapter 4 as the Old Testament and ordinances of the Sinai covenant), and how even some good Christians like Peter were carried away into the doctrine that Jews are separate from Gentiles. He then emphasizes in this chapter that we are not saved by the law, but by faith. In chapter 3, he again speaks of the fact that we are saved by faith, teaches that those who believe are the children of Abraham and not the fleshly Jews, and explains the purpose of the law as bringing us to a knowledge of sin. Chapter 4 deals with being under bondage to the Old Testament law and the difference between the children of the bondwoman and the children of the promise. Chapter 5 deals with the danger of believing that the law can save us, and explains that we serve God now in the spirit. Chapter 6 wraps up the matter, dealing with glorying in the flesh and the unprofitableness of the flesh.

The book of Galatians is one of the most powerful testimonies to the falsehood of the Hebrew Roots movement, attacking every main doctrine which they hold: salvation by the Torah, keeping the Old Testament carnal ordinances, and lifting up the unbelieving Jews and Israel. This shows that indeed the heresy existed in the first century, but it was not the beliefs of the true Christians who followed Christ, rather, heretics who had crept into churches. Therefore, it is utterly ridiculous to quote from some theologian two hundred years later in a vain attempt to make the point that your doctrines aren't new. There is nothing new under the sun.

Despite the fact that Christianity had already been corrupted by the time the Apostolic Age was over, some still love to vainly cherry-pick quotes from the so-called "church fathers" in an attempt to prove their doctrines. I used to do so myself in reaction to the Roman Catholics, who love to claim that their church has existed since the 1st century. I counteracted these claims with quotes from saints from their church, usually from the 2nd and 3rd centuries. The Hebrew Roots movement, just like a lot of cults out there, do the same.

However, it is possible to show as well that this is simply cherry-picking evidence. As many quotes you can show from people who didn't believe in the Trinity, you can find quotes from people who did believe in the Trinity. If you find quotes showing observance of the Sabbath, you can find also quotes of people saying the Sabbath is abolished. Let me give a few examples. I recall using historical quotes from ancient theologians in an attempt to disprove the doctrine of the Trinity. However, you can also find statements from the 'church fathers' which show the opposite: that the believers confessed the Father, Son, and Holy Ghost, and that Jesus indeed is God. Consider the following:

> "Ignatius, who is also Theophorus, unto her which hath been blessed in greatness through the plentitude of God the Father; which hath been foreordained before the ages to be for ever unto abiding and unchangeable glory, united and elect in a true passion, by the will of the Father and of Jesus Christ our God; even unto the church which is in Ephesus [of Asia], worthy of all felicitation: abundant greeting in Christ Jesus and in blameless joy (Ignatius of Antioch, c. 110 AD, *Epistle to the Ephesians,* introduction)."

> "But our Physician is the Only true God, the unbegotten and unapproachable, the Lord of all, the Father and Begetter of the only-

begotten Son. We have also as a Physician <u>the Lord our God, Jesus the Christ</u>, the only-begotten Son and Word, before time began, but who afterwards became also man, of Mary the virgin. For "the Word was made flesh." Being incorporeal, He was in the body, being impassible, He was in a passible body, being immortal, He was in a mortal body, being life, He became subject to corruption, that He might free our souls from death and corruption, and heal them, and might restore them to health, when they were diseased with ungodliness and wicked lusts. (Ignatius of Antioch, c. 110 AD, *Epistle to the Ephesians*, chapter 7)."

"<u>For our God, Jesus the Christ</u>, was conceived in the womb by Mary according to a dispensation, of the seed of David but also of the Holy Ghost (Ignatius of Antioch, c. 110 AD, *Epistle to the Ephesians*, chapter 18)."

"Now may the God and Father of our Lord Jesus Christ, and the eternal high priest himself, the Son of God Jesus Christ, build you up in faith and truth...and to us with you, and to all those under heaven who will yet believe <u>in our Lord and God Jesus Christ and in his Father</u> who raised him from the dead (Polycarp, c. 110 AD, *Epistle to the Philippians*, chapter 12)."

"the Father of the universe has a Son; who also, being the first-begotten Word of God, <u>is even God </u>(Justin Martyr, c. 150 AD, *First Apology*, chapter 63)."

"As you wish, Trypho, I shall come to these proofs which you seek in the fitting place; but now you will permit me first to recount the prophecies, which I wish to do in order to prove <u>that Christ is called both God and Lord of hosts</u> (Justin Martyr, c. 160 AD, *Dialogue with Trypho*, chapter 36)."

"<u>And that Christ being Lord, and God the Son of God</u>, and appearing formerly in power as Man, and Angel, and in the glory of fire as at the bush, so also was manifested at the judgment executed on Sodom, has been demonstrated fully by what has been said. (Justin Martyr, c. 160 AD, *Dialogue with Trypho*, chapter 128)."

"Christ Jesus [is] our Lord, <u>and God</u>, and Savior, and King, according to the will of the invisible Father (Irenaeus of Lyons, c. 180 AD, *Against Heresies*, book 1, chapter 10)."

"For I have shown from the Scriptures, that no one of the sons of Adam is as to everything, and absolutely, called God, or named Lord. But that He is Himself in His own right, beyond all men who ever lived, God, and Lord, and King Eternal, and the Incarnate Word, proclaimed by all the prophets, the apostles, and by the Spirit Himself, may be seen by all who have attained to even a small portion of the truth. Now, the Scriptures would not have testified these things of Him, if, like others, He had been a mere man...He is the holy Lord, the Wonderful, the Counselor, the Beautiful in appearance, and the Mighty God, coming on the clouds as the Judge of all men;—all these things did the Scriptures prophesy of Him (Irenaeus of Lyons, c. 180 AD, *Against Heresies*, book 3, chapter 19)."

"This Word, then, the Christ, the cause of both our being at first (for He was in God) and of our well-being, this very Word has now appeared as man, He alone being both, both God and man—the Author of all blessings to us; by whom we, being taught to live well, are sent on our way to life eternal...The Word, who in the beginning bestowed on us life as Creator when He formed us, taught us to live well when He appeared as our Teacher that as God He might afterwards conduct us to the life which never ends (Clement of Alexandria, c. 200 AD, *Exhortation to the Heathen*, chapter 1)."

This is just scratching the surface of quotes from early authors (notice how they're all from the 2nd century) which taught that Jesus is God along with the Father. And yet some of these, such as Justin Martyr and Irenaeus, I would use, cherry-picking quotes out of context, with no knowledge of these other statements by the same, in an attempt to deny the Trinity. It's the same way with the Hebrew Roots doctrine of keeping the Sabbath and continuing to obey the Torah. Consider these additional quotes:

"For He hath made manifest to us by all the prophets that He wanteth neither sacrifices nor whole burnt offerings nor oblations, saying at one time; What to Me is the multitude of your sacrifices, saith the Lord I am full of whole burnt-offerings, and the fat of lambs and the blood of bulls and of goats desire not, not though ye should come to be seen of

Me. or who required these things at your hands? Ye shall continue no more to tread My court. If ye bring fine flour, it is in vain; incense is an abomination to Me; your new moons and your Sabbaths I cannot away with. These things therefore He annulled, that the new law of our Lord Jesus Christ, being free from the yoke of constraint, might have its oblation not made by human hands. (c. 100 AD, *Epistle of Barnabas*, 2:4-6)."

Finally, He saith to them; Your new moons and your Sabbaths I cannot away with. Ye see what is His meaning ; it is not your present Sabbaths that are acceptable [unto Me], but the Sabbath which I have made, in the which, when I have set all things at rest, I will make the beginning of the eighth day which is the beginning of another world (c. 100 AD, *Epistle of Barnabas*, 15:8)."

"Be not seduced by strange doctrines nor by antiquated fables, which are profitless. For if even unto this day we live after the manner of Judaism, we avow that we have not received grace ... If then those who had walked in ancient practices attained unto newness of hope, no longer observing Sabbaths but fashioning their lives after the Lord's day, on which our life also arose through Him ... how shall we be able to live apart from Him? (Ignatius of Antioch, c.100 AD, *Epistle to the Magnesians*, chapter 8)."

"But we do not trust through Moses or through the law; for then we would do the same as yourselves. But now--(for I have read that there shall be a final law, and a covenant, the chiefest of all, which it is now incumbent on all men to observe, as many as are seeking after the inheritance of God. For the law promulgated on Horeb is now old, and belongs to yourselves alone; but this is for all universally. Now, law placed against law has abrogated that which is before it, and a covenant which comes after in like manner has put an end to the previous one; and an eternal and final law--namely, Christ--has been given to us, and the covenant is trustworthy, after which there shall be no law, no commandment, no ordinance. (Justin Martyr, c. 160 AD, *Dialogue with Trypho*, chapter 11)."

"The Lawgiver is present, yet you do not see Him; to the poor the Gospel is preached, the blind see, yet you do not understand. You have now need of a second circumcision, though you glory greatly in the flesh. The new law requires you to keep perpetual sabbath, and you, because you are idle for one day, suppose you are pious, not discerning why this has been commanded you: and if you eat unleavened bread, you say the will of God has been fulfilled. The Lord our God does not take pleasure in such observances: if there is any perjured person or a thief among you, let him cease to be so; if any adulterer, let him repent; then he has kept the sweet and true sabbaths of God. If any one has impure hands, let him wash and be pure. (Justin Martyr, c. 160 AD, *Dialogue with Trypho*, chapter 12)."

"But if we do not admit this, we shall be liable to fall into foolish opinions, as if it were not the same God who existed in the times of Enoch and all the rest, who neither were circumcised after the flesh, nor observed Sabbaths, nor any other rites, seeing that Moses enjoined such observances; or that God has not wished each race of mankind continually to perform the same righteous actions: to admit which, seems to be ridiculous and absurd. Therefore we must confess that He, who is ever the same, has commanded these and such like institutions on account of sinful men, and we must declare Him to be benevolent, foreknowing, needing nothing, righteous and good. But if this be not so, tell me, sir, what you think of those matters which we are investigating." And when no one responded: "Wherefore, Trypho, I will proclaim to you, and to those who wish to become proselytes, the divine message which I heard from that man. Do you see that the elements are not idle, and keep no Sabbaths? Remain as you were born. For if there was no need of circumcision before Abraham, or Of the observance of Sabbaths, of feasts and sacrifices, before Moses; no more need is there of them now, after that, according to the will of God, Jesus Christ the Son of God has been born without sin, of a virgin sprung from the stock of Abraham. For when Abraham himself was in un-circumcision, he was justified and blessed by reason of the faith which he reposed in God, as the Scripture tells. (Justin Martyr, c. 160 AD, *Dialogue with Trypho*, chapter 33)."

Of course, it was of the general opinion of these authors, who all lived within a hundred years of the apostles, that the Old Testament laws, such as the sabbaths and the circumcision, have no purpose under the New Testament, but that we are under a new law. Of course, as already pointed out, I am not saying this is true simply because they said so; but because the Bible says so. The point is that it is utterly foolish to conclude, by picking and choosing quotes from early church fathers, any belief, especially that of the Hebrew Roots doctrine. Some of these men taught strange doctrines elsewhere; it is because false doctrines and heresies had already crept into churches.

Therefore, it is useless to try to use church history as a way to defend their doctrines. Those in the Hebrew Roots movement have demonstrated themselves to be abundantly ignorant of religious history. It is not just so that they twist texts written in the 2nd and 3rd centuries to defend their doctrines; but they will falsely claim that Christianity as we know it today was invented by Constantine, and almost entirely comes from paganism. The mistake made here is that they, like I did, have this bizarre and uninformed opinion that all denominations of Christianity are the same, and all come from the Roman Church, as if nobody believed the doctrines which I profess in this book before the 4th century.

The "Constantinian" lie mainly comes from Michael Rood, who propagates it using information which comes from a book called *The Two Babylons*, published by Alexander Hislop in 1853. Even though Hislop was a Presbyterian who mainly attacked the Roman Catholic church, the Hebrew Roots often lumps all other Christians in with the Catholics. The premise of the book and the Constantinian lie is that the religions of the world were created at Babylon through worship of Nimrod and his wife Semiramis. They assert that Semiramis had a son named Tammuz, and that pagan worship evolved from the worship of these three figures at Babel. The idea is that this continued into the Roman religion through figures such as Mithra.

In 312 AD, Constantine made a fake conversion to Christianity and legalized it in the Roman Empire. Following this, Constantine called for the first ecumenical council at Nicaea in 325. The Hebrew Roots movement believes that Constantine's conversion and his subsequent support for a universal church is what brought Roman paganism into Christianity: that it was him who brought in Easter (supposedly a pagan holiday), Christmas (also a pagan holiday), the Sunday sabbath (pagan), and all kinds of other objects of sun worship. Thus, the claim is that Roman Catholicism is nothing more than a hybrid between Christianity and sun-worship. However, even though many Christians in the United States, especially Baptists, do not participate in the traditions and idolatry of Rome, they still will call us pagans for the same reason.

The tale of the Constantinian corruption of the Bible is heavily exaggerated. While it is true that Constantine had a great impact on the establishment of the Roman Catholic Church, it is false to just blame everything on him. As already demonstrated, there were so-called Christians who believed in Sunday worship before Constantine, as shown by the above quotes supporting the abolition of the seventh-day Sabbath. Constantine simply established the 'no work on Sunday' idea, and made it law in the empire in 321 by his decree to rest on the "venerable day of the sun."

Another strange claim of these historical ignoramuses is that Constantine worshipped Mithra, and that this god was the basis of the Catholic religion. For some odd reason, Michael Rood and others use the term "Sol Invictus Mithra" as if this is one god. Sol Invictus, the god which Constantine did truly worship, as evidenced by coins bearing the image of this 'Invincible Sun,' was a separate deity from Mithra. Mithra was an ancient Persian god who was worshipped by a small cult in Rome which was heavily based on Zoroastrianism. Iconography associated with Mithra include his birth out of a rock, the killing of a sacred bull, and a banquet feasting on the bull.

Sol Invictus was a separate god which was brought into the Roman empire by an emperor named Elagabulus in 218 AD, which was based on a Syrian god, whose name means "god of the mountain." The cult of this god became official only in 274 AD during the reign of Aurelian. However, even though Sol Invictus and Mithra were separate gods with separate origins and descriptions, they did play a close role together in the Mithraic mysteries. I encourage you to examine the artwork of Mithra. In many scenes Sol is with Mithra; there are two persons. For example, in the banquet scene, Mithra and Sol eat together. It is not so that there is one god who Constantine worshipped called "Sol Invictus Mithra." Mithra had nothing to do with Constantine's religion, and there's no evidence of such.

We could talk about Constantine all day, but it's not just Constantine which is the problem: but also the myth about Nimrod. The idea is that Nimrod invented this pagan system of worship, and that Constantine, part of the Babylonian system, brought it into Christianity. However, the claims made in Alexander Hislop's book are utterly false, and the fact that people still take it seriously is absurd. *The Two Babylons* was published in 1853, which was right as excavations at the city of Babylon even began, but much of Mesopotamia had not been excavated, nor had the finds been analyzed. Thus, Hislop had to base most of his claims on writings of Greek historians who came centuries after Babylon had fallen. However, modern archaeology, having uncovered plenty of texts from Babylon, shows that Hislop and Rood's understanding of the Babylonian religion is in error.

For example, the claim that Nimrod was married to a woman named Semiramis, and their son was Tammuz, has no basis in fact. The marriage is based on the legend of Ninus and Semiramis, first written by Ctesias of Cnidus, a Greek physician from the 5th century BCE. There's no doubt that the Greeks had failed in their interpretation of Babylonian records (which was common, just read Herodotus and see how ridiculously inaccurate it is). The story of Ninus is that he was the son of Belus, or Ba'al, and that he established an enormous empire in the ancient Near East. He subjugated all the kings of the surrounding countries, and upon moving into Bactria, took for himself a wife, named Semiramis. Nothing in the records by Ctesias, Diodorus Siculus, or Castor of Rhodes on Ninus say anything about a son named Tammuz; all give their child's name as Ninyas.

The problem is that there's only evidence for a queen named Semiramis as the wife of the Assyrian king Shamshi-Adad in the 9th century BCE, not thirteen centuries prior. Semiramis, whose Assyrian name was Shammaramut, was considered to be a powerful woman because she briefly ruled as a co-regent with her son Adad-nirari III after the death of her husband, and helped expand the empire. The fact is that Semiramis was an Assyrian queen, and that even the Greeks claimed that Ninus and Semiramis were Assyrians (the name of Ninus is connected with Nineveh). Yet the Bible tells us in Genesis 10 that it was not Nimrod, but Asshur the son of Shem who founded Assyria and built cities such as Nineveh. Thus, not only are anachronisms used in the Greek histories, by Alexander Hislop completely mistakes Assyrian rulers with Babylonian ones.

What about Tammuz? Tammuz, also known as Dumuzid, was indeed a Babylonian god. Tammuz was the son of the Sumerian goddess of sheep, Sirtur, and the wife of Ishtar. Hislop and Rood claim that Ishtar is equivalent with Semiramis, who is supposed to be his mother. Much of the stories of Tammuz involved his marriage to Inanna (Ishtar), and his rescue of his wife from Kur, the underworld. Inanna dies, but escapes from the underworld, and allows the demons of this world to drag Tammuz down into the underworld to be her replacement. The story goes that following this, Inanna allowed Tammuz to arise from the underworld for half of the year, but to go back down for the other half of the year. This is nothing like anything written in Genesis, nor is it mentioned whatsoever by the Greek accounts of Ninus and Semiramis.

It's not difficult to figure out who Nimrod was when one looks at Mesopotamian history. He is to be equated with the ancient king of Uruk, Enmerkar, the son of Meshkiangasher, the son of Utu the sun god. There are several reasons for this identification. Firstly, the suffix '-kar' means 'hunter' in Sumerian, and Nimrod is described as a great hunter in the scriptures (Gen. 10:9). In addition, the Sumerian stories of Enmerkar say that he is the builder of the city of Uruk, which is the Biblical Erech, which Nimrod built (Gen. 10:10). The cuneiform text *Enmerkar and the Lord of Aratta* also gives a narrative of a 'confusion of tongues' which is very similar to the tower of Babel story in Genesis 11.

The possible confusion concerning the identity of Tammuz may come from a conflation between Dumuzid the Shepherd (the god called Tammuz), and a king of Uruk named Dumuzid the Fisherman. The Sumerian Kings List separates between these two; the former ruled before the flood, and the latter after the flood as the successor to Lugalbanda, the general who succeeded Enmerkar and father of Gilgamesh. However, there's no evidence that this Dumuzid was in any way related to Enmerkar; rather, the kings list states that he came from a different city in Mesopotamia, called Kuara.

Alexander Hislop is right to claim that the Roman Catholic Church is based in paganism. Their bishop, the Pope, takes the name of "Supreme Pontiff," a title used in the Roman religion for the head of the college of pontiffs, or priests who oversaw the worship of the gods in the city of Rome. The veneration of Mary as the queen of heaven undoubtedly has its roots in the worship of pagan goddesses, especially the "queen of heaven" mentioned in the book of Jeremiah (Jer. 7:19, 44:17-19, 25), which was most likely the Canaanite goddess Astarte, who bore the title. The Catholics probably got the title from a similar goddess, Juno, the wife of Jupiter, who bore the same title of Queen of Heaven. The Roman Catholics use numerous objects and symbols in their worship which have their roots in Roman sun worship; that's undeniable.

However, what is unsubstantiated is saying that this all comes from Nimrod. This is undoubtedly a mistake by Hislop based on the lack of available sources from Mesopotamia at the time he wrote. However, Rood and others, like Yahweh's Restoration Ministries, are inexcusable for their errors. The former flat-out lies in his RoodAwakening program, claiming that "everybody in the east knows this." This is simply untrue. The Nimrod and the Constantinian myth is greatly exaggerated. It's true that Nimrod began pagan worship, and Constantine initiated the ecumenical movement which centered Catholicism in Rome, but to just start making stuff up in order to support this is dishonest.

Another piece of dishonesty is just the ignorance of Christianity and its history in general. The Hebrew Roots movement has an attitude of "we're God's real followers and Christians are pagans." Based on the assertions of people like Michael Rood, I honestly believed that all denominations of Christianity had been given into pagan worship. However, no independent Baptist worships or venerates Mary. No Baptist bows down to a Pope. No Baptist prays to saints, nor has idols in their churches, nor uses sun imagery, nor refers to Sunday as a 'new sabbath', nor adheres to the traditions of the Roman Catholic church which is not based on the Bible. To just lump all of Christianity in together is dishonest and stupid.

The Hebrew Roots will sometimes argue that true believers are not Christians, but Nazarenes. This is based on a single mention of the word "Nazarene" in the Bible as referring to followers of Jesus, in Acts 24:5, where Paul is accused of being a ringleader of the sect of the Nazarenes. However, the word Christian is also used in the scriptures, not just by the heathen to describe the believers (as in Acts 11:26 and 26:28), but also by Peter in 1 Pet. 4:16, showing that this title was embraced by believers. And it's no wonder: there's nothing wrong with the title of "Christian." It simply means "Christ-like" or "belonging to Christ." If you belong to Christ, then you are a Christian.

In addition, as pointed out earlier, accessing early documents is not a reliable way to determine what the apostles believed and practiced. Heresies, seditions, and false teachings had already corrupted churches within decades of the foundation of the first New Testament church in Jerusalem in 30 CE.

Nazarene was indeed a title used for Christians in the 1st century, but this does not mean that later groups which bore the same name were the same. This faulty logic is the same that the Roman Catholics use: they see that there was a church in Rome in the 1st century, and just because their church is also the "Roman Church," assume that this means their religion goes back to the time of Jesus Christ.

However, the next historical mention of Nazarenes indicate them as a separate sect from Christians, which adhered to the Sabbath and Old Testament carnal ordinances, as already pointed out in chapter 2. As shown from what the Bible says, this is not what Jesus and the apostles believed or taught. If we are to rely purely on what the scriptures say, the conclusion is that the religion of the New Testament include the doctrines of salvation by grace alone through faith alone in Christ alone (John 3:16, 36, 5:24, 6:40, 47, 11:25-26, Acts 10:43, 16:30-31, Rom. 3:21-22, 28, 4:5-8, 10:9-17, Gal. 2:16, 3:11, Eph. 1:12-14, 2:8-9, etc.), that this salvation is eternal life, meaning that it cannot be lost (John 3:16, 36, 6:40, 47, 10:28-29, 11:25-26, Rom. 8:38-39, Eph. 1:12-14, 4:30, Titus 1:2), that the Old Testament carnal commandments, such as meat, drinks, and sabbaths are done away with (2 Cor. 3:6-7, Eph. 2:14-16, Col. 2:14-17, Heb. 9:10), that there is one God, who is three persons, including Jesus Christ, who is God (John 1:1, 14, 8:58, 10:30, 20:28, Rom. 9:5, Phil. 2:6-11, Col. 1:16, Heb. 1:8, 1 John 5:7), and that the Jews are not God's people, but believers in Christ (Matt. 21:42-44, Rom. 2:28-29, 9:30-33, 11:1-32, Gal. 3:9, 26-29, 4:22-31, 6:16, Eph. 2:11-19, Phil. 3:3, 1 Pet. 2:8).

CONCLUSION

My journey through the Hebrew Roots was a mess. I, like thousands today, was sucked into this because it's the new cool fad and trend in theology. The doctrines of these Messianic teacher is nothing but something to scratch the itching ears of those who are carried about with every wind of doctrine. Being a 14-year old at the time, and already having been deceived by false Bible versions and lack of instruction in the Gospel and principles of the scriptures, already had come to the spiritually blind conclusion that we are saved by our obedience to the commandments of God, which included even the things that Christians did not do: such as keep the sabbath and abstain from pork.

The fact of the matter is, the Bible teaches that those who are unsaved do not have the ability to understand God's word. In 1 Corinthians 2:14, it says "The natural man receiveth not the things of the spirit of God: for they are foolishness unto him, neither can he know them, because they are spiritually discerned." Without the spirit of God to discern spiritual truths, one cannot know the things which the Bible teaches. Being unsaved and in the world, false prophets often come to the conclusion that we need to work our way to heaven, or that we have to be good enough. This is the conclusion reached by all religions of the world: whether it be Roman Catholicism, or Islam, or the Jehovah's Witnesses, or Zoroastrianism, or Judaism, among others. The conclusion is that our status in an afterlife all has to do with whether or not we are good enough to attain that afterlife, and whether we've done more good than bad.

But the Bible teaches that all have sinned (Romans 3:23), and that Jesus Christ came into this world to save sinners (1 Tim. 1:15). It teaches that we cannot be justified by the deeds of the law (Romans 3:20), but only by faith of Jesus Christ. It is declared, "Believe on the Lord Jesus Christ, and thou shalt be saved (Acts 16:31)." Only the righteousness of Jesus Christ can make us children of God, and can reconcile us to the LORD and save us from the wrath and judgment of hell and the lake of fire. This is the truth, the great mystery of the gospel, that only through the sacrifice of the Lamb of God, slain on the cross, buried, and raised bodily to justify and make intercession for us, can we be saved.

Two years is not that long of a time, even when compared to the short vapour in which the earth has been in existence. Many people fall into false religions and cults for an even longer amount of time. For me, the two years felt like a long time. The Hebraic Roots mindset completely defined who I was. Many thought I was a Jew, having seen me with my unshaven beard and tzizit; my refusal to eat any unclean meats, and my refusal to do any work whatsoever from Friday at sunset to Saturday at sunset. I was afraid that breaking these laws intentionally would cause me to end up in the lake of fire; that God would judge me, since I knew the "truth" and refused to keep it.

Why did I leave the Hebrew Roots movement? It is because of the gospel of Jesus Christ. The one key which unlocked the scriptures was salvation. If you were to ask me in early 2018 whether I knew for sure I would go to heaven, my answer would be no, or if I did say yes, it would be based on my own obedience to the Torah. Through the light of the preaching of the word of God on June 25th, 2018, the Holy Ghost revealed to my heart the outstanding truth of the simplicity of Christ, and reproved me of my sin. I understood that I was a wretched sinner, unable to come to righteousness by my own ability. That night, I put my trust on the name of the Lord Jesus Christ and what he did, and asked the Lord to save me.

From that point on, through careful study of the scriptures, now having the spirit of God indwelling me, I began to slowly tear away the false deceptions which had been built up in my mind for the last two years. I began to understand more about baptism, the word of God itself, the Godhead, and many other Biblical concepts and doctrines. Just like any other false religion, through searching the scriptures, the lies were cast down.

Made in the USA
Monee, IL
23 July 2021